Dramatic Psychological Storytelling

Dramatic Psychological Storytelling

Using the Expressive Arts and Psychotheatrics

Rob Allen and Nina Krebs

palgrave
macmillan

First published 2007 by
PALGRAVE MACMILLAN
Houndmills, Basingstoke, Hampshire RG21 6XS and
175 Fifth Avenue, New York, N. Y. 10010
Companies and representatives throughout the world

PALGRAVE MACMILLAN is the global academic imprint of the Palgrave Macmillan division of St. Martin's Press, LLC and of Palgrave Macmillan Ltd. Macmillan® is a registered trademark in the United States, United Kingdom and other countries. Palgrave is a registered trademark in the European Union and other countries.

ISBN-13: 978-0-230-50681-7 hardback
ISBN-10: 0-230-50681-X hardback

This book is printed on paper suitable for recycling and made from fully managed and sustained forest sources.

A catalogue record for this book is available from the British Library.

A catalogue record for this book is available from the Library of Congress.

10 9 8 7 6 5 4 3 2 1
16 15 14 13 12 11 10 09 08 07

Printed and bound in Great Britain by
Antony Rowe Ltd, Chippenham and Eastbourne

Roslyn Medaris, wife and soul-mate

Carey Allen, son and comrade *Rob Allen*

To the memory of a most amazing storyteller,
Mary Geoghegan Bolton. *Nina Krebs*

Contents

Acknowledgements

Roslyn Medaris has been an essential part of the process. Not only was she willing to test the *Dramatic Psychological Storytelling* process in her own work situation, her honest feedback and contributions along the way have been invaluable. Carey Allen added his performance and playwrighting skills to make an outstanding contribution to the DPS process. Trish Ludgate contributed major editorial intelligence. Dave Krebs cleared space for work time and travel, essential aspects of any creative process. Graduate students from Charles Sturt University – Australia have researched the DPS model and have all contributed to its understanding and use. Their careful work lends not only broad experience with the process, but the academic credibility that is essential to assure professionals who will use DPS that it is valid and reliable. In addition, special thanks to all the professionals who have shared their knowledge after attending our workshops and conference presentations and also those who are now actively involved in the DPS process – we appreciate your support and contributions. Thank you! YOU!!!!

Contributors

Carey Allen
Loraine Anderson
Bill Blaikie
Cherie Borosh
Anna Bray
Mixhuca Cervantes-McBride
Brigette Conway-Dobson
Karen Lattouf
Roslyn Medaris
Tamlyn Philips
Tandi Pickard
Amanda Rouhliadeff
Julie Simon
Carol Tutchener
Jo (Joan) Willis

www.dramaticpsychologicalstorytelling.com

Preface

Guideposts: Dramatic Psychological Storytelling

Meaning comes into our lives, not so much because we search it out, but because we recognise it when it emerges, or even more often, through hindsight. An intentional journey increases the possibilities. When truth and intention meet, we gain new ground in enriching our existence.

Dramatic Psychological Storytelling (DPS) is significantly different from other change processes because it involves dramatic expression using the expressive arts in a psychological intersubjective orientation as well as meaning reflection or making through enactment storytelling. Workshops designed to test DPS generated high energy and rich interaction, with many participants describing their experience as moving and profound. What had been theory became practice with good results.

As more people engage DPS, questions will arise that require creative responses. A website will include questions, critiques and contributions from around the world creating the connection that DPS promotes: dialogue and exploration of the expressive arts to reflect and create meaning in Clinical and Counselling, Human Resources and Educational settings. Research will be made available utilising DPS, including numerous theses, with many more now in progress – and all this will be available on the website:

www.dramaticpsychologicalstorytelling.com

Part I: the first three chapters lay the **conceptual foundations** as they relate to DPS. This includes the steps necessary in a search for meaning that involves new perspectives in psychology, the rediscovery of storytelling and the unique Dramatic Enactment of the Expressive Arts. This ancient but radical combination results in a dynamic and productive union. The spotlight is then focused on the relevance of the Expressive Arts and the action method Psychotheatrics for dynamic intersubjective exploration and the establishment of Meaning. Chapter Four offers a detailed explanation of the DPS model.

Part II: explores the relevance of **the seven Expressive Arts** – Narrative, Film, Theatre, Music, Visual Art, Dance and Kinaesthetics, and Ritual and Epic and their direct application to DPS. Entering DPS through one's personal connection with the Expressive Arts, rather than a more traditional conservative approach, provides a creative openness to one's own story in a social context, as well as to new experiences. Each of the chapters in this section describes the application of a particular art type for DPS and includes an interview with an authority in the field directly linking this art type to DPS. In addition, a demonstrative case using DPS with that art type is provided.

Part III: provides details for application of the seven Expressive Arts with the three action methods **Psychotheatrics**: Imaginal for groups; Playwright for individuals and couples; and Montage for individual transformation in a collective setting.

Part IV: describes practical **applications** of DPS in Clinical and Counselling, Human Resources and Educational settings. Discussion for individuals engaged in their personal search for meaning is also included. Each chapter contains case studies and examples that apply to that particular domain. This section also addresses the need for competent facilitator skills providing specific information and steps necessary for effective practice.

Part I
Conceptual Foundations

1
Introduction: Destination or Journey

The journey gives the destination worth.
The letters ASAP form a familiar command: 'As Soon As Possible', yet the importance of the journey, weighed against the arrival at the destination, is interesting to consider.[1]

Dramatic Psychological Storytelling (DPS) presents a flexible seven-step model for insight and change. Anchored by Expressive Art and the action method, Psychotheatrics, DPS combines **drama** (expression through seven different Expressive Art types), with **psychology** (experiences of the individual and the collective), and **storytelling** (the content, the expression of an experience or situation). DPS creates a visual phenomenological, intersubjective framework as it depicts challenges, strategies and outcomes, whilst developing a dynamic storybook.

DPS's seven steps are explained and demonstrated throughout the book. Following is a list to introduce the terms used:

- Expressive Arts (seven types)
- Element (Psychotheatrics: Imaginal, Playwright, Montage)
- Craft (Rhetorical Analysis, Expressive Writing, Method of Physical Action)
- Story Map
- Dramatic Enactment
- Meaning
- Touchstone Story

If you have ever wished that you could see a complex personal, interpersonal or organisational dynamic broadly portrayed, in order to better understand or modify that dynamic, DPS offers a systematic process for doing just that. Using Expressive Arts and Psychotheatrics, DPS is effective for counsellors, psychologists, human resource practitioners, educators and other helping professionals. In addition DPS is utilised for personal awareness and self-discovery. This book is designed as a teaching tool, a manual for people who want to learn about and use DPS.

'State of the art technology will change. State of the heart, storytelling, will never change', Sid Ganis proclaimed as he presided over the previous year's big screen storytelling at Hollywood's Academy Awards in 2006.[2] As it reflects state of the heart, storytelling offers factual or metaphorical communication for building personal, interpersonal and collective comprehension. Combined with Dramatic Enactment, as it is in DPS, storytelling becomes a powerful visual connection for deep meaning. An uncomplicated case example outlines the model at the end of this chapter.

The mythic power of DPS resides in its connection with universal stories. When Touchstone Stories, distilled through group (and family), organisational or personal experience, assume the shape of familiar myths, they create a powerful connection with others, through time and space. Discovering that you are not the first – or the last – to face expulsion from Paradise contains solace when you realise that the dilemma which consumes you fits that mould. If you carry the story forward to see that it deals with coming of age, growth, or moving on, you then become free in a new way to explore solutions and to consider the next steps in your journey.

Drama can have a narrow definition as related specifically to theatre or, as used here, it can have inclusive and expansive connotations. To be dramatic is to be connected, active, vivid, striking or exciting and this energy can be expressed through many channels. The channels employed for reflecting and enacting stories in DPS are these seven Expressive Arts:

Narrative
Film
Theatre
Music
Visual Art
Dance and Kinaesthetics
Ritual and Epic

DPS invites a sense of fun and play, relaxing the constraints within which we hold ourselves. Creating stories using the Expressive Arts promotes a fresh, sometimes even humorous, look at life's challenges. Freed from the need to hand over a product, imagination can be spontaneous. Where in real life can we play out the future with little to no risk? DPS promotes exactly that kind of experience. Through Dramatic Enactment, scenes from the future can be created and those from the past revisited and revised. Relationships can be tested, old wounds opened and healed more effectively. By consciously producing and absorbing imagery that is simulated from life experience, the client reveals options. New awareness forms around the possible outcomes that may be chosen. Unconscious actions or motivations may become apparent, thus giving the client control that did not exist before.

Many of our current leaders are people who can't get enough: wealth, power, acclaim or freedom from personal responsibility. For ordinary individuals who experience having no potential for making a difference in world politics, the complexity of life in these times can become overwhelming and depressing. Many people face a crisis in meaning, reflected by the rise of depression as a major health concern in so-called first world nations.[3] The old gods are dead and mainstream religions escalate holy wars in this modern scientific age. Many people have nothing left to believe in or to join with and feel disconnected and alienated. Others, in an attempt to flee that sense of alienation, embrace religions that refute spiritual questioning. This fragmentation has isolated and polarised us.

A sense of identity and community is not easy to establish, even when one recognises the need. In contemporary culture we are diminishing connection with our deep roots in favour of looking good, having the best, or taking the most trips. DPS offers an alternative to this depletion, with access to the mythos, deep history in fact and spirit, as it relates to ordinary life.

Numerous disciplines are responding to a call for meaning, a spiritual connectedness to something more than just one's self. There is rediscovery and a new appreciation for the fundamental relevance of storytelling and the dramatic power of the Expressive Arts to explore, to discover and to connect. DPS focuses on **Meaning**. It provides a vehicle for the missing link: **connection.**

Most individuals, regardless of class, culture, or level of ability, can benefit from DPS as it is used to connect with personal meaning.

Feeling empowered in one's own experience impacts the immediate social environment. Connection with stories and ideas bigger than one's own knowledge and personal experience, offers hope and energy to engage challenges and create options for making the world a better place, one individual at a time.

The DPS process offers:

- Access to personal or group dynamics that are usually not forthcoming by employing an action method based on Storytelling and Dramatic Enactment of the Expressive Arts.
- Psychological protection for those involved and the enhancement of self-esteem through the detached witness approach.
- Cooperation and team building among people in conflict. By allowing 3D dynamics, it becomes possible to *see* how it is in others' shoes.
- Perspective on self and interpersonal relationships through the detached witness and by 'the other' approach.
- Fun in discovery and observational learning.
- Life experience with minimal risk to explore psychological insights through behavioural/cognitive/affective rehearsal.
- Personal, interpersonal and mythic connections. This is the very foundation of storytelling, drama and sacred psychology and the underlying structure of DPS.

According to Albert Einstein 'imagination is more important than knowledge'.[4] However, when it comes to making sense of personal and work life we need both artistic soul and rational intellect. Expressing personal, group and organisational stories in dramatic form can be deeply healing, challenging and transforming.

Sigmund Freud's 'talking cure' was founded on the idea that telling the story, confessing, relieved the person who carried a painful secret. James W. Pennebaker, in his book *Opening Up: The Healing Power of Expressing Emotions*,[5] describes his findings that writing authentic feelings about one's personal trauma for just a few minutes can reduce blood pressure. Transforming personal trauma or organisational angst into story or drama that can be comprehended from a distance, rather than experienced with overwhelming emotion, allows a sense of control. With the forest on stage, so that individual trees and bushes become visible, information needed for choices and decisions is more accessible than when scrambling around in the underbrush of immediate emotion.

Using DPS with groups and organisations experiencing conflict or working at cross-purposes can relax defences, explore sensitive areas and find common themes where none seem to exist. With Imaginal Psychotheatrics each group member can contribute to the story by adding a link, which in turn creates a powerful 'chained out' group story using Rhetorical Reality Analysis[6] that all members relate to and own psychologically. This group story can be further explored and developed through Dramatic Enactment; individuals gain fresh perspective on conflicts and their own contributions to the process. Seeing one's personal or organisational issues portrayed at a psychological distance, through the detached witness process, then discussed, reviewed and enacted by others, makes it possible to absorb information without having to protect self-esteem from direct encounters or influences.

DPS is engaging and active. It requires participants to tell their story – or a piece of it – and, depending on the Psychotheatrics Element in use, the client then utilises one of the Expressive Arts as a vehicle for storytelling. There is no need for grand production here; just the essence of the experience is sufficient. Everybody in a group or in an organisation has a point of view, an understanding of the team or the company. Rarely are most people asked for this point of view, nor would they feel safe sharing it. Problems arise because people act out covert feelings and attitudes, due to lack of opportunity to express authentic thoughts and feelings in a positive framework. People who barely speak to each other on the job site can find themselves working together to solve common problems after working with DPS.

If you work in counselling, education, human resources, or, if you are a person who is interested in expanding awareness of self and others on your own, DPS offers an accessible approach to information about the human condition. Professionals can utilise DPS in their repertoire and bring the skills they have to the process. For people exploring awareness and deepening consciousness, much of the process is accessible and useful. DPS enhances creativity due to its very special relationship to the world of the Expressive Arts, both for application as well as exploration. The pages that follow will demonstrate this approach and its specific applications. Although this is not a linear model, a linear map offers guidelines that can later be adapted to more circuitous applications. The following example shows the use of DPS in an uncomplicated case with a single client, supported by a Facilitator.

Dramatic Psychological Storytelling (DPS)

EXAMPLE

You are a therapist (the Facilitator) who has been seeing Mandy (the client) for some time. She has had a dream that feels important and exciting to her and she wants to explore it with you. (Setting and subject matter vary infinitely). Some of the dream's message seem obvious and helpful, but some elements remain veiled. The two of you decide to employ DPS. Here are the steps you might follow (streamlined for demonstration purposes):

1 Expressive Art

Although she is not accomplished as an artist, Mandy decides to try drawing a few significant aspects of the dream content and feeling. She will also be on the lookout for existing Visual Art or a Film that reflects her dream. (She could just as well have chosen to create a brief Theatre scenario, a Dance piece, or to reflect on a piece of Music. She could also utilise one or more of the other Expressive Arts.)

2 Element

Playwright Psychotheatrics will be the approach with Mandy as an individual. (For a group it would be Imaginal Psychotheatrics or, for an individual working in a collective setting, for character/personality transformation it would be Montage Psychotheatrics.)

3 Craft

In addition to creating the drawing, the client engages in a 20–30 minute Expressive Writing[7] session in which she writes as much as she can, associating with the dream and the drawing, allowing herself to write without censoring, as much as possible. (Here, the group would engage in Rhetorical Reality Analysis,[8] or the individual in a collective setting would utilise *Stanislavski's Method of Physical Action*[9]).

4 Story Map

The client follows the Story Map in Chapter 4, and briefly outlines the elements of the story as it has emerged, through her reflections on the dream, her drawing and writing.

5 Dramatic Enactment

With the Facilitator in a supportive role, the *client* brings all the previous steps to bear in working with the original drawing, re-engaging and expanding it, or by actualising the dream by utilising one or more of the other Expressive Arts. The Dramatic Enactment will be how Mandy chooses to express herself in relating to her experiences up to this point. She could create a Theatrical scenario, or choose a Film that demonstrates this for her, or an existing Visual Art piece – or more than one of these. She may or may not choose to return to the work she did with the original Expressive Art type – the drawing.

Overview on how to actualise and utilise the Expressive Arts in Dramatic Enactment is provided in Chapter 4 and full details are provided in each of the seven Expressive Arts chapters. Dramatic Enactment provides the client creative 'projection', observation as a **witness**, providing emotional safety and rational objectivity.

6 Meaning
Using all that has emerged in the previous steps, the client, with the Facilitator in a supportive role, discusses the material that has been revealed. Of course she may also take notes, record or collect the material in some way that is helpful to her.

7 Touchstone Story
Reflection, discussion, and perhaps more Dramatic Enactment, help refine the material so that a Touchstone Story emerges. (Note: More than one theme or Touchstone may surface here).

2
Intersubjective Meaning

The union of dramatic action, psychology of meaning and creative storytelling

The difference between the birth and the origins of something is the difference between the cry of new life and the song of the collective chorus; the difference between the beat of a new heart and the pulsating drumbeat of our ancestors. Birth, pink and rosy, looks forward. It does not need to justify itself, for it is full of strength, discovery, dance and laughter. Life does not ask such promise to justify itself. Yet, in times of challenge, of the abyss, the '*me*' is not enough. The collective, psychological, spiritual, '*we*' is necessary. Drama and storytelling offer us this union.

Dramatic Psychological Storytelling (DPS) combines **drama** (expression through seven different Expressive Art types), with **psychology** (experiences of the individual and the collective), and **storytelling** (the content, the expression of an experience or situation). Like nesting Russian dolls, each of these pieces contains elements of the other. Psychology and storytelling inhabit drama. Drama and storytelling inhabit psychology and so on. The DPS model spotlights and combines all three, displaying and clarifying scenarios from life experience to help us understand our relationship and connection with self, others, and the universe – past, present and future.

Dramatic

We need our myths and fairy tales, our legends and dreaming. We can take these dreams of the imagination and turn them into a material form through magic and illusion, and for a short time really believe they are true. Like with a play, a musical or an opera we can be transported into another reality and leave the theatre with a sense of wonder.

Ross Skiffington, Bell Shakespeare Company[1]

Dramatic methods use all three dimensions of time: past, present and future. Other educational, therapeutic and human resource procedures can tend to simply analyse the past or prepare for the future, missing important information and processes that can be found in the present moment.[2]

Dramatic methods make use of space, setting, environment, movement and all of the characteristics of humans (including voice, smell and/or physical presence). They can also work productively with intangible objects such as emotions, imagination, the energy of objects, symbols and meaning (Fox, 1987).[3] They can make these qualities tangible and workable. Therapists, educators, human resource professionals and individuals using dramatic methods are not constrained by content or by structure, in that the source of our possibilities is our imagination. Dramatic methods can physically engage these important aspects of self for educational and therapeutic use.

Dramatic methods, with their Expressive Arts base, can also recognise, engage and support the whole person. Of particular relevance is the way that dramatic methods use the whole body in the process. The approach using dramatic methods treats humans as whole beings, without an artificial separation of mind and body. Schutzenberger (1991),[4] for example, uses drama therapeutically with seriously ill cancer patients. She points to the findings of the new sciences of psycho-neuro-immunology and psycho-neuro-endocrino-immunology, the medical and scientific community and her own experience, to emphasise the importance of the influence of the mind/body.

Dramatic methods can also include the spiritual and metaphysical aspects of being and connect them when working on personal issues. For example it is possible to work, in a concrete and physical way, with personal symbols and dreams to externalise the internal world. This encourages exploration of spiritual and metaphysical aspects which can be connected and explored through dramatic action, reflecting on many different issues and concerns.

The Performance Continuum developed by Michael Wilson[5] highlights intensity levels of communication and performance and is directly relevant to the practice of DPS.

Conversation .... Cultural performance
Low intensity.................................... High intensity

Informal.. Formal
Subconscious................................. Conscious (performer)
Low risk.. High risk
Low rewards.................................. High rewards

Sharing stories would be a good example of a conversation at low intensity level. DPS uses all aspects of the Performance Continuum to assist, clarify and enhance the expression of Meaning for the client. A good example of DPS utilisation would be the client experiencing a cultural, high intensity, formal performance (case study '*Some Rooms*' in Chapter 10) involving high risk and rewards to the performers but low risk and high rewards to the client. Another example would be the client exploring their search for meaning in a low intensity, informal safe environment but with high rewards (case study *Changing Scenarios, Changing Lives* in Chapter 15).

Dramatic methods can offer the opportunity for fuller expression. Marcia Karp has been using dramatic action methods for many years. She states that the most important benefit of dramatic action is that it fulfils in people 'the need to have encouragement and time to tell their truth about what happens in life; to risk looking at what didn't happen, to uncover opportunities and to test alternatives'.[6] These aspects of dramatic action are also inherent in DPS and are very valuable tools for exploration and healing.

Psychological

> *A method that fits the small work and not the great has obviously started from the wrong end ...the commonplace may be understood as a reduction of the exceptional, but the exceptional cannot be understood by amplifying the commonplace. Both logically and causally the exceptional is crucial because it introduces...the more comprehensive category.*
>
> Egar Wind[7]

Passion for our work, compassion for others and imagination for the soul really matter in life. These three qualities are meaningful and are the areas that contemporary psychology should embrace. After years of wandering in the scientific psychological wilderness, more and more psychologists are finding nourishment in metaphorical psychology firmly based on meaning, using the mytho-poetic approach.[8]

The World Health Organisation recognises depression as one of the most significant health problems worldwide.[9] Many link this epidemic to an absence of meaning, the loss of soul and spirit. We need to understand that the soul is the core issue, not a 'phantom limb'! Possibly a key to the soul and our spiritual dimension is to recognise that we are part of the earth, not separate from it. We might appreciate more ancient ways of knowing, such as the practices of indigenous Australians who call on their ancestors and the spirits of the earth, an effective coping strategy in their culture to assist in grief and loss.

In looking for ways to understand human behaviour and alleviate mental and emotional pain, it seems that scientific psychology has focused on the commonplace and tended to ignore the sacred, providing partial explanations but shying away from the centrality of meaning. There is a tremendous need now for the appreciation of integrity and of wholeness, for the totality of the person rather than a reduction to bits and pieces. Anti-depressants will only help so much; science can only go so far. Instead there is a need to discover meaning through symbols, rituals and myths: the avenue to spirit and soul. There seems to be a profound link between the spiritual exile of the soul and a psychological exile in developmental terms. Religion brings with it a package: experiences, prayer, rituals, repentance, but it also brings a sense of righteousness that defines one group as true believers and others as outsiders. The essential spiritual dimension may be nurtured within organised religion but it can also be developed without the necessity of religious institutions or of ownership of a particular religious faith.

Lynda Sexson believes that 'religion is the creation of an imaginative...universe... Peculiar moments in ordinary lives, saturated by metaphor or personal symbol-making, are the stuff of religion'.[10] What is needed is the reparative experience of the soul. We need a fuller humanity with the recognition that healing involves much more than just the medical/scientific world.

Michael Whelan, Director of Aquinas Academy in Sydney and a Roman Catholic Priest, Dr Russell D'Souza, Senior Fellow, Mental Health Research Institute in Melbourne and Dr George Halasz, a Sydney Psychiatrist,[11] have much in common: meaning and spirituality. In their view there is an imbalance with the ascent of reason and intellect and the decline of the soul: a polarisation between science and religion creating a dichotomy between faith and reason. This has led to a stern world with a dualistic notion of what it is to be human. The 'scientific expert' knows best approach has focused on the expert's view rather than the client's experience. 'Carol Gilligan (1994, p. 19) asks how it was possible for thousands of psychotherapists over the years before the 1970s to spend countless hours treating, observing and diagnosing men, women and children in difficulties and "still not know about the incidence of incest and prevalence of domestic violence now deemed epidemic in the United States" by the conservative American Medical Association'.[12] This is quite simple to understand if we accept the expert imposing their paradigm on to the client's experience. They were not listening, only lecturing or talking at their clients. This denial of the client's reality is a form of positivistic oppression and violence. DPS joins with the client by the metaphorical use of the Expressive Arts, to reflect the client's experience and reality in order to allow the client to create their own meaning.

Scientists are not separate from the domain they study and professionals are not separate from their practice. Instead there is a need for critical thinking and reflexivity to recognise monologic assumptions and embrace dialogic influences. Furthermore, it is an error to only regard subjective experience as existentially and phenomenologically relevant. Equally, it is an error to emphasise the 'genetic' or diachronic view, that all can simply be explained in terms of natural positivistic law of past events or causes resulting in certain effects. Instead, subjective psychical space interprets experience as meaningful only through intersubjective experience with others. The hermeneutic model is particularly relevant as it recognises that we need to have our preconceptions challenged in order to develop. Our learning, therefore, is based on the effects we have on others and which they, in turn, have on us.[13] DPS is based on the supra-individual synchronic nature of simultaneous meaning, not the positivistic Newtonian clockwork universe of past and present causal relations. Meaning is shared and not purely subjective; rather, psychical space is intersubjective.

The union of intersubjective meaning with psychology means that our individual unique story joins with the emerging (global) story to become one. Meaning in psychology is valuing storymaking and storytelling. This is the art and practice of soul making, requiring that 'we die to one story to be born to a larger story'.[14] Our spiritual DNA contains our cultural Great Story(s). These timeless myths and fairytales are imprinted in our individual psyche and form our collective soul. Psychology needs to recognise the importance of the spiritual. Together, we create a richer story.

Our Great Story is from patterns, a commonality, which connects us across categories that bind cultures together. There is power from the archetypal world, an energy that comes from our soul, which helps us to **see** patterns, establishes our commonality and creates our meaning. If we listen to our soul, our inner voice, we will find our way!

The arts offer us keys to worlds of the exceptional, the creative, and to purpose, with real healing qualities. We can have a glimpse of this world by imagining the ancient Greek city Epidaurus, home of Asclepius, the God of healing. His tools were theatre, music, dance and dream. Serpents were the living symbol of this God (still surviving in the Caduceus, the symbol of modern medicine). Philosophy and athletics were spiritual practice. Mind, body and spirit were one; art, science and mystery were all valuable and harmonious. Together, each made a contribution to a fuller life.

'Science without religion is lame; religion without science is blind' (Albert Einstein). We can substitute sacredness for religion here, as religion needs the sacred but the sacred does not need religion to be relevant. We can be sacred/spiritual without belonging or seeing ourselves as members of a particular sect. Sacredness is a feeling or state of mind, which is personal and transpersonal. Religion is the way that state of mind gets codified into law and institutionalised. Therefore: 'Science without sacredness is lame, sacredness without science is blind.'

In DPS the created work contains personal material that carries a high degree of Meaning for the client. The individual places parts of his/her inner life on view to be turned and examined, reshaped and then re-internalised. From the point of view of object relations psychology, the work, or pieces of it, may become an 'internalised object', a part of its client/creator's psychological makeup. Viewing this process through the lens of intersubjective meaning, the work offers a place for soul baring and exploration.

In the song, *Somewhere, Over the Rainbow*, Judy Garland sings the last haunting line, 'Why, Oh why, can't I?' The answer is: you can! There is no place like home. Just click your heels. Sacredness is bigger than just 'me' It is about 'we', found through rituals requiring involvement. It is connectedness and generosity, the direct opposite of selfishness and narcissism, which lead to alienation, depression and aggression. DPS using Psychotheatrics and the Expressive Arts is unique, as it marries storytelling and the dramatic illustration of the Expressive Arts. It facilitates direct active 3-Dimensional, subjective and affective involvement. At the same time it offers cognitive rationality and psychological protection through distance as a witness.

This sacred component is connectedness and is important in DPS to explore psychological experience, as it is described through storytelling and expressed through dramatic action using the expressive arts. This process helps to reveal personal and interpersonal essence and Meaning.

Storytelling

> *The destiny of the world is determined less by the battles that are lost and won than by the stories it loves and believes in.*[15]
>
> Goddard

'Once upon a time....' These four words still return magic to our hearts, no matter if we are seven or seventy. Storytelling brings enchantment and anticipation and embraces that kaleidoscopic quality: imagination. Storytelling is the transmission of imagination, weaving our complex connections with each other. We tell stories to share, to teach, to bond; stories are our life force; stories are our existence. *The Elder Edda*, the bible of the ancient Vikings, taught that our immortality was our 'name'. Story keeps the name alive. In fact all bibles are our collective very special stories, encapsulating our values and culture. In *The Moor's Last Sigh*, by Salman Rushdie,[16] one of his characters comments that when we are dead, all that remains are the stories.

Jean Houston, the godmother of Sacred Psychology, believes that storytelling is the oldest form of teaching, fundamental to transmitting culture. Jesus taught through parables. We need to return the 'story' to our lives! Our fast food style, electronic culture with short, edited sanitised stories, creates bored people following meaningless advertising slogans for direction. The story needs to be living and dynamic; stories exist to be exchanged, to be the essence of human development. 'Myths orchestrate the culture and consciousness of entire civilizations.'[17] The rebirth of storytelling is a reaction to formula/jargon, which heralded the death of connection and meaning.

Our personal storytelling, according to James Hillman,[18] the father of Archetypal Psychology, is the way we remember; it is vital to our existence. Stories offer the images we need for a sense of personal calling, a reason for living. We need the BIG picture. We need romantic themes, beauty, mystery and myth. Our life story is beauty – and beauty, according to Thomas Aquinas in *Summa Theologia*, arrests motion; it is the cure for psychological malaise. This does not deny the ugly and the mean-spirited aspects of human nature, or the tragedy that strikes without warning. Without a personal story that holds beauty within it, linking into the Great Story that connects us, we are isolated and alienated. We have lost our way. 'Death is all around us, as it has always been. We need shamans and storytellers to help us make sense of it all'.[19]

Jack Zipes[20] believes that storytelling has, and always will have, two basic functions: (1) to enculturate by expressing the norms and customs of a group/culture in order to survive and, (2) to challenge and question the establishment, or dominant value system, with the intention of transforming and improving it.

'A real story touches not only the mind, but also the imagination and the unconscious depths of a person, and it may remain with her or him through many years, coming to the surface of consciousness now and then to yield new insights.'[21] The 'me' focus is boring; the experiences are monotone, singular, alone. If a person's story is shallow, with the same old view, same old time, same old things, there is no depth. A rut has occurred, stuck like a broken old phonograph record, on and on, the same old tune. Make the story rich, deep, flowing with possibilities. This is the difference between dis-ease and ease; illness and wellness. Expand and enrich the story. The song by Roberta Flack, *Killing me Softly with his Song* is the imposition of one story on another. It is flattening, deadening, maiming. Sometimes other cultures do this when they conquer. To impose a story is to maim and destroy. To live a story is to be; to create a story is to be divine. No 'ur-text'[22] with a fixed meaning should be imposed on a client's story by 'experts' deciphering and misinterpreting Carl Jung or Joseph Campbell in a rigid authoritative manner. Rather, story needs to be an emancipatory force not an oppressive one that is fixed. It needs to have direct relevance to client experience and meaning and thus can be changed and transformed by the client.

Francis Howard, an anthropologist at Ojai Foundation Conference on Storytelling stated: 'Sharing stories builds a sense of community. It triggers, it informs, inspires and gives the psyche strength, the courage and the connection to take action in the world'.[23] If we want to connect and nurture, then we share our story with others, which in turn, helps to nurture our self, along with others. A sense of community occurs when we realise we are not alone, that others have endured, triumphed and that we have commonalities; our isolation and alienation is transformed with other kindred spirits.

The very basis of human intimacy is storytelling. We are all capable of sharing a story; we just need the encouragement and opportunity for this experience to occur. The more we do, with real dialogue (not just the 'me' monologue) then the more we develop and grow. When we share our stories, we discover more about ourselves and others and they, in turn, learn about us. It is an enriching experience for a teacher, parent, or colleague to share their stories. Enriching for them and for us! Learning by experiencing through story is more powerful than any textbook. How wonderful when both are combined with the story enriching dry technical manuals, bringing them to life.

Storytelling is implicit drama; it is exciting. Story engages; it is demanding. It requires our attention. Great teachers and especially our friends use stories to reveal. We learn about values, expectations, and intimacy. Special bonds are created between a storyteller and listener, because stories connect us. Real storytelling requires dialogue and this leads to meaning, the essence of relationship, of existence. We have our modern storytellers; they work in schools, hospitals, and organisations. They help us to connect with one another and to understand that we are not alone. These new storytellers use traditional material but in new and creative ways. All the stories have commonalities. This is why they connect. They tell of triumphs, tragedies, heroes and villains, hope, love, betrayal. They weave an understanding that keeps us warm in chilly times, like the Grand Stories, or folktales of old.

Stories help to teach discipline; fairytales, for example, have critical moral codas. Stories help us to handle difficult emotional experiences; they inspire and we try to emulate those we admire. Effective storytelling is the foundation for powerful observational learning. Just read the biographies of achievers. This definition is not restricted to the rich and famous. Instead it means real achievement of the self – at ease with self. You will find many examples: someone you know personally perhaps, or inspirational individuals like Mother Teresa or Fred Hollows,[24] whose achievements are recognised the world over, through their memorable stories. Stories allow us to explore, rehearse, take risks and learn in a safe and comfortable environment.

John Dewey believed that learning should start with experience. This is only the beginning however, as it opens the doorway to enquiry.[25] Storytelling is a perfect vehicle in education to share experience and then use reflexivity to critically analyse the meaning of the experience for developmental purposes. The 'sense of storytelling that we try to instill in children cannot be accomplished if we do not explore all the arts.... which involves all the skills and talents of the children and opens their eyes to their potential'.[26] Dramatic expression using the arts allows one to experiment with possibilities and attain an almost 'Brechtian distancing effect that enables the children to step back from themselves, to step out of themselves and to become someone new'.[27] Storytelling has been shown to be effective for educational programs against bullying, for health promotion and social inclusion and is the very foundation on which Sesame Street bases its success. The relating of personal stories in therapy has been demonstrated to raise self-esteem and assist in dealing with demons through externalisation. In so doing, telling personal stories has been particularly effective in improving mental and physical wellbeing. In Human Resources, storytelling has been very effective for staff development purposes.[28] Organisations develop their own folklore, and storytelling becomes a very useful tool to illustrate and explore this further.[29] George Burns, a psychologist from Western Australia writes on the use of stories in therapy, *101 Healing Stories* (2001)[30] and offers some basic guidelines for storytelling to be effective: enthusiasm, experience, not just techniques; a story that fits; realness; flexibility, let the story change as needed; and maintain awareness of others, their need for interaction and dialogue.

The purposes of storytelling are: tradition, education, cultural identity, entertainment, therapy and spirituality. When storytelling is democratic and about community building, it is affirmative. Most stories have multiple characters and situations, therefore allowing clients to dynamically identify possibilities on many different levels. There can be a very dark side too, when story is imposed to control and manipulate others by those in power.[31] DPS is client-centered, with the client in conscious and rational control; professional assistance is designed to reflect the client's story not to impose expert interpretation. The Container Model of Storytelling suggests stories heal by acting as containers for intolerable affect and conflicting impulses, paralleling object relations. Storytelling and storylistening have been found to provoke an altered state of consciousness, or a 'story-stoned' state that seems to promote healing by creating a more receptive and less threatening environment in which to encounter and explore issues and purge demons.[32] Projective identification occurs when clients use stories to project unwanted and undesirable experiences or characteristics on to fictional others.[33] DPS, using the Expressive Arts, is ideal to utilise the Container Model and projective identification in conjunction with the client for developing and enhancing a feeling of wellbeing.

Conclusion

Learning how to use the Expressive Arts to dramatise our story is a joy. It is a discovery of the self: the interpersonal and the collective. Storytelling enlightens life's journey, its triumphs and trepidations. In our lives we fulfil dreams that transform into stories. Our legacy resides in the stories that remain after we are gone.

3
Expressive Arts

Tell me and I may forget.
Show me and I may remember.
Involve me and I will understand.
Confucius

The Expressive Arts channel creativity and offer diverse pathways for forming, sharing and appreciating human experience. Individuals gravitate toward art types that are comfortable and/or attractive to them as means of expressing themselves, communing with others, escaping the daily grind, or resonating with an aesthetic experience. This identification and connection holds a special place in *Dramatic Psychological Storytelling* (DPS). By entering the model through one's personal connection with the Expressive Arts rather than in a more linear, logical mode, openness to one's own story, as well as to new experience, is encouraged and enriched.

Expressive Arts are based on **story** and conveyed through **dramatic** action. In addition, each is **psychological** as it is expressed through the individual(s) in a social context. The seven Expressive Art types employed in DPS include:

1 Narrative
2 Film
3 Theatre
4 Music
5 Visual Art
6 Dance and Kinaesthetics
7 Ritual and Epic

The Expressive Arts hold the reflection of stories, created to convey Meaning. This is true for both the artist as creator and the participant as client. Both psychologically experience, identify with and establish connections to this phenomenon. Each Expressive Art type has a unique style in which the stories are dramatically presented in relation to the particular individual and the social/psychological context.

Each Expressive Art type can be arbitrarily divided into four components (adapted from Schechner, 2003):[1] **Performance** is the entire 'happening', the complete setting, before, during and after the action and involves performers as well as spectators. **Script** is the story, the information, the message. **Drama** is the reflection of the story through the particular Expressive Art type used. **Method** is the Expressive Art type used: Narrative, Theatre, Film, Music, Visual Art, Dance and Kinaesthetics, or Ritual and Epic.

The Expressive Arts share core commonalities and some obvious differences in their particular expression:

- All seven are public **performances** in differing degrees. Theatre, Film, Dance and Kinaesthetics, Music, Ritual and Epic offer easy illustrations as public events. Even though some forms of Visual Art and Narrative could be exclusively solitary events, this degree of isolation is rare. Other than private journaling, at some point the work is likely to be read or viewed by people beyond the artist or writer and becomes a public performance that involves other people.
- All seven share conventions of one type or another designed to facilitate and enhance the pursuit of the artist (creator) and participant (client) in the particular Expressive Art type. These conventions, or traditions, recognise and actually help create a special world quite different from everyday life. This special world is not superfluous but indispensable to purpose and meaning in human life.
- All seven are founded on **storytelling**. In fact, the very essence of each Expressive Art type is centred in a story, which is its heart.
- All seven are **dramatic** as they involve expressive action. DPS expands the definition of drama from its theatrical origins to include the actualisation of artistic/social dramatic life proceedings that are memorable, significant and vivid.
- All seven are **psychological** as they are about the phenomena of meaning to the individual in a social context and assist in establishing collective identity.

Seven Expressive Arts	**Seven Multiple Intelligences***
Narrative	Linguistic or verbal – language
Film	Intra-personal – self understanding
Theatre	Inter-personal – social understanding
Visual Art	Spatial – mental maps
Music	Music
Dance and Kinaesthetics	Body and Kinaesthetics
Ritual and Epic	Intra-personal and Inter-personal
All 7 Expressive Arts in DPS use the rational/objective witness approach	Logical and mathematical*

* The DPS model is paradoxical as it is both non-linear and intersubjective in process, and also it is rational in the use of the objective witness approach to ensure protection. The key is to promote meaning; reason is critical, moving beyond the pure emotional feelings of Aristotelian catharsis. Instead, a dynamic is created to make choices. There is detachment, a witness process. From the outside looking in, one can alter viewpoints and take different sides in the issue being explored. The process facilitates 'point of recognition' and promotes insights – rationality is paramount.

The seven Expressive Arts are complementary to the work of Howard Gardner in multiple intelligences.[2] His view is that intelligence is practical and is an ability or set of abilities to solve complications or create products related to cultural contexts.

Intra-personal and Inter-personal intelligences are found to be highly related to emotional intelligence.[3] This is the ability to understand and control one's own emotion as well as to understand what others are feeling.

The above chart relating the seven Expressive Arts to the seven Multiple Intelligences only highlights the dominant relation, whereas there are also secondary relations. For example, Film is individually oriented so it would have dominant intra-personal aspects but it also has a strong inter-personal connection. The same applies, but in reverse, for Theatre. Most of the seven Expressive Arts would reflect more than one of the multiple intelligences.

Expressive Arts in Dramatic Psychological Storytelling

Each of the Expressive Arts described below is applicable to DPS from the point of view of both the artist/creator and client or, in other words, the performer and the viewers who are engaged and active participants in the process. Whether in a therapeutic, educational, organisational or personal setting, one can be the artist/creator or the client in DPS.

Narrative

Have you ever heard a friend tell a story about something you experienced, and you barely recognise the event? What you remember as mildly interesting has become thrilling and magical in the telling, complete with dramatic gestures and sound effects. Narrative can be anything from the most boring lecture to an action-packed cliffhanger, but the common ground is the transmission of information, imagery and emotion from one person to another, through descriptive speech or writing. We can only speculate about the origins of narrative storytelling, but we know the art is ancient and universal.

Anne Pellowski has written an analysis of the history of narrative storytelling in her book *The World of Storytelling*.[4] She has suggested that narrative storytelling had its origin in play activities, with gifted but ordinary folk entertaining their particular social group informally. Gradually these activities were included in religious rituals, historical recitations and educational functions. Christina Baldwin tells us, 'Life hangs on a narrative thread. This thread is a braid of stories that inform us about who we are, and where we come from, and where we might go...when the power of story comes into the room, an alchemical reaction occurs that is unique to our kind...'.[5]

William C. Menninger used literature[6] – books, poetry, newspapers and magazine articles for adjunctive homework to enrich the therapeutic environment. According to Menninger, literature serves therapeutic, educational, recreational and social purposes. Literature has immediate gratification, provides externalisation of issues and problems and facilitates social interaction through discussion and review.

Narratives reveal the meaning people give to life experiences and the subsequent development of these into storylines. These storylines have significant ramifications on our life and relationships. Reality depends on the perspective we have and our interpretation of experience. Thin storylines tend to be rigid and oppressive. It is important to explore other life experiences that can then be interpreted with positive meaning and see if these can be incorporated into the storylines to add breadth and healing.[7]

DPS also utilises the power of Narrative to unveil, illustrate and convey meaning in therapeutic, educational and human resources settings.

DPS is an ideal vehicle to alter perspectives by re-authoring experience and therefore changing the meaning we attach to our relationships and subsequently to our life and the way we live it.

Film

Film includes cinema, television and photographs. An art type that began as electronic theatre has evolved to include interactive games that give even very young children access to highly complex interactive entertainment and information technology. The capacity to store data and repeat it limitlessly broadens the scope of anything that becomes its subject. An audience viewing a film shares an experience with another person who may see the same movie at home on a DVD, or by watching the same television program, universalising that experience at a global level.

Film can also be used to record actions or artistic performances that can then be re-viewed by the artist/creator and the client and can become part of future performances.

Films have a close relationship with metaphor. They provide safe distancing from actual life experiences and allow the client to become the protagonist in their own story. Each provides a vehicle to rehearse possible solutions to situations. Film, like metaphor, bridges the gap between what was, is now and future possibilities. Film provides both affective as well as cognitive insights necessary for change. Cognitive insights tell what to do but affective insights provide motivation to enable change. Film provides identification as it deals with stories of individuals not philosophical abstractions. In so doing, it is a perfect vehicle for reversing negative world views by reframing techniques. Individuals emotionally distraught or with learning difficulties seem to find films much more accessible than other media such as written narrative for instance.[8]

Photo-voice[9] is a process that allows people to illustrate how they see their world through the use of photographs. This 'voice' is empowering and can be the basis for conversations concerning their life, or their personal story. It can also be an ideal vehicle to use in therapeutic, human resources and educational settings.

Films represent a wide variety of different types of media that impacts on their direct use. Cinema and television direct broadcasts do not allow stopping the action to discuss or review, but this seems to be a minor issue when revisited later. Obviously videotapes, DVD and photos do allow direct intervention at key points to highlight aspects.

Use of Film with DPS as stimulus material for individuals and group interaction is almost limitless. Simulation, as seen on the 'cold' medium of Film allows for safety as a witness but is very 'hot' with identification. It can seem more real than life and because of its static and repeatable nature, is more accessible for review and study.

Theatre

Theatre's unique offering is the interaction of live players with an audience that creates a particular type of intersubjective space – the presentation of the human condition to a group of people who carry their feelings and impressions away into their own lives. Interpersonal connection and understanding form the fundamental base of theatre. Community ritual and theatre have strong historical links founded on the oral tradition of storytelling.

According to Phillip Moore in his work *Acting Out – Therapy for Groups*,[10] theatre draws upon the imagination, creativity, cognition, verbal skills and perhaps, most importantly, the life experience of participants who are empowered to explore issues directly relevant to them and to express their doubts and fears in a safe and supportive space. Theatre is experiential and may provide a deeper learning experience on both the cognitive and emotional levels. Theatre is about extending boundaries of time and place as far as they can go, including our emotional responses to them. Performing life issues makes it possible to isolate an event or to compare one event with another. We can look at situations that have happened to other people in other places and times perhaps, or look at one's own experience after the circumstance within the safety of knowing that just at this moment it is not really happening.[11]

Theatre has a long tradition as a forum for exploring controversial issues, confronting difficult situations and for generating and facing disturbing emotions. Dramatising metaphorical stories is effective as it distances the client from the difficult experience but allows them to re-experience this in a safe environment, which can then be used for integration.[12]

Augusto Boal's work utilises Theatre to examine individual, internalised oppressions and then illustrates these in a larger social context. His view of catharsis is especially significant as he views the Aristotelian catharsis as coercive by urging the purging of emotions and asocial tendencies by the establishment. Instead he advocates a rational catharsis that challenges the controlling group by exposing and then removing the blocks of social external control imposed by them. He points out that these are then internalised in order to oppress by institutions such as the school, family and church. Boal's 'cop in the head' and other theatre techniques challenge the external imposition of control on our psyche.[13]

Theatrical processes can assist in spotlighting disruptive and persistent ways of being that are dysfunctional. These same theatrical activities according to Alida Gersie[14] can also facilitate exploration of other possibilities of being and in so doing help to explore more satisfying ways of living.

The work of Renee Emunah[15] emphasises using theatre with clients to allow them to try and achieve something that in real life was too difficult or frightening. Once this barrier has been broken, it is less difficult to then actualise this experience in real life. There is a powerful relationship between stage life and real life. Theatrical behaviours unite the cognitive and affective; these then become part of the client's repertoire and can now be used in real life. Applying Theatre is a good way to try new experiences and also reveal and face our shadow side.

DPS uses Theatre to express experience, develop story, try new possibilities, face the shadow side and integrate new aspects of self and meaning in a safe place provided by the witness perspective. It emphasises cognitive control with affective integration. In DPS the client never role plays self directly, portraying only others, in order to ensure distance and control. This is similar to Robert Landy's[16] 'aesthetic distance' based on theatrical and psychological principles, which retains the cognitive over-distanced observer, with the under-distanced participant. DPS offers the possibility of understanding and relating to complex emotional and cognitive states using Theatre in a simple and comprehensible manner.

Music

The art of moving feelings by combinations of sounds is half of the definition of music. The other half has to do with the expression of those feelings by combinations of sounds. We can only imagine the origins of music. Vocal expression imitating human or animal sounds, rhythmic expression of love, fear, pain, or the simple beating of the human heart. Music offers capacity for expression and connection at a non-linear, non-verbal level.[17]

Music has been shown to produce a positive dynamic influence on the psychological, physical, cognitive and social functioning of individuals and on groups. In addition, positive therapeutic changes have occurred to individuals experiencing health or educational problems. Music can act as a positive coping mechanism for those under intense pressure. It is a way to create your own environment when you have little control of your circumstances.[18] In particular, listening to and/or performing music can enhance emotional wellbeing, physical health, social functioning, communication abilities and cognitive skills through musical responses.[19]

The ability to process and express experience solely through words is rare in children and also in many adults, due to lack of cognitive or language sophistication. Music is a creative and symbolic form of engagement and communication that can enhance the processing and expression of experience for those clients who may have difficulty doing so otherwise.[20]

In therapeutic, educational or corporate settings, DPS can utilise Music in the design of programs for individuals and groups based on client needs. This model is ideal for therapists, educators and human resource professionals, who may incorporate the use of Music for identification and exploration of significant issues and important topics as well as emotional and cognitive states. In particular DPS can utilise Music through improvisation, receptive music listening, song writing, lyric discussion, music and imagery, music performance and learning through Music. Professionals using the model in this way may incorporate music even as they participate in interdisciplinary treatment and planning, on-going evaluation and follow up.[21]

Visual Art

The power of Visual Art to connect the individual with the inner self as well as with the energy of the collective and the collective unconscious speaks to those who are open to taking in the experience. When art comes through a flow state, it contains unconscious form, the parts that the artist does not necessarily intend – brush strokes, accidents of form, unintentional colours or objects, in addition to the more obvious aspects of colour, form and content. It may well be the unconscious form emerging through the work that connects in a powerful way with the viewer, triggering a shift from the analytical, linear, verbal left side of the brain to the less organised sensual, non-verbal right side. The resulting experience may be pleasurable, 'oceanic' immersion or connection with other strong feelings such as joy or fear.[22]

Visual Art can be used as a magical gateway for expressing experience. A good example is the connection we have with our environment, what better way to express this connection than through original Visual Art using natural materials. The Environmental Education Conference held in Adelaide found 'sculptures and prints describe more powerfully than words how students forge connections with their environment'. Visual Arts were an integral part of life in ancient times and reflected people's connections to each other and their environment. In today's world there is a re-discovering of visual arts for expressing experience, communication and identity building.[23]

Visual artists work from as many perspectives as there are artists – some meticulously creating their works to fulfill a vision, some working with the material to be surprised by what evolves, and others engaging the process from every step along this continuum. The work may be mainly self-expressive or intended to be evocative for the viewer. Viewers bring their own perspective and may be in synchronization with the artist's intent or have a powerful experience or interpretation that is not at all what the artist intended.

Sharing this artistic experience with others through DPS has the power to unveil feelings and motivation that have been hidden, or are barely in the artist's or the participant's awareness. Bringing these feelings into the open not only allows revelations for the individual, but for others who may have a related experience with the work of art or the art-making process. Utilising DPS opens the possibility of refining the experience so that clarity of Meaning may emerge from what may otherwise have been a powerful but incoherent experience.

Dance and Kinaesthetics

Bodies sharing movement in space create their own energy mass. Reaching back to the beginning of time, tribal ritual dancing is hypnotic, leading to altered states. The most formal ballet tells a story. Social dancing has been a significant part of human conversation throughout the ages. Dance has been used by people of many cultures to express powerful emotions, tell stories, treat illness, energise for battle, celebrate important events and maintain communal bonds.[24]

Mind and body are inseparable and there is a strong need for non-verbal means of expression, reflected in the growing use of Dance and Kinaesthetics in therapeutic, human resources and educational settings.[25] Memories formed during highly significant moments, positive and negative, are stored in the body and are much more accessible through physical expression.[26] 'While verbal utterance of emotion may be withheld or disguised, its non-verbal expression cannot be entirely controlled. An action as simple as walking may reflect the prevailing mood'. Human emotion is mainly a body experience and this concept has implications for mental and physical health, as well as educational ramifications.[27]

DPS can harness this power of movement in a therapeutic, educational or organisational setting and use it to promote personal growth, health and wellbeing. The key assumption that the body and mind are interrelated has extremely important ramifications – personally, organisationally and globally. Mind and body are one. We are one with others. We are one with the earth. We are connected. Dance and Kinaesthetics are about being one: the unity. DPS recognises and supports the views of many dance therapists and practitioners of kinaesthetics, that mental and emotional problems are often held in the body. Conversely, the state of the body can affect attitude and feelings, both positively and negatively.[28]

Ritual and Epic

'Definitional ceremonies' are collective meaning autobiographies according to Victor Turner. These are enacted during rites and rituals, where a group continues or creates its identity by marrying the living present to the vibrant cultural past. This super-ordinary state is in stark contrast to ordinary day to day life based on left brain cause and effect positivism. Instead ritual and rites tend to engage the right hemisphere brain – intuitive, holistic and synthesising. Meaning is not objective, fixed or rigid, but intersubjective and selective and can be created or continued through enactment of Ritual and Epic events.[29]

Welfare State and many other groups use Ritual and Epic events to create intersubjective meaning to enrich individuals, groups, and entire communities. 'In a world where the shared culture of human beings is increasingly threatened by largely imposed electronic culture, myths and archetypes have to be discovered and re-made not simply revived ... To mark moments of ceremony in ways that would honour their importance, *Welfare State* began to devise for particular groups of people, new ceremonies, using the talents, personalities, images and ideas of the people for whom they were made ... These events have ritualistic elements in which reason, reflection and awareness are heightened'.[30]

Whether it is the international crowd attending the Olympic games or a small group gathered to watch a Ritual like a marriage ceremony, a funeral, or a baptism, or an epic event like the *Live8* Concert to ameliorate world poverty and hunger, this shared experience is worthy of exploration. The ritualised wedding ceremony is a classic example of the importance of a Ritual that is part of all cultures. Even if all members of a particular culture do not have their own wedding, everyone knows what the occasion signifies. Both participants and observers are changed by these proceedings as they reflect common hopes, fears, dreams and experience. Often we walk away from events of this nature, knowing we have been part of a meaningful experience. We have difficulty, however, obtaining much clarity about the meaning in any way that we can articulate or use to make sense of the ritual. Exploring the intersubjective space created at Ritual and Epic events using DPS shows us the path into a more personal and social understanding of these experiences.

Conclusion

From the beginning of time people have expressed themselves in artistic ways, involving themselves in activities that offer pleasure and meaning but may have no 'practical' application. Such activities have transporting qualities that offer freedom, with the focus shifted from the cares of everyday life. This brief overview is intended to highlight the Expressive Arts as they relate to DPS and stimulate thinking about the art types and their possibilities as conduits for finding and creating Meaning. Each will be developed in depth later with accompanying case studies and interview material.

4
Dramatic Psychological Storytelling

Dramatic Psychological Storytelling (DPS) is an accessible and powerful tool for exploration of human experience in the hands of a skilled Facilitator such as a therapist, educator or human resource professional. Through the Expressive Arts, story and dramatic expression, DPS creates a vehicle for exploring experience(s) or psychological dynamics that seem significant and important. DPS also provides a process for reviewing and managing conflict.

DPS utilises **Psychotheatrics**, a method based on rational, witness objectivity that enhances internal locus of control.[1]

There are three Psychotheatrics Elements that are designed for different client configurations:

- **Imaginal Psychotheatrics** which focuses on the target **group** (Chapter 12)
- **Playwright Psychotheatrics** is designed for the **individual**, or pair (Chapter 13)
- **Montage Psychotheatrics** has been specially created for personality and character transformation in a **collective** setting. (Chapter 14)

Briefly, however, Psychotheatrics is a vehicle that further develops and explores material from Step 1, the seven Expressive Arts (Chapter 3) to dramatically express the story of the client. It forms Steps 2 and 3 of DPS. In Step 2, there are three Psychotheatrics Elements, allowing for individual, group or collective work. Step 3, Craft, differs for each of these three Psychotheatric Elements in order to allow for the individual, group or collective to create and actualise their stories. Furthermore DPS is based on a rational foundation that allows the client to always be in the position of an objective witness rather than to be subjectively overwhelmed.

All three types of Psychotheatrics are about change, with the client in charge but supported by the Facilitator. Although the three types of Psychotheatrics share a common theoretical foundation as dramatic action methods, the framework for each that arises out of this shared foundation is quite different. DPS selects the appropriate Psychotheatrics Element for a particular application, using one or more of the seven Expressive Arts (Narrative, Film, Theatre, Music, Visual Art, Dance and Kinaesthetics, Ritual and Epic) outlined in Chapter 3.

This chapter will address the commonalities of DPS shared by each Psychotheatrics Element. Later the particular unique framework for each Psychotheatrics Element will be elaborated.

The seven action steps of DPS include:

1. **Expressive Arts** (Narrative, Film, Theatre, Music, Visual Art, Dance and Kinaesthetics, Ritual and Epic)
2. **Element** (Imaginal, Playwright, or Montage Psychotheatrics)
3. **Craft** (Rhetorical Reality Analysis, Expressive Writing, Method of Physical Action)
4. **Story Map** (Guidelines charting the important features of the story)
5. **Dramatic Enactment** (Using any one or more of the seven Expressive Arts)
6. **Meaning** (Clarifying the significance, implications, essence, substance of revealed material)
7. **Touchstone Story** (Key aspects, model, patterns, paradigm, blueprint, benchmark, distilled essence)

This brief outline of the seven action steps in DPS overviews the process and can serve as a quick reference as you plan and activate your experience with DPS.

1 Expressive Arts

Ask the client to list relevant examples in as many of 7 categories as possible for later exploration and storytelling possibilities.

Narrative – oral, informal writing, book, poem, news article
Film – cinema, television, video camera, photographs
Theatre – formal play, performance, or an informal scenario
Music – song, concert, composition, group practice
Visual Art – painting, drawing, collage, installation, performance

Dance and Kinaesthetics – choreographed or informal; designed movement, sport, viewing performance
Ritual and Epic – ceremony (birth, marriage); spectacle, happening (Olympics), organisational ritual

What is the type of story? Is there a foundation that reflects the structure of the story? Any one or more of the seven Expressive Arts may assist to reflect the story. Here are formats to think about – all of these can be bittersweet:

Coming of age	Life crisis
Succeeding against all odds	Dreamings
Creation	Initiation
Conflict	Epiphany
Marital struggle or marital bliss	Joy of discovery
Addiction	Loss

For example, with Narrative you could tell the story of coming of age. This could simply be an oral story of a personal experience, or there may be a poem or novel or even a parable like the *Garden of Eden* (Chapter 5, Narrative) that you have heard or read that has aspects that represent your story as a starting point. Or, you may find your story of succeeding against all odds represented in the Film, *Whale Rider* (Chapter 6, Film). Possibly seeing a Theatre production of *The Jester* by Carey Allen (Chapter 7, Theatre) could bring to the surface some uncomfortable psychological aspects of your story. Similarly, seeing a theatre performance of *Face to Face* by David Williamson reminds you of a bullying episode that was significant in your life (Chapter 17, Education and Awareness). A Visual Art experience like *Portent and Portal: The Soul and Spirit of Everywoman*, at the Gregory Kondos Gallery (Chapter 9) may also express important parts of your story. In Music, a certain voice or instrumental piece may speak to you psychologically by helping to express something meaningful to you. The lyrics or composition may relate to parts of your story (Chapter 8, Music). Possibly a Dance performance, like the Sydney Dance Company production of *Changing Rooms*, may express a challenging experience to assist you in coming to terms with significant past periods in your life story (Chapter 10, Dance and Kinaesthetics). Experiencing an event can have a very profound impact on you, like seeing *Kelso High School* (Bathurst, NSW, 2005) *after* it was totally destroyed by fire (Chapter 11, Ritual and Epic).

Any one or a combination of these seven Expressive Arts can be harnessed to help explore a personal, group or collective story. This experience and involvement with the Expressive Arts can portray aspects of a story, or assist in the further exploration of the story, or clarify which story will be the focus of the work to come.

2 Element (*Psychotheatrics Method*)

The context for DPS determines which Psychotheatrics Element will apply.

- For a targeted group that shares a common variable use **Imaginal Psychotheatrics** (Chapter 12).
- For an individual, couple or very small group use **Playwright Psychotheatrics** (Chapter 13).
- When working with designed character/personality transformation use **Montage Psychotheatrics** (Chapter 14).

Each of the Psychotheatrics chapters, Imaginal, Playwright and Montage, describes that Element in detail, providing the information to guide you through the process. Chapter 18, Facilitator Skills, adds suggestions for facilitating DPS using Psychotheatrics and the Expressive Arts in Clinical and Counselling, Educational and Human Resource settings.

Psychotheatrics was originally developed in 1979 and was designed for psychotherapy, awareness and behaviour change, based on theatrical and therapeutic principles. Even back then, Psychotheatrics was heralded as a significant contribution based on rational perspectives to allow the client to stay in control: 'Psychotheatrics goes far beyond the usual psycho-dramatic techniques and it is much more therapeutic in scope', stated Albert Ellis, Director, Institute for Advanced Study in Rational Psychotherapy, New York City.[2]

Since then Psychotheatrics has been seamlessly incorporated into Dramatic Psychological Storytelling, which focuses on the seven Expressive Arts. DPS is quite different from psychodrama which emphasises the subjective, emotional, spontaneous approach driven by the therapist. In stark contrast, DPS highlights objective, rational, planned action driven by the client, with assistance from the professional facilitator. It focuses on individual responsibility in a social context and the discovery of options for structuring and re-structuring behaviour patterns in Clinical and Counselling, Human Resources and Educational settings.

3 Craft

Each of the three different Psychotheatrics Elements uses a different Craft for implementation.

- Imaginal Psychotheatrics uses Rhetorical Reality Analysis.
- Playwright Psychotheatrics uses Expressive Writing.
- Montage Psychotheatrics uses Method of Physical Action.

Imaginal Psychotheatrics – Rhetorical Reality Analysis

This Psychotheatrics Element is designed to work with a group that shares a common characteristic, like driving under the influence of alcohol. The Facilitator has identified some key goals and objectives for this group and now encourages a volunteer, or recruits a group member, to share an experience (a scenario/story) related to the goals of the group. This story can be based on any one or more of the seven Expressive Arts. For example the client may simply tell of an experience that happened to them related to driving under the influence, or how a particular movie affected them related to alcohol or drug abuse or... Next this story is *chained out* by other group members, one by one. One critical requirement is that each person's contribution must relate to the original story experience told by the first member and then modified by the other group members. It must be real for the group member adding to the story. As each group member adds a link to the growing story chain the story continues; it grows stronger and more powerful. Each link in the chain segment should only be a short scenario; otherwise we tend to lose the energy created. This story only needs to be a short illustration of a group member's experience that relates to the developing story. A complete description of the Rhetorical Reality Analysis process, based on the work of Ernst Bormann[3] is contained in Chapter 12 – Imaginal Psychotheatrics. Case study examples of Imaginal Psychotheatrics are in Chapters 5 Narrative, 7 Theatre, 15 Clinical and Counselling, 16 Human Resources and 17 Education and Awareness.

Playwright Psychotheatrics – Expressive Writing

Expressive Writing, based on James Pennebaker's work[4] creates the groundwork for the Dramatic Enactment using one or more of the seven Expressive Arts. Expressive Writing is a very easy process to use. The only necessary rule is to spend at least 20 minutes and no more than 30 minutes writing the experience from Step 1 in DPS, the Expressive

Arts. The story reflected in one or more of the seven Expressive Arts is chosen because it is personal (with possible links to interpersonal and transpersonal) and particularly relevant to the individual so touched. The process is deceptively simple, but incredibly powerful and pertinent. A full description is contained in Chapter 13 Playwright Psychotheatrics. Case study examples of Playwright Psychotheatrics are to be found in Chapters 6 Film, 8 Music, 9 Visual Art, 10 Dance and Kinaesthetics, 11 Ritual and Epic, and 17 Education and Awareness.

Montage Psychotheatrics – Method of Physical Action

We have adapted the Method of Physical Action created by Konstantin Stanislavski and later modified by Jean Benedetti.[5]

Using the Method of Physical Action to actualise the new character role chosen, is a detailed and powerful process that requires several phases to implement. The Real 'I' is sustained (your centre of self) but incorporates the thought patterns (cognitions), feelings (affective domains) and behavioural actions of the new character to create the transformation. A full description of the Method of Physical Action is contained in Chapter 14 Montage Psychotheatrics. A case study example of Montage Psychotheatrics is in Chapter 16 Human Resources.

4 Story Map

To develop the story, use the illustrated Story Map[6] by following the signposts on the left and writing and/or drawing notes in the right column. The Story Map can be used with any of the Expressive Arts as each reflects a story (as many stories, actually, as there are perspectives!)

Title Succinctly describe your story.	
Orientation Who is in the story? When is it happening? What is going on? How will you start your story? What will your first sentence be? Where is it happening? What will the setting look like? What words will you use to describe the setting and how can you help paint a mind picture?	

Initiating Event What specific event inspired you to create this story?	
Complication What challenge(s) does the main character need to overcome?	
Sequence of Events What events happen first, next, last? What does the main character do? Does he/she act and react in a believable way?	
Resolution How will things work out? What issues need to be confronted? How will your story end?	
Coda The message or moral of the story.	

5 Dramatic Enactment

The Dramatic Enactment of the story, using any one or more of the seven Expressive Arts, may come at several different times. A suggestion is that it is utilised after the original scenario is developed by the Story Map, but it may come later after the Meaning and Touchstone Story steps. Dramatic Enactment may be used more than once throughout the process, depending on the needs of the client(s) and may be dramatically expressed through any one or a combination of the seven Expressive Arts: Narrative, Film, Theatre, Visual Art, Music, Dance and Kinaesthetics, and Ritual and Epic.

The key is to choose situations or combinations that reflect the story or aspects of it – brief, condensed thumbnail illustrations that highlight and represent this. It is not really important to be exact here, or to be a perfectionist, just to try and do it. The process will then flow as the client and others explore and identify these significant moments. Dramatic Enactment is firmly based on the principles of *Epic Theatre* developed by Bertolt Brecht.[7] 'The process seems to need only parts of the story, not the story as a whole.'[8] 'Work is based on a highly selective use of certain aspects of the story.'[9]

The Dramatic Enactment process is fluid; it combines open-ended storytelling with dramatic expression rather than following a rigid, fixed plot. The key is to promote Meaning; reason is critical, moving beyond the pure emotional feelings of Aristotelian catharsis. Instead, a dynamic is created to make choices. There is detachment, a witness process. From the outside looking in, one can alter viewpoints and take different sides in the issue being explored. This process facilitates 'point of recognition' and promotes insights. The purpose is to develop a fluid process that is flexible and responsive, not to have a fixed-point story. The Dramatic Enactment can be emotionally cathartic as well as rational. However, the emotional aspects of catharsis should not overwhelm the logical as, in this process, rationality is paramount.

Applications of Therapeutic Enactment[10] are complementary to our use of Dramatic Enactment in DPS. Like DPS, the work of Marvin Westwood, Patricia Keats and Patricia Wilensky address aspects of Moreno's model of psychodrama that jeopardises the possibility of resolution and repair for clients due to four main factors: individual safety, role of spontaneity, purpose of catharsis and lack of attention to the group/social context.

Psychodrama does not prefer to engage the client in careful planning involving reviewing events. Instead the therapist in psychodrama is in full control of the situation and makes strategic decisions without the client's conscious consent. Spontaneity is actively pursued and encouraged in psychodrama as a successful end product, under the direction of the therapist. Psychodrama focuses on a subjective catharsis, in order to encourage an Aristotelian purging of emotions. Finally, there is a very individual, protagonist focus in psychodrama.

DPS unlike psychodrama engages the client in careful planning involving revisiting past, engaging present and envisioning future situations in order to enhance positive outcomes. The client is in full conscious control of the situation in DPS, assisted by a professional facilitator. Spontaneity in DPS is used as as a bridge to transformational learning and is the starting point of change, enabling the client to carry this forward and apply it to specific life situations. Catharsis in DPS is enhanced through the objective detached witness perspective, which leads to rational/emotional epiphanies. Finally DPS emphasises that Meaning for an individual is in an intersubjective/social context.

Examples of Dramatic Enactment can be found in the case studies illustrated in Imaginal Psychotheatrics: Chapters 5 Narrative, 7 Theatre, 15 Clinical and Counselling, 16 Human Resources and 17 Education and Awareness; Playwright Psychotheatrics in Chapters 6 Film, 8 Music, 9 Visual Art, 10 Dance and Kinaesthetics, 11 Ritual and Epic and 17 Education and Awareness; Montage Psychotheatrics is in Chapter 16 Human Resources.

6 Meaning

The classic power of the sacred is of particular relevance here and is found in the poetic/literary combination of drama, storytelling and psychology. The work of Bill Blaikie, academic in Theatre Arts at Charles Sturt University reflects this creative combination. He comments: 'When drama, through storytelling and (phenomenological) psychology, breaks the metaphor of our self-centred construct and allows us access to a relationship with the larger picture based on selfless values, then something sacred has probably happened. Breaking a restrictive metaphor and replacing it with a grander one, makes us realise that we belong to something far bigger than the family, the nation or the gender construct into which we have been socialised.'[11]

This step, finding Meaning, is the time to review what has taken place through the journey up to this point. Reflect on each of the steps: the Expressive Arts, the Psychotheatrics Element used, the Craft method which assisted in reflecting the developing story, the Story Map which helped frame the story developed through the Craft, and then the Dramatic Enactment which helped to further illustrate the story. What is the Meaning of all this? What values and attitudes were expressed? What is known and what has been discovered? What is disturbing and what is precious? Where will this lead in the future? What will happen? In which areas can I/we make choices?

7 Touchstone Story

Once the original story has been transformed through the Craft type utilised, then further developed through Story Map, and illustrated through the Dramatic Enactment, there is time for reflection of Meaning. A transcendence of new understanding has occurred, resulting in the Touchstone Story. Each Psychotheatrics Element has a different method of arriving at this very important stage, highlighted primarily through the Craft type and then illustrated through the use of one or more of the seven Expressive Arts in Dramatic Enactment. For Imaginal Psychotheatrics this point is reached in a group setting. Using Rhetorical Reality Analysis, each group member adds a link to form a powerful story chain. Playwright Psychotheatrics uses written summary scenarios that then form a pattern. Montage Psychotheatrics uses character rehearsal to arrive at a transformation. It should be emphasised that there is no final Touchstone Story; rather there could be one or more that are reflective and fluid. The Touchstone Story is the nugget that the client as creator takes from the process, a succinct reminder of what has transpired that can resurrect the power of the experience in the future.

Assimilative integration[12]

- The DPS theoretical orientation is consonant with many other models and may effectively be used with behavioural, personal construct, feminist, cognitive, systems approaches, existential and phenomenological processes. Essentially DPS employs the Expressive Arts and storytelling to dynamically implement desired outcomes through the action method of Psychotheatrics.
- DPS complements the behaviourist[13] approach by providing alternative perspectives and vicarious learning. The opportunity to rehearse and try new behaviours in a safe environment leads to an improvement in the overall situation.
- The personal construct model[14] focuses on revealing client constructs to life circumstances. DPS assists in developing alternative personal constructs leading to client change.
- Like the feminist approach,[15] DPS is collaborative and focuses on establishing Meaning and the rejection of labels.
- With the cognitive model,[16] DPS assists to illustrate cognitive schemas and distortions and then reframe these, leading to new ways of thinking, behaving and feeling.
- DPS is congruent with systems approaches,[17] as it always highlights the individual in relation to the social context and can help to illustrate particular boundaries and hierarchies.
- DPS is existential[18] and phenomenological[19] in orientation as it focuses on the construction of Meaning but in an intersubjective space. Less importance is placed on the content of experience than on the Meaning attached to it. In addition, DPS is very congruent with the approach of positive psychology[20] and emphasises the necessity to focus on positive strengths rather than pathology and victimology. DPS assists in identifying our most positive traits or 'signature strengths' that will assist in our most important areas of life: relationships, health, career and spirit.

Mapping the process

The following table presents DPS in graphic form. You may want to isolate and expand the column that is relevant for your work and use it for preparation and note taking.

SEVEN STEP DRAMATIC PSYCHOLOGICAL STORYTELLING			
	GROUP	**INDIVIDUAL**	**COLLECTIVE**
DRAMATIC	**1 Expressive Arts** The story developed through: 1. Narrative 2. Film 3. Theatre 4. Music 5. Visual Art 6. Dance and Kinaesthetics 7. Ritual and Epic	**1 Expressive Arts** The story developed through: 1. Narrative 2. Film 3. Theatre 4. Music 5. Visual Art 6. Dance and Kinaesthetics 7. Ritual and Epic	**1 Expressive Arts** The story developed through: 1. Narrative 2. Film 3. Theatre 4. Music 5. Visual Art 6. Dance and Kinaesthetics 7. Ritual and Epic
PSYCHOLOGICAL	**2 Element** Imaginal Psychotheatrics	**2 Element** Playwright Psychotheatrics	**2 Element** Montage Psychotheatrics
	3 Craft Rhetorical Reality Analysis	**3 Craft** Expressive Writing	**3 Craft** Method of Physical Action
STORYTELLING	**4 Story Map** 1. Orientation 2. Complication 3. Sequence of events 4. Resolution 5. Coda	**4 Story Map** 1. Orientation 2. Complication 3. Sequence of events 4. Resolution 5. Coda	**4 Story Map** 1. Orientation 2. Complication 3. Sequence of events 4. Resolution 5. Coda
DRAMATIC	**5 Dramatic Enactment** **Imaginal Psychotheatrics** using one or more of the **7 Expressive Arts**	**5 Dramatic Enactment** **Playwright Psychotheatrics** using one or more of the **7 Expressive Arts**	**5 Dramatic Enactment** **Montage Psychotheatrics** using one or more of the **7 Expressive Arts**
PSYCHOLOGICAL	**6 Meaning** Values and attitudes explored and expressed	**6 Meaning** Values and attitudes explored and expressed	**6 Meaning** Values and attitudes explored and expressed
STORYTELLING	**7 Touchstone Story** Essence of the experience	**7 Touchstone Story** Essence of the experience	**7 Touchstone Story** Essence of the experience

Adjust 7 Step Model to fit circumstances © Rob Allen and Nina Krebs 2006
™ Psychotheatrics ™Dramatic Psychological Storytelling

Part II

The Seven Expressive Arts

5
Narrative

Thou shalt not might reach the head, but it takes
Once upon a time to reach the heart.
Phillip Pullman[1]

Once upon a time, in many parts of the world, stories of ancient origin carried the people's wisdom and were gifted to the young as their sacred heritage. The recipient of such a gift, David Mowaljarlai, writes of his father's narrative skill on behalf of his people: 'He was a peacemaker who would talk all night. He counseled reason with stories ... in a parable kind-of-way. That made people quiet. People listened and when they could see the scene, then they grasped the message.'[2]

The powers of Narrative, both oral and written, to hold, soothe, teach, address, resolve conflict and create new vision reside in this short example. From times before history, leaders have told stories to soothe and unite people. Storytellers have been honoured community members, appreciated for their abilities to entertain and help people transcend their daily cares.[3] Great teachers tend to be great storytellers, who find artistic expression, often in metaphor, to make their points.

Chances are if you are reading this narrative, some form of expressive reading, writing, or speaking plays an important part in your life. You could even be one of those strange people, a bibliophile.

> Ever since there have been books, there have been bookworms. That's more than 4000 years of voracious reading... The making of books was a scary new technology: marks made on clay or silk or paper became time capsules of knowledge. They conveyed secrets.

> They ignored distances. No wonder that, early on, books became sacrosanct in ways we cannot even imagine.[4]

Narrative as an Expressive Art embraces the use of language beyond mere description. We frequently reach for metaphor to find or create connection. As Howard Stein writes, 'The function of metaphor serves an exalted human dynamic: it communicates multiple, over-determined meanings and desires, while remaining a universal instantiation reflective of our shared humanity.'[5] In other words, metaphor, describing one thing in terms of another, communicates complexity and, at the same time, helps us see our shared humanity. Narrative, the accumulation of metaphor as well as mundane or theoretical information, assumes diverse forms. Books, poems, personal journals, periodicals and electronic media of all kinds offer information, education and escape.

Narrative is, and always has been, the world's most popular teaching tool and purveyor of knowledge. Narrative takes the form of scholarly treatises, practical information and entertainment. It is used to put forth an idea, describe a situation or a process, give instructions and tell a story. Or, it can be utilised to help us chase our fantasies. Whether stories fall into the category of true romance and fantasy, or others such as science fiction, drama, or mystery, they pull us away from the mundane into other worlds through the writer's imagination and our own. Even in the electronic age, readers turn to recreational reading to enrich life. Narrative as entertainment, whether through listening to a story or curling up with an entrancing novel, opens windows on real and imaginary worlds that are far beyond the physical reach of the listener or reader. A library card is a ticket to any place you choose.

It is not just reading or listening to narrative that enfolds human experience. A whole industry flourishes around helping us tell our stories through personal journal, memoir and speech.[6] Typing 'personal journal writing' into the Amazon.com search window brought up 619 results, instructive books about journal writing as well as the journals of others. Deena Metzger describes this impetus for self-reflection through journal writing:

> The inner world is for each of us...the essential territory where everything that might be known resides until it can be called forth into the public arena...the images, inspirations, dreams, nightmares, intuitions, hunches, understandings that arise from the inner world are the *prima materia* from which everything, including ourselves, is constructed. To be willing to live within the imagination is to commit

> oneself to the gathering together of the pieces that might begin to form a self. To avoid this territory is to avoid the encounters that might validate, inform, or enhance one's experience.[7]

As James Pennebaker's research suggests,[8] when people write about emotional upheavals in their lives, improvements in physical and psychological health can result. Writing reduces stress by helping people to acknowledge an experience and enables them to put together the pieces of an event and understand what happened. Expressive writing is the Craft used in Playwright Psychotheatrics and is described further in Chapter 13.

Poetry holds a special place in narrative tradition. Having started writing poetry through some workshops based on Pennebaker's research, Connie Gutowsky shared her thoughts about the drama inherent in poems:[9]

> Poetry evokes the senses – color, taste, touch vision, hearing – and makes language organic. The surprise in a poem can pull the reader into it – like Visual Art, or Music – and outside himself or herself. Through line breaks, rhyming, or sounds, poetry can completely surprise the reader. You think you are going someplace, and then there can be a word – leaves or pear/pair – used in such a way that it means two things at the same time, bringing a whole new twist in direction.
>
> What poets choose to write about is psychological, though they may not exactly sit down to write about their traumatic childhood or feelings of grief, how life has impacted them shows in their themes, the forms they choose, the way words appear on the page. One thing I've noticed is that people who write poetry often do other forms of art and delight in thinking a little differently. I think people choose the form out of a deep desire to be heard and understood. Almost all poems tell stories, or you can find a story in them. I wanted to write a narrative poem about a long flight, and when I showed it to my colleague, he said it was a metaphor for life. So there can be big stories in little poems, or little stories in big poems but they have special qualities of imagery, rhythm, and sound.

Brigette Conway-Dobson writes:[10]

> The telling of narratives and the enactment of narratives is something that has traveled with us through the ages. Stories have allowed us to

> connect and learn, escape, relax, transform and heal. How we interpret this world and how we communicate that interpretation is through the use of story. Humans have a tendency to describe and express events in their lives in story form. Whether we are describing what we did last summer, or our hopes for the future, we often organise our thoughts into story form. It is suggested that stories are more easily stored in memory and are more easily retrieved from memory, especially when the story includes a goal, followed by action, perhaps some conflict and a resolution.

The **dramatic** aspects of Narrative emerge through the creation of vision and experience by using words, whether they are written or spoken. One person transmits an image or experience to another by telling or writing about it. Although the experience is indirect, it becomes shared. The more the teller dramatises the narrative with gesture, detail, inflection and colourful language, the more the listener or reader is able to comprehend.

Narrative is **psychological** both in telling or receiving. The psychology of the writer or storyteller determines choice of topic, material, style and medium. The listener's psychology receives the narrative and shapes it in a way that is meaningful to that person. A story may have powerful emotional impact on one person and not another, depending on the individual's life experiences, capacity for openness, and interests.

Narrative **is** story, the great connector among people of all kinds, through the ages. **Storytelling**, the art of forming and delivering the narrative content is the qualitative process of transmitting the experience, belief, or information from originator to audience. It is this art form that enlivens narrative and is as important as the content.

Listeners, readers and writers all follow narrative threads into other worlds, more deeply into themselves, or on paths to information or the experiences of others. Narrative is a container that holds us all.

Interview conducted by Nina Krebs with Dr Heather Folsom[11]

Just to give you a broad framework, here are the questions I'd like to put to you: What is dramatic about Narrative? What is expressive in an outgoing way, and then what is psychological about Narrative? How can we talk about Narrative from the point of view of storytelling?

I was thinking about the topic before you came over and I realised that all art is Narrative, no matter what the form, whether it's a painting or music. In a way what art *is*, is narrative. It's something psychologically meaningful to the person who created it and sometimes to the receiver. But, speaking particularly of words and that which is written down – which is the area that I'm going to talk about – it's more obviously narrative because it's a story in words. It doesn't matter how abstract it may be.

Part of what is **dramatic** and expressive is that one finds metaphors and elements which represent an idea. As opposed to saying, 'I hate my mother', if you say, 'The rabbit destroyed the carrot', then you may have a different form of expressivity. Another thing I think about is what I call overtones. That is if you take a sentence, or a paragraph, or a whole book, there's both what's written and then there are the overtones that are set up in expression. It's almost like harmonics in music that reverberate and create cross resonances in terms of stimulating a sense of meaning and a sense of emotion. To me that is, really, what art *is*; it's not just a statement of fact, but it creates associations, it creates the combination of ideas that leads to a broader, deeper and more complex experience.

In relation to **psychological** – when you come to Narrative and storytelling specifically, what's psychological about it comes from a very ancient human tradition, which is an impulse or a need to create meaning and order out of experience and to use language to do that. Although, as I said before, you can do cave paintings or you can beat a drum. That's also psychological, but in terms of just using words and telling a story, it's an absolutely ancient human tradition in all cultures through all time and will always be true. What's psychological about it is that I actually think the human mind is wired for story. The way we understand things is to create a little arc of meaning with a beginning, middle and end and even if what we're doing is absurdist or, in a sense there is no end, nonetheless the human mind makes a little story because that's how we come to understand experience. So in a certain way, Narrative is psychological, an encapsulated and obvious form of something we do all the time. Every time you have a conversation with another person, you tell a little story and that's how the other person understands the meaning. They understand here are the characters, here is the setting, here is what happened and either you tell them or they glean from it the meaning.

And Storytelling?

For **storytelling** I will use a story as an example, one of my very favourites, that I think embodies everything I've talked about: the dramatic, the psychological and it very much embodies the story and the use of narrative to tell a psychological truth. One of the things I was also thinking of in terms of my understanding of what you're discussing, is the relationship between narrative and a sort of psychological process. There are two wings to it: one is that which we do ourselves, the writing that we create, and then there's the writing that we read or that we hear from another person. There are differences and similarities and I could talk about both, but for my example I'll use one that I have read and that your readers can read also, a story called *The Judgement* by Franz Kafka, perhaps my favourite short story ever.[12]

I call it a cautionary tale short story because it's an example of what not to do, and although in no way does Kafka say to the reader, or to himself, 'don't do what this character did', you walk away kind of resolved that you will not do that. The story is about a young man who is incredibly worried about other people and about doing better than they do. It starts out with his friend, who he feels is sort of a failure, and he is afraid to tell his friend about his own life because he's doing rather well. His business is going well. He's become engaged and so he's feeling quite pleased with his own life, and he does not want to hurt his friend's feelings by telling him of his own good fortune. On the other hand his fiancé would like the friend to know that they're engaged and invite him to the wedding and so forth. So in the end the young man decides that he will do so, because he also doesn't want to hurt his fiancé's feelings and he's caught in between. Meanwhile, the real essence of the story has to do with his father, whom he lives with since his mother died. He goes over to show his father the letter that he's written to his friend although he doesn't even want to do that. He actually is so worried about everybody that he's a little worried about intruding on his father. Despite this, he shows his father the letter. Well, at first it looks like his father is very weak and frail and the son is chiding himself for not taking better care of his father and thinking 'when we're married ... my father has to live with us and I have to take better care of him'. But then the father somehow rises up and begins yelling at the son and says A: 'I know your friend and I've been in secret communication with him', B: 'He's a much better young man than you are and he's basically the son I never had', C: 'Your fiancé is a tramp', and, D: 'You ought to drown yourself'.

This is very Kafkaesque because, in many senses, Kafka's main characters are somehow imperiled. There's some way which prevents them from taking the action that would be the right action. They're paralysed! And so what actually happens is this young man, who has gone from feeling good about his life but worried about what others may think, leaves the house and jumps off a bridge and kills himself. So, the cautionary tale is, don't do what he did and give up. To me it's so brilliant because, although Kafka never tells you the actual meanings of any of these things, the story reads in such a gripping and dramatic and humorous and outrageous and insane, absurdist way that it clutches at you and I believe it changes you. This is a story that I felt changed me when I read it and made me feel more committed to my own path and to not be stopped by other people, whether they intentionally or unintentionally threw up obstacles in the way. So I think it's just one of the great, great examples of how Narrative has this incredible resonance, power and meaning to change us and to influence us.

Can you talk more about how this Narrative lives in you?

This particular story lives in me because I think one of my own issues is guilt and worrying about being successful or injuring other people, being perceived as someone who is callous and self-centered and looking to my own happiness and not thinking about others. I don't think it is actually true that I'm like that but somehow my neurotic issues are that I worry about that a lot and so the story just spoke to me.

End of interview

Research Project – Narrative, Sacred Story[13]

Description: This research project explored the underlying meaningful elements in common to a group of five university students, one psychology academic, and two research assistants who engaged the sacred story: *the Garden of Eden.*

DPS (modified to fit the circumstances of this situation, as it is always).

1 *Expressive Art type*
Narrative: *Garden of Eden.*

2 *Element*
Imaginal Psychotheatrics – DPS – designed for a group that shares a common characteristic(s).

3 *Craft*
Rhetorical Reality Analysis: This example used a Bible story known to almost everyone in the Western world. Group members added their own

interpretation links about the meaning of the story of human beings in relation to God, for instance that the story symbolises the relationship between parents and their children. Other observations were that the temptation of the forbidden fruit could have been provided as a means of encouraging Adam and Eve to become independent and that the journey to self-discovery often involves taking risks and challenging authority. These interpretation links by each participant then developed into a powerful chain representing a shared group story.

4 *Story Map*

Orientation: Adam and Eve in the Garden of Eden. Everything is perfect and beautiful. They have all that they need. God has told Adam the only thing he is not allowed to do is eat of the fruit of the Tree of Knowledge.

Complication: The Devil, in the form of a snake, tries to tempt Adam and Eve to eat the forbidden fruit. The challenge: whether to obey God and not eat of the fruit of the Tree of Knowledge.

Sequence of events: The snake puts doubt into the minds of Adam and Eve about whether what God says is actually true. Eve listens to the snake. She eats the forbidden fruit. She tries to convince Adam to eat it as well. Adam eats the fruit. As a result of eating the forbidden fruit, Adam and Eve receive the knowledge of good and evil. They immediately become aware that they are naked and cover their nakedness. For the first time Adam and Eve see opposites, distinctions, are conscious, able to make judgements, have their own values, make their own decisions – develop a *self*. When God sees that they have covered themselves, he knows that they have eaten the fruit. God casts Adam and Eve out of the garden.

Resolution: Adam and Eve must now live with the knowledge of suffering and death. They must live their lives in accordance with God's will in order to be reunited with him in heaven after death. They now realise the consequences of disobeying God.

Coda: To be or not to be – that is the real question!

5 *Dramatic Enactment*

Rob Allen facilitated the enactment of the story, setting the scenes which provided the opportunity to explore the underlying meanings of this story. Group members directed the action and represented the roles of God, Adam, Eve, the snake and the Tree of Knowledge.

6 *Meaning*

Group members experienced the power of this story and spoke of the meanings they perceived. For example: knowledge brings the danger of risk; the unknown is perilous and God is trying to protect his children. You cannot be fully alive without knowledge or without suffering; with maturity and knowledge come aloneness. Yet people don't want to be alone, they want to share their experiences. Being safe and protected can be boring. Being free means you have to look after yourself which is difficult and you don't always make the right decisions. To recreate, both Adam and Eve need to be fertile. Creativity is an interconnected productive act. Eating the fruit from the Tree of Knowledge enabled the birth of consciousness, expulsion from the protective womb, the creation of self and the ability to be fertile!

7 ***Touchstone Story***
There is a tension between protecting your children and letting them take enough risks to be able to grow and form their own personalities and build their own lives. The experience of life is about the choices that one makes in order to experience growth and change from the known to the unknown. The outcomes of these choices determine who we are and who we think we are. The more aware we become, the more we experience a yearning for growth and fulfilment and the stronger we become. This journey is not always easy or pain-free. Sometimes there are obstacles and these obstacles may be in the form of those who would control, oppress, or even protect. Meaning for life can be found through all of these experiences.

Narrative and DPS

The utilisation of Narrative art types such as books, short stories, poetry, journal/diary, and oral storytelling, with DPS, touches the heart as well as the mind. We can use personal Narrative or the great sacred stories to illustrate, explore, discover or highlight Meaning. Whether the story is ancient and universal or immediate and deeply personal, working through the steps of the DPS model bring it into the immediate, rational and emotional present for exploration and development. Through stories, old or new, we can see ourselves in the context of our lives and imagine new realities.

6
Film

I believe much of our awareness of the world around us has been mediated through film. The question is not 'if' it happens but rather 'how much' of our meaning and our responses to visual images have their basis in film. What is real memory of an experience? What is a film memory? Have they become blurred or interchangeable?
Robyn Medek, Artist[1]

Film can freeze action. It can examine minute details of expressions and gestures. It can rewind and fast forward. It is immortal and may be repeated to review again or share with others. These aspects have reshaped **dramatic** expression.[2]

A good example is the screening of the *Wallabies versus the Springboks* on the big cinema screen – at the Metro Cinema in Bathurst.[3] A rugby match is turned into a dramatic communal event: 'Book now to avoid disappointment – Bathurst Burs Junior Rugby Tri Nations Charity Evening – formal wear or rugby attire – Tickets $45 each.'

The expressive dramatic quality that film is able to use is very special. We are now able to revisit the action. If an interesting aspect happens we can go back and see it again, or from different angles, and interview authorities on the game while the play is going on.

The emotional turning points today are very similar to those thousands of years ago. Film allows us to explore this **psychological** archaeology in relation to our contemporary psyche. We see how our personal unconscious blends with our collective unconscious. This helps to establish that we are not alone. We have connections!

Film is an important personal, interpersonal and transpersonal psychological reference point:

> My greatest achievement is creating work that speaks out for marginalised people. The 'Finished People' began when I was asked to teach a workshop at Open Family, which is a youth services organisation in Cabramatta (Sydney). I was asked to make a short film and it ended up a full-length feature movie. We were nominated for the AFI (Australian Film Industry) awards. Every now and then, I have a person come up to me that saw this film and it changed their life. That is a great feeling. That is success. Khoa Do, Aged 26, Film-maker, 2005 Young Australian of the Year.[4]

Film is ideal for **storytelling**, as it is a medium for both personal and interpersonal discovery. Basic stories need to be told again and again to different generations. Film uses mythological concepts that can help you find your individuality but also realise you are part of a larger community. Everyone has a chance to be a hero or not, every day of our lives. Film demonstrates these universal themes in a variety of portrayals that we can experience at will to refresh or illuminate ourselves.

The movie *Motorcycle Diaries*[5] represented the 'journey', about discovery and change. It captured the imagination of many who viewed it, and its website invited you to share your story: 'Has the World Changed You? If your travels have given you a life changing experience, or if you have a reaction to the film, we invite you to join in and share them here:

- Click here to share your story.
- Click here to view a few shared stories.'

Following is an interview by Rob Allen with David Stratton, film critic with *The Australian* newspaper and Australian Broadcasting Corporation-TV's *At the Movies*, which will help to illustrate our cinematic connections:[6]

David, would you please highlight the dramatic, psychological and storytelling aspects of cinema as an expressive art form?

Without wanting to be too pretentious about all this, I suppose my feeling is that the cinema usually reflects stories, or tells stories about individuals, rather than collective stories. I mean, most stories – and films

– are about battlers of one sort or another, whether it's Buster Keaton, facing all kinds of odds, or whether it's even the hero of something like *The Grapes of Wrath,* where there's a collective story going on in the background, but the film itself focuses on an individual and his struggle. So, almost always …I think that cinema generally deals with more individual stories from a dramatic and psychological point of view.

For example then, cinema is much more an individual hero's or heroine's journey?

Yes. It's difficult to come to terms with anything bigger than that. Even in the Soviet Union films which are a collective experience to a degree still, nevertheless, focus on individuals within the crowd. For example, in the *Odessa Steps* sequence they all the time focused close-ups or medium close-ups on individuals, because they mean much more, I guess, to an audience. The director knew that would be the case. So even in a collective film like that, there was still a concentration in the images on individual characters … the current debate about asylum-seekers here in Australia, you know, if you just say 'asylum-seekers' and you don't individualise them or humanise them, it doesn't mean anything very much, but once you start talking about individual people then it means a lot more.

Yes, I do see what you mean. If you look at cinema as an Expressive Art type, particularly the ***dramatic*** *qualities of expression, can you comment on what makes it unique among the arts?*

Well, I think the first thing that makes cinema unique as far as the dramatic arts are concerned – at least if you discount television for the moment – prior to the cinema, we have no idea, really, what the actors of previous generations were like, how they performed, or the style of theatre. We have some ideas about what the theatre was like in the 18th century and the early part of the 19th century, but we don't really know for sure because we can't now see it. Since the cinema – and that's what makes it so important in my view – we can. We can see the young Greta Garbo, we can see the young Laurence Olivier, we can see the young Clint Eastwood and we will always be able to see that. Future generations will always be able to see that and this is something that never happened before the cinema came along. So that's one area of its uniqueness, but it's also, of course, a combination of all the other arts. It's a combination of drama, music, photography, and movement.

Sam Fuller says it beautifully in *Pierrot Le Fou*[7] when he says the cinema is 'conflict, violence, sex, in other words, emotion' and that's true. It is an emotional art, it plays on our emotions and I'm not sure it's unique in that because the theatre does that too, but it does it very powerfully because it can use close-ups and because it can use editing and the combination of those devices: the exhilaration that the combination of all those elements can bring.

Let us take an example to illustrate the dramatic, psychological and storytelling aspects of Film?

I think films like *Million Dollar Baby*[8] and *Sideways*[9] are both examples of storytelling: contemporary examples of the power of cinema in completely different ways. You have two completely different approaches to the cinema in those two films and I think the impressive thing with *Million Dollar Baby* is that on the one hand it delivers psychologically as a boxing drama and the audience is manipulated in a positive sense to side with this incredibly brave and talented young woman. Then the film turns on its head in the last part to tackle an extremely controversial subject, euthanasia. All this without the audience being aware of where they have been taken and I think it says a lot for the craft, not only the craft but the craftiness, too, perhaps, of Clint Eastwood and the people who made the film, that it succeeds so well on those levels and has succeeded in getting people who maybe didn't think about the question of euthanasia to consider it in those terms. You can say it's manipulative, it is manipulative, but then the best cinema is manipulative, it just depends how you want to be, whether you want to be manipulated or not. A film like *Sideways* takes a very humanistic approach, a much gentler approach to the foibles of its characters who are, on one level, quite reprehensible people and yet the film is generous towards them and towards all the characters in the film. Actually it's like a Renoir film, where you really feel that the director cares about all these people, warts and all, flaws and all. He wants you to love them and you wind up loving them, and this is the power of film, dramatically and psychologically. To take characters that you may not normally respond to and find the good in them to allow you to respond to them in a very positive way.

End of Interview

We have focused on cinema as a significant, artistic representation of film. Television is considered by many as unworthy or too pedestrian, a faulty and biased view that fails to recognise the vital impact of television on us personally and collectively. Television has archetypal figures also, which 'speak' to us psychologically, tell our stories, and act as personal and communal reference points.

In addressing this question, Martin Esslin has argued that *I Love Lucy, Kojak, Archie Bunker* and *The Fonz* 'might cut pale figures side by side with those of Odysseus, Achilles, Arthur, Lancelot and Guinevere, but their genesis as the outcrop of the collective unconscious has not been so different. The pantheon of archetypal characters in the ever-recurring situations in television serials', he has contended, 'accurately reflects the collective psyche, the collective fears and aspirations, neuroses and nightmares of the population, as distinct from the factual reality of the state of the nation'.[10]

The collective psyche that television taps into and represents is not a monolith; there are many diverse ethnic, cultural and even 'clan' psychological identities that are represented by different features on television. The next day we can talk about a television show, what it means and exchange thoughts and viewpoints. Some of these may be superficial while others, quite important and revealing. The dramatic expressive medium of television allows an audience to watch and share the same experience, whether this is a small cable channel or a major commercial network reaching millions. This becomes even more impressive when we realise that television shows can be seen in many other countries and these are then blended into their culture with unique psychological and storytelling reference points.

The Whale Rider

There is a universality of storytelling in the film *The Whale Rider*, which has an international resonance. These same themes are relevant in all sorts of societies and cultures throughout the world. This movie is about a community faced with problems of ancestry and succession, about women and their place in society:

Synopsis[11] In a small New Zealand coastal village, the Maori people claim descent from Paikea, the Whale Rider. In every generation, for more than 1000 years, a male heir born to the Chief succeeds to the title.

The time is now. The Chief's eldest son, Porourangi, fathers twins – a boy and a girl. But the boy and his mother die in childbirth. The surviving girl is named Pai.

Grief-stricken, her father leaves her to be raised by her grandparents. Koro, her grandfather who is the Chief, refuses to acknowledge Pai as the inheritor of the tradition and claims she is of no use to him. But her grandmother, Flowers, sees more than a broken line: she sees a child in desperate need of love.

And Koro learns to love the child. When Pai's father, Porourangi, now a feted international artist, returns home after twelve years, Koro hopes everything is resolved and Porourangi will accept destiny and become his successor.

But Porourangi has no intention of becoming Chief. He has moved away from his people both physically and emotionally. After a bitter argument with Koro, he leaves, suggesting to Pai that she come with him. She starts the journey but quickly returns, claiming that her grandfather needs her.

Koro is blinded by prejudice and even Flowers cannot convince him that Pai is the natural heir. The old Chief is convinced that the tribe's misfortunes began at Pai's birth and calls for his people to bring their 12-year-old boys to him for training. He is certain that through a gruelling process of teaching the ancient chants, tribal lore and warrior techniques, the future leader of their tribe will be revealed to him.

Meanwhile, deep within the ocean, a massive herd of whales is responding, drawn towards Pai's and their twin destinies. When the whales become stranded on the beach, Koro is sure this signals an apocalyptic end to his tribe. Until one person prepares to make the ultimate sacrifice to save the people: The Whale Rider.

Research project – Film[12]

Description: This research project explored the underlying meaningful elements in common to a group of four university students and one academic of a cinematic experience: *The Whale Rider* movie. Drama and storytelling tap into the sacred world of the collective, where symbol and myth reside. The *Dramatic Psychological Storytelling* (DPS) – Playwright format creates a method of revealing the underlying meanings and allows for creation of a composite description of the dramatic experience.

Seven step DPS (modified to fit the circumstances of this situation, as it is always).

1 ***Expressive Art type***
Film: *The Whale Rider*

2 *Element*
Playwright DPS: – designed for the individual, couple or very small group. This method creates a vehicle for revealing underlying meanings and themes, plus allows for an overall description of the experience.

3 *Craft*
Expressive Writing (Pennebaker, 1997):[13] where the writer explores the relationship between the experience to their own life – you sit alone and just write about your experience, minimum 20 minutes, maximum 30 minutes – the act of writing allows the thought processes to slow down and actually alters the way the experience is represented and understood in our minds, leading to greater insight and clarity. Each participant completed this process, after the cinema experience, alone and without discussing the movie with others.

4 *Story Map*
Each of the five participants then developed their Expressive Writing into a story using this process. Again, this was completed after the cinema experience by each participant, alone and without discussing the movie.

5 *Meaning*
Each of the five participants identified meaningful aspects individually, according to Playwright Psychotheatrics.

6 *Dramatic Enactment*
Expressive Art type, Narrative – written and oral. In a departure from the normal individual/couple format of Playwright, in a group session the next day we all met and shared our Craft – Expressive Writing, Story Map and Meaning. We then discussed these experiences and developed common meanings from looking at this group experience of *The Whale Rider* movie.

7 *Touchstone Story*
Each of the five participants had previously identified their own individual Touchstone Story. In the preceding Drama Enactment we shared our individual work and were able to develop and identify significant statements, common meanings and overall themes and hence create a group Touchstone Story.

Themes

Statements were identified collectively from our individual work, through collaboration from the Craft (Expressive Writing) and Story Map. Key summary headings then formed our group composite Meaning that we shared. These were then summarised and became our

Touchstone Story. We found this to be a very revealing and enlightening experience of discovery for everyone involved in the process. Themes are identified below, made up of many individual statements, however we have only provided a very brief summary here to illustrate:

Expectations: 'How do we know what we are meant to be and who decides if it is good enough?' 'The judgements we make as parents and the potential for harm from the child's perspective.' 'Expectations can both smother and ridicule.' 'I have learned that there have been positive and negative aspects gained from the high expectations set for me.' 'I want my own children to learn about the world themselves, to make their own choices about their lives.'

Power Struggles: 'I could understand Koro wanting to maintain cultural ties but felt that he lacked insight into how to maintain them in the present day, without trying to rigidly keep the ones from long ago.' 'It highlighted the need for a progressive way of thinking on both sides of the generations.' 'All parents struggle to find this balance.' 'I wanted Rawiri to succeed. I wanted him to discover his own power within.'

Cultural Conflict: 'Idealism may be a noble attribute but it has a high price to pay in the real world.' 'The core values of society (for example, respect for others and nature) are the important parts to be maintained.' 'We hold onto faith and values which guide us in our daily lives.' 'The introduction of western culture brought with it a new way, where the youth are no longer required to respect their elders and where life is about the moment.'

Self-Identity: 'It made me question my own role as a parent.' 'Standing in the face of adversity and growing despite it.' 'Acceptance validates the individual.' 'To have a strong sense of my own self-worth and celebrate my achievements, despite not always meeting the high expectations of the person closest to me.'

Communication: 'If only we could take the time to hear the narrations of our children.' 'As individuals, we need to be heard.' 'Maybe they need to yell to make us understand and maybe they have no choice but to defy us.'

The Spiritual Journey: 'The Whale Rider brings hope to our world. It brings hope that we do not have to live with "warrior" violence. That a real warrior is nurturing.' 'All the time they were looking for answers, for a saviour – and she was there the whole time.' 'Rather than looking out for a saviour, we all need to realise perhaps it is within us to find, but only if we continue to question, to listen and to learn.'

Leadership: 'A good leader is one who is connected, leads by inclusion, integrity, kindness, generosity and brings out the strengths in others.' 'We need a leader with a vision of hope for the future.'

Film and Dramatic Psychological Storytelling

The utilisation of Film with DPS is limitless. It provides a safe, witness aspect, but it is also extremely involving and revealing as it is a very creative process for exploring important issues. The focus is flexible, depending on whether there are therapeutic, educational or human resources concerns. This process can be used with individuals and couples (Playwright Psychotheatrics) or groups (Imaginal Psychotheatrics) and provides a useful vehicle for transformation in a collective setting (Montage Psychotheatrics).

7
Theatre

In other arts the audience sees the result of the creative process.
In theatre the audience is present during that process.
Sonia Moore[1]

Theatre is **dramatic**. It is a 'live' form that 'enlivens' by bringing life to the community and the individual. Theatre began as religious ritual, with performers making their art a spiritual practice. Theatre is spiritually based as it taps our collective unconscious and nourishes our personal consciousness. It gives us energy. It is relevant in the present but also timeless.[2] This living quality sets theatre apart from other art forms, particularly film that records 'forever' but does not require direct audience involvement.

Both film and theatre are effective in their own manner. Theatre's duality, its mirroring quality, offers direct immediate reflection. Shakespeare believed that theatre's purpose was just this: to mirror life, throw back an image so we can 'see' ourselves. Theatre has immediacy, present vitality and is ephemeral. It is limited in size, a living art form, provocative, entertaining and truly magical with its 'active construction of meaning in regard to human experience'.[3] A good example of the ephemeral but eternal nature of theatre is *Morning*, a play directed by Carrick O'Connell which featured Rob Allen's son, Carey, as the main character, Daniel. Rob notes 'Now when I hear the sounds of birds at daybreak, I flash back to the play. I "see" my son on stage in this "other" character. I cannot replay this performance like a film but it will be with me forever.'

Theatre is **psychological** – soul and psyche: theatre is at the heart of both. The term *Persona* in ancient Greek means 'sounding through' masks – representing happiness, sadness and other emotions. Performers behind the masks were not personally identified. We think of the modern psychological 'mask' as the sense of 'self' we wish to project as we keep our real self hidden. Thespis, the 6th century Greek poet, regarded as founder of tragic drama, took off the mask and declared identity. We can have both, the collective mask and the personal psyche through theatre. We are both. Furthermore, theatre reflects the sacred. Since ancient times it has served as one of the main paths to the divine.

Theatre, with no intention of being therapy, is a powerful agent for change. Playgoers experience involvement at a personal level just by being in the audience. When we hear a story, view a play, we take it in. The play becomes part of us. We gain insights, make connections, form new ideas. The more closely the drama speaks to our own needs, interests, fears or wishes, the more it is likely to affect us.

Theatre is **storytelling**; it is called the 'seeing place'. It is alive, confronting, demanding of attention. As it involves the viewer, it is the porthole for collective and personal transformation. Since the dawn of time it has been a medium for spiritual alchemy in the exploration of meaning and purpose. In the modern age, with all our sophisticated technology, we seem to have lost our way. We need the magic of ancient times; we need the power of the personal dynamic. We need to listen to our soul; storytelling **is** our soul listening. Theatre is implicit storytelling through the 'seeing place': a magical combination. Theatrical storytelling is collectively nurturing and personally transforming.

The following **interview with Rob Allen and Bill Blaikie**, academic in Theatre Arts at Charles Sturt University in Bathurst NSW, will help to illustrate individual and collective connections with theatre.[4]

I really appreciate you sharing your expertise with us Bill. Please talk about your views on how theatre is dramatic: how it is psychological and how it is storytelling? First can we focus on the dramatic expressive aspect of theatre? What are some of theatre's unique dramatic qualities of expression?

Theatre is **dramatic**, as distinct from spectacular, in that it is made up of a series of instances in which individuals are in very particular moments of crisis. These moments make the plot. So the drama is in our watching the clash of wills or the clash of desires or the clash of goals of the characters as they oppose each other. Each character is an obstacle to the other and we probably identify with one character and not with another. So we identify with Iago or with Othello or with Desdemona in that play and join in their struggles. Theatrically though, what we see are instances selected from the whole story, that the playwright has chosen to activate. From these enacted moments we, the audience, can construct the story in our head. But it's really the selection of those intense moments of life, where action is compressed into a few moments, which are significant. Lorca said: 'Theatre is a platform, a passion, and two people.'

Now for the psychological aspects of Theatre?

It is **psychological** in that we gain an understanding of the human condition. It is good theatre, through a particular instance of human interaction or human decision making. Theatre has to be concerned with the particular, right down to the intake of breath, the action of a hand, the turn of a head. This is the body language that is unique to a very, very particular moment between two people. So, in preparing the scene, the actors have to arrive at a considerable depth of understanding about people who would make those particular claims about themselves and their social status, their age, their education, their appetites, their ambition. If the actors achieve this we, the audience, see this as true to the human condition. We see the truth of Oedipus, we see the truth of Macbeth, we see the truth of Lear, but we also see the truth of Macduff and Edgar and Iago. And then you watch as those individual egos clash with each other, bringing the dramatic moments that reveal the story, because in theatre the real storyteller is the audience.

The audience make sense of these snapshot moments out of people's lives and if the playwright is good, he has chosen them so we leap from one moment in the story to another moment to another moment. We construct the story as we go and see the pattern and the way in which it all ties together in a psychologically satisfying way.

Your answer certainly illustrated the psychological aspects of Theatre and also touched on storytelling, which was my third question. That was interesting about how the audience is the storyteller. Would you please elaborate further on the storytelling aspects of theatre?

Theatre is **storytelling**, the search is always for the good story, the appropriate story, and the one which is right for the time. So in Ancient Greece they were looking at stories that people knew. However, they were telling them from a different viewpoint, or revealing the story in a different way or reinterpreting, so that the audience is surprised by the interpretation of the story. They have revealed to them aspects of their personalities and their characters, the flaws that lead to their downfall. For example, in a very good man like Oedipus, one character flaw will lead to his downfall. This is a warning to us, as the audience, to watch out for the flaw in ourselves. As a storyteller you have to have the psychology of the character right, in order to create the tensions between the characters. That psychology may be worn on the inside in a naturalistic play, where we're driven by circumstance and our social conditioning and the sort of places we live in. Or, it can be externalised as it may be in the Commedia or in the Ancient Greek theatre, or in Brechtian theatre where the actor actually stands as separate from the character. He or she stands in the position of commenting on the character's choices so that we see the contradictions that the character has been caught in because of his particular social upbringing and inability to resolve the conflicts that exist inside him.

That is very interesting, concerning catharsis and Brecht, in a psychological sense. Would you describe Brecht's and Aristotle's views of catharsis in theatre?

There are real differences, absolutely, because what Brecht does is reveal the story up front so that you watch the reasons for the story being the way it is. It's not storytelling in the traditional sense in which we are kept interested by the unveiling of the next set of relationships in the story. What should capture us are the ways in which the contradictions in the characters are worked out. This happens in such a way that we are surprised by the decisions that they make, but we see the social necessity, at the same time, of the decision that the characters make. The catharsis in Brechtian terms is a freeing of us from the social conditioning that has made us hold contradictory viewpoints at the same time.

So it is rational?

Absolutely! It's rational; he wants us to think as much or more than he wants us to feel. But I would say in Aristotelian catharsis we are purged by pity and terror, but at the same time we are forced to think about the problem of overweening pride, of hubris, of whatever the character flaw is, so that we identify it in ourselves, and that requires cognitive realignment, I suppose.

So Theatre tells a story, but it tells it almost like the three dots and people will see a triangle, so you're trying to choose those three dots that will reveal the triangle or the square or, however many dots will reveal the circle. And it is only the dots. You do not draw the line because the audience will provide the connections that make the dots become the circle or the square or the rectangle or whatever.

The audience then is the storyteller in theatre because they make sense of the story and relate to it?

Yes. They make the story from a series of enacted and enactable moments from the play.

Would you carry the concepts of theatrical storytelling and the audience a little further please?

When you get to something like *Waiting for Godot*, what Becket does is play on our desire to make a story out of it. Knowing that the audience is attempting to make a story out of it, he will lead us off on other tracks, which are tracks that help us understand the predicament that we are in as a society that has lost its way.

For example, the play you recently directed, Dreamings, *certainly made me reflect on my developmental life journey, our communal story. As a member of the audience, I understand that I became the storyteller. Can you use* Dreamings *to illustrate the dramatic, psychological and storytelling aspects of theatre?*

Through research and improvisation we sought to invent a story, or series of stories, about what attaches young people to Bathurst.[5] In asking people about their relationships to Bathurst and the Central West we were seeking to arrive at some theatrically useful stories through their particular understandings. These individual stories revealed individual psychologies providing a level of dramatic variety. In storytelling terms we drew on the old story of the eternal return: birth, initiation, consummation, repose, death and rebirth. We then built a dramatic plot structure from those moments we felt we could enact effectively. This could be seen as a fairly conventional introduction, development, climax and resolution. It became more circular in that it was from birth to death and back to rebirth, but rebirth in spirit rather than of the body. From the outset and at the end it was also operating at a metaphorical level, which we tried to lay in right at the beginning through using the circus techniques of the tissue to represent foetal sacs and birth. We made this theatrical in that there were three of them and one of them had two people inside it, so there was a surprise in it based on variety. We used theatrical techniques inside a dramatic structure which was attempting to be poetic and work the metaphor as well as the surface level of story. We were using Aboriginal storytelling as a guide here. The very simple surface of their stories usually is an entry to a complex web of relationships based on Aboriginal knowledge and lore.

Thank you for sharing your expertise with us.

Sacred aspects of Theatre by Bill Blaikie

Rituals are to do with maintaining the order of things, the culture, the society, the religious observances and therefore of the metaphor that those rituals are associated with. Sacred theatre has something of mysticism about it, a direct knowledge of the sacred, a recovery of lost knowledge, the answering of spiritual questions that have no ritual answers. There are a whole variety of ways that the sacred has been approached across cultures: sweat lodges, isolation, chanting, drumming, meditating, physical exercise, fasting, narcotics, hallucinogens, alcohol, tantric sex, vision quests, sleight of hand magic by shamans, initiation ceremonies, smoke, fire. The mask is one of many tools that may be used alone or in conjunction with any of the above. The variety of means to the sacred experience indicates that it is perhaps a common human need and experience. Normal theatre today has to be commercial. Theatre was commercialised during the Renaissance: Shakespeare and the Commedia dell' Arte are examples. If you worship Mammon then I suppose this theatre might be sacred for you. Yet there is something in theatre that often helps us transcend temporal concerns and allows us to see universal values, or that heals deep emotional and physical wounds. And the sacred can appear anywhere unexpectedly and so it might in the most unlikely theatre performances. Sacredness is, in part, a right relation to the world and when we feel rebalanced by theatre then something sacred has happened. This might happen in something as commercialised as *The Lion King* or a *Circus Oz* show, for example.

The work of *Bread and Puppet Theatre* in the States has been one of service rather than profit and John Schumann bakes and distributes bread made with yeast he has kept alive for thirty or more years to his audiences. There is a communion behind this that has a sacred purpose. Dario Fo's one-man show Mistero Buffo is unmasked in the literal sense, yet its retelling of Biblical stories from the fool's point of view reveals much that is sacred. One of Fo's pieces is about the feeding of the beggar or the stranger because you never know in what disguise the divine will appear to you. In our economically rationalised world most shows are just diversions, breaks from the economic grind, but one day you can be suddenly transported by a performance to that grander perception of life. Under the right circumstances in the protected theatrical womb we allow ourselves to become entralled. Perspective wobbles and shifts opening onto something beyond our selfish preoccupation as it expands to behold a larger picture based on selfless values. A scared moment occurs. By framing, re-framing and broadening our view we emerge onto a plane beyond the familiar and glimpse something more than ordinary life.

Research Project – Theatre[6]

Description: This research project explored the underlying meaningful elements in common with a group of five university students, one academic, one teaching assistant and one actor/playwright of a theatrical experience of a short play *The Jester* by Carey Allen.[7]

It is interesting to note the work of Joel Schechter on 'fools' and 'jesters' whose role it is to challenge and subvert the established order.[8]

Seven step DPS (modified to fit the circumstances of this experience, as it is always!)

1 *Expressive Art type*

Theatre: This piece could be called *Reflection* because the Jester character speaks to his audience about themselves, their lives and their situations. In the discussion following the performance, it was noted that the Jester wore a mask, which is often seen to be a way of hiding one's true identity. Yet the Jester speaks as though he is the voice or the true identity of each member of the audience. The Jester challenges the social façade which people create in order to give themselves a sense of security, value and identity in the world. He challenges their belief in themselves and their relationships, in the social rules which they have created and also in religion as a way of giving meaning to life.

The Jester's purpose in the story is to reflect (expose) the imperfections and contradictions of society by challenging the audience, who represent those in charge. In addition the challenge is to confront the authentic self, both the light and dark sides!

2 *Element*

Imaginal Psychotheatrics is utilised, as it is designed for a target group that shares a common characteristic(s). This format creates a method for revealing those underlying common meanings and allows for creation of a composite description of the dramatic experience. This method facilitates group exploration of the individual and collective relevance and meaning of a particular phenomenon – in this case a theatrical performance.

3 *Craft*

Rhetorical Reality Analysis: *The Jester* is an original piece of writing and performance using the archetype of the Jester which occurs throughout literature and theatre. Each group member added interpretation links of this performance, which soon grew into a powerful chain reflecting an overall group story, identifying some of the meanings this archetype has within our culture. One group member felt that the Jester challenges people to take responsibility for themselves and to recognise that materialism is not the answer. The group discussed the necessity of removing the façade. Life should be lived truthfully, honestly and to the fullest – no pretense. An interesting paradox! It was noted that at times the Jester appears to be sinister, but at other times, the fool or comedian as he shows us the truth about ourselves and the world through humour, which makes it easier to absorb. Group members commented that the Jester is a part of everyone, and that this straightforward honesty about the social façade mirrored a childlike honesty in a complicated adult.

4 *Story Map*

Orientation: A character appears from nowhere, with no obvious props other than his mask. He is identified in the title as *The Jester* and he presents a soliloquy. He refers to himself as 'joker' and 'judge' and he addresses the audience initially as 'dear nobles'. The use of the words 'joker' and 'nobles' suggests a court in another century. The implication is that this commentator is outside time and place and that the court and Jester images are symbolic of human life.

Complication: The Jester challenges the audience's assumptions about life, relationships and religion and about their own 'nobility' and importance in the world.

Sequence of events: The Jester appears and begins to mock and strongly challenge the audience. He says that he will dig out the audiences' 'darkest secrets'. He attacks the symbols of security that many value –

spouse, child, and job. He attacks the materialism of society. He produces a gun. He talks about 'karma' and asks the audience if they want him to shoot himself. He shoots himself but then appears to be alive at the end of the soliloquy.

Resolution: If you see this scenario as a metaphor for life, the protagonist (the Jester) dies and yet appears to be alive at the end. This could represent the ambiguity of religious belief in such questions as: 'Is there life after death?' and 'Is there something meaningful that goes on after we leave this meaningless existence?' In keeping with the nature of the piece, there is no clear resolution.

Coda: The following ideas came out of the group discussion on *The Jester*: individuals die but life continues; be authentic; be true to yourself; you have to face certain challenges and maybe if you were in the Garden (of Eden) you'd never have to face those things; there is no hiding behind masks and false selves.

5 *Dramatic Enactment*

Consisted of three phases: informal Theatre reconstruction by our group, where we re-enacted certain aspects of the 'Jester' by gestures or facial expressions; Kinaesthetics/movement, to see how it felt and looked to be the Jester – putting on the mask, using the gun; Narrative, occurred when we had an overall review and discussion of *The Jester.*

6 *Meaning*

Group members identified the Jester as an archetype, variously characterised as an innocent observing human life; a part of each of us, which retains that childlike innocence even when we take on the trappings of maturity and society; or a cynical commentator on the falseness of the social game. It was noted that an outside observer can more easily identify society's shortcomings, make judgements and tell the truth about the value of what we do. Comedians often take on and are allowed to play this role, and in doing so, they act like a safety valve for society – because they are comedians, or fools, they do not need to be taken too seriously. Therefore, although they are rebels, it is a safe rebellion to some extent. The danger is that if the rebel goes 'too far' in holding a mirror up to society, he or she will be destroyed.

One group member drew comparisons with corporate life, in that no one would dare to be authentic and say what they really feel as 'your future would be finished in most corporations if you did'. It was stated that: 'If organisations had a Jester they would get rid of him.' There were parallels too about Jesus rebelling against the mores of his day –

'Jesus was crucified for not conforming; that is what happens when someone challenges the establishment'. Since Jesus is said to have risen from the dead, there is also a parallel between that story and the end of *The Jester*.

7 *Touchstone Story*

As always, there can be more than one Touchstone Story. This is a one man show in which the single character can represent an innocent observer, a more cynical observer, or an element of the personality of every human being. This character masquerades as an entertainer, but what he has to say is confronting. He calls into question the value of most of the things which make up our social structure. He points out that we are all weak and mortal. He punishes himself for being a rebel by shooting himself but, like Jesus, he comes back to life, perhaps making the point that all of these elements of humanity (and possibly, of divinity) are endlessly repeated in the cycle of life.

The truth about life can be presented in the most confronting and engaging way and yet it is not easy to face. People who desire to live authentic lives will embrace the truth, despite the difficulty and the cost and will achieve inner happiness as they listen to the voice within. Those who are afraid of being genuine hide behind 'masks' in order to conform to society's norms, and seek their happiness in materialistic pursuits. They disregard the message of truth as foolish, and lack responsibility for the self. Those who are open to authentic living will recognise opportunities to develop and embrace it.

Theatre and DPS

The effective use of Theatre with DPS is endless. First seeing a theatrical performance for entertainment still speaks to us. Possibly it may trigger something wonderful or disturbing and this response can then be reviewed. A particular play may be shown for educational, therapeutic or human resource issues (for example see *Face to Face*, Chapter 17: Education). Or a short scenario could be enacted by the local theatre troupe for these purposes or could even be performed by students, staff or clients. Certainly for the Dramatic Enactment stage of DPS, Theatre has many applications (numerous examples are given throughout this book). We are not speaking of formal or refined acting here, just simple portrayals in short scenarios. Simple, easy, effective, creative and fun.

8
Music

The last time I saw Joe Campbell, a few months before his death in 1987,
he was as enthusiastic and entertaining as ever,
inviting me to his house in Hawaii
so we could finally sit down and crack open the
mystery of shamans, the animal powers, and the drum.
Mickey Hart[1] *Drumming at the Edge of Magic*

The opening line in *Curiosities of Music*, Louis C. Elson[2] tells us, 'Music has been broadly defined by Fetis as "the art of moving the feelings by combinations of sounds"; taken in this broad sense it may be considered as coeval (beginning at the same time) with the human race.' Moving through time, geography, culture, faith, and now, even space, music is an ancient and universal language. In her book in which drumming practices of women in antiquity are described, Layne Redmond writes, '...transforming practices such as rhythmic drumming or meditation can put us in touch with the archetypal patterns of consciousness inherent in human beings'.[3] From sharing the simplest rhythmic tapping to sophisticated multi-media productions involving sounds from space, music weaves connection within and among people. Musical choices and preferences become key parts of identity and significant ways in which we learn about and communicate who we are. Melodies, remembered from the past, flow into the present, bringing with them their attendant emotions and images.

Anna Bray,[4] a veteran of more than 60 professional and non-professional performances in musical theatre writes:

> Music has been called an emotional language without words. Not only does it have universal appeal from the cradle, it can express and

evoke a range of emotional states that other art forms can only aspire to encompass. Devoid of visual form, it requires no understanding to appreciate: one can hear a piece of music and not know anything about its construction, context, purpose, or even what instruments are playing and still have a moving dramatic experience.

Performing music can also be a powerful mind/body experience. From my own experience the closest analogy would be a sensation of mental and physical levitation. This experience I suggest can be equated with what is termed 'spiritual', 'sacred' or 'ecstatic', as it touches on something inexpressible, universal, and archetypal.

Dramatic

The dramatic qualities of music, its expressiveness both for audience and performer, require no understanding of language or technique to be powerful. In an **interview with Roland Peelman**,[5] Director of Sydney's *The Song Company*, Rob Allen asked:

Roland, could you comment on the dramatic, psychological and storytelling qualities of Music?

The way the harmonies move through the piece is both very abstract and very **dramatic**. The dramatic rationale, though, the way it becomes dramatic, is because it's related to a particular ritual. In a recent work we created a kind of a new ritual simply by doing what we did. The singers sang and moved at the same time and it was highly choreographed so that the music and the movement would be one and the same. That doesn't happen very much in dance. Usually the dancers move and the music plays; you hear through the loudspeakers. Here there was very much an attempt to keep them together, so that both would be dramatic and, in a sense, without telling an obvious story, without giving the words to the audience. It was dramatic because of that ritualistic aspect. In a sense, a concert by a string quartet playing a late Beethoven quartet in the concert hall of the Sydney Opera House, is a ritual. The audience comes there and by quarter past eight everybody is seated and ready to partake. The fact that the performers come on stage, take their bow, sit down, look at one another and start and at the end acknowledge all those people who have been listening to it, indicates we are all sharing the same music. The playing of the music is not the music. The music is what is created, so in a sense, the audience and musicians are on an equal **psy-**

chological level there. We don't necessarily need those words and all those other references for something to be dramatic. There is something inherent and a lot of people have taken heart from that, particularly in this day and age when so much music is reproduced on disc, which can't be done for a dance company or for a theatre company. You can look at a video but you don't have the same experience. Music is so elusive, it happens in time, it's totally abstract. Even the score, that's not the music, that's just a piece of paper, that's a code, a message that somebody put on a piece of paper which is then left for the performers to read, to interpret how it should be.

*What about **storytelling** and Music?*

Music always tells a story in some form. I remember when a composer whose work we did came to Sydney two or three years ago. We were working through the piece and it's really not easy. The way it starts, for example, for the girls, it's very hard technically, the way the voice has to invent the sound. It took quite a while and we nearly got there, before the first performance. I remember one day, Julian, the composer, took the girls aside and said: 'You have to be both the birds, the little bird that goes wandering, and you have to be like the one who is looking for the bird. You have to be all of that' and then they understood the story and it made all the difference. I've always remembered that, because the music is both the bird and the one who looks for the bird. It's both the player and the audience.

End of Interview

Psychological

From singing in the shower, to performing or listening to the ritual qualities of music at the opera, music is not only dramatic, but it is psychological. It is evocative, expressive, and impossible to adequately describe with words. Whether you are the singing bird or the one who goes wandering, listening to the song, music is a common denominator. With no knowledge of either the opera or the language, the profound grief of Aida's aria enshrouds the listener. Singing, playing or whistling the blues, may not erase pain, but does provide relief. Regardless of religious preference, George Frederic Handel's *Halleluiah Chorus* communicates joy. From the beginning of time, babes have been soothed by crooning. Dance music promotes expression of joy, sexuality, preparation for battle, a complete range of strong or subtle emotion.

Attending a concert by 88-year old jazz pianist Dave Brubeck and his quartet, Nina Krebs, on her recent wedding anniversary, remembered her excitement at going to two concerts he gave, first when she was in college 45 years before and then about 10 years ago:

> I have listened to and loved this musician's work all my adult life. The outdoor concert under the stars entranced me, as Brubeck played the complex music he had composed just the year before. No sign of frailty in the intricate and demanding piano work. At the concert ten years ago, I was shocked to see an old man step on stage and sit down at the piano. In my mind, he was still the youngster who had played at Arizona State University in the 1950s, but my perceptions shifted, abruptly. The musician is aging, and so am I, but the music offers a reliable, pleasurable continuum, which will remain after both of us depart. Brubeck's music is like a special friend to me in the way that it connects my past and my present through memory and all that the music evokes in me.

In addition to very personal psychological qualities, music is transpersonal. Festivals featuring diverse musical forms abound worldwide. People come together to play, listen, learn, dance, share or just be entertained. Even when no other communication exists between nations, cultural exchanges may allow musicians to cross borders, making them diplomats without portfolio in dangerous times. Celebratory communication through music has a special place in all cultures, with holidays being especially rich in musical storytelling.

> On Christmas Day, *Compass*[6] celebrates the season with a profile of a range of Australians who bestow upon others the joy of the gift of song. For Christians and non-Christians alike Christmas has become a time for family celebration and the giving of gifts ... sometimes quite expensive gifts. The gift of song costs nothing, yet for both giver and receiver it is a gift beyond value that for many encompasses the true meaning of Christmas.
>
> Jonathon Welch is a former principal tenor with Opera Australia who founded a choir for homeless people. He's now passing on the joy of song to members of the *Sydney Street Choir*.
>
> The female a cappella quartet *Blindman's Holiday* draws from many languages to build empathy and bridges between cultures.

In rural Victoria the all male *Acafellas* choir sings for social justice and the environment. All share a belief that the experience of singing with others promotes peace and goodwill between people and evokes a sense of connection and sheer elation not easily explained to others.

Storytelling

Among indigenous people, song and chant tell cultural stories and teach the ways of their ancestors. In the Middle Ages, troubadours roamed Europe bearing their interpretations of current events through song. Music is the mainstay of liturgy, giving form and rhythm to long ritual passages in virtually all the world's religions. Throughout history, oppressed people have embedded messages in song in order to communicate with peers, unbeknownst to oppressors. Music both tells stories without words or pictures and accompanies stories, told through those media. Musical jingles and commercials become annoyingly indelible as mini-stories in our brains. Cinematic scores foreshadow, heighten and predict action without diverting audience attention from the screen.

Moya Henderson[7] is a distinctive and impressive Australian composer whose work is motivated by a concern with society's myths and cultures. Her clear vision, prophetic spirit and idiosyncratic musical style stand out in the Australian musical world. She reveals the process and the poignant story at the heart of her new radiophonic composition, *I walked into my mother*, which is her personal response to reading the testimonies of so many Aboriginal women and men who were taken away from their families and homeland. This musical setting is drawn from the evidence presented by one of these witnesses, and recognises the anguish suffered by a child whose only meeting with his mother was brief and tantalising, the memory of which still fills him with yearning. His statement, 'This was my first feeling of love, and it could only have come from my mum', is from the text she uses for this production, found on page 156 of *Bringing Them Home*. It is the testimony of someone identified only as 'Confidential evidence 139'.

Award-winning northern California composer and folksinger Linda Book[8] shares the power of storytelling in a song she wrote. As artist-in-residence for local elementary schools, she performed for sixth graders throughout a spring semester. One of the songs she did for them was *Someday I'm Gonna Have a Horse*, in which she bewails the fact that as a child her mother wouldn't let her have a horse, no matter what scheme she created to make that happen. There was no place to keep a horse. The family couldn't afford a large animal – and on – and on – which she soulfully portrays in song. At the end of the semester, one of the teachers came to Linda and said, 'Linda, I think you should know this before it goes too far. The sixth graders are taking up a collection to buy you a horse'.

Music and DPS

When Freud described the 'oceanic experience', he referred to religion, but he could well have been referring to making or listening to music. When the experience of 'levitating' as Anna Bray described it or total entrancement occurs, the effect is profound. That experience, in and of itself, can be moving beyond words, and may well be more than enough. By continuing the episode through DPS, a new container can be created that enhances clarity and may bring deeper understanding. The same can be true of the simple question: 'Why does that piece of music touch me so?'

A Case Study by Nina Krebs – *Sun Rings*

1 *Expressive Art type*

Music: In April, 2005, I attended a performance of *Sun Rings*[9] at Mondavi Center, Davis, California, later described in *Sacramento Bee* Newspaper, as *An Otherworldly Night with Kronos*.[10] The pre-season brochure description had attracted me: '*Sun Rings* is a major new work celebrating human space exploration. The renowned Kronos Quartet shares the stage with the University of California, Davis, Chorus, all to a spectacular set of lighting and video. Written by famed Northern California composer Terry Riley and co-commissioned by NASA (National Aeronautics and Space Agency), this evening-length program unites the artistry of Kronos and Riley with the wonder of technology, bringing the music of the sphere to life for the new millennium.'

2 *Element*

Playwright Psychotheatrics

3 *Craft*

Expressive Writing excerpt: Incredible! I felt completely surrounded by and absorbed in the experience. I want to learn more about the composer and hope there is a CD of the music. There isn't, yet. Something about it touched me deeply. I'm glad we stayed for the post-concert interview and were able to see the musicians and the composer up close and hear their comments. My sense is that Terry Riley wrote the music from his heart, finding ways to access sounds from space and embrace the material in such a way to make it speak to all of us. The quartet and the visual artist who created the video that played on the screen had everything to do with the moment as well as the 100-voice UC Davis chorus seated behind the screen. As I write this, I can feel my writing energy come back and know that I can focus to do the work I want to do. I feel excited...

4 *Story Map*

Orientation: I am attending a concert of the Kronos Quartet playing *Sun Rings* at University of California, Davis, Mondavi Center. Michael Tilson Thomas, conductor of the San Francisco Symphony and others, described this resonant hall as an 'instrument' in and of itself.

Complication: I am feeling overwhelmed, behind schedule, bogged down by studio remodel in progress, sad about personal losses...

Sequence of Events: On a spring evening, I walked into the auditorium illuminated at the level of twilight, to my seat about 30 rows from the front. The stage was set for the Kronos Quartet – four chairs, music stands and an embracing semi-circular forest of thin poles varying in height. The deep blue backdrop glowed slightly and offered a credible rendition of an uncluttered night sky. Intermittent squeaks, tweets, booms and whistling sounds bathed the gathering audience who added hushed murmurs and rustling programs to the mix.

After a time, the quartet members walked on and, nodding to light applause, assumed their spaces. The violinist passed his hand in a waving motion through the air. A strange choreography. Another of the musicians took up the gesture and did the same. They began playing, all four musicians, from time to time, interspersing the string music with single hand waving. Recorded squeaks and whistles as well as musical strains and other noises formed part of the composition. Twinkling lights in random order flickered from the poles around the musicians.

The ten 'space-scapes' are largely atonal woven with recognisable themes and rhythms, unfamiliar but not unpleasant; each of the pieces with its identifiable differences. Images began floating across the backdrop – formulae, clouds, spacecraft, images of planets and moons. Voices entered. The lighting shifted to reveal a portion of the 100-member

University of California, Davis, Chorale, seated behind the scrim. At a point late in the program the light show escaped the scrim and covered the arched ceiling and walls in the front part of the auditorium with colourful wheeling letter symbols, pulling audience, quartet and chorale into the magical space experience.

Kronos Quartet, along with NASA Art Program and a long list of other agencies, commissioned composer Terry Riley to take the sounds of space, which had been collected over a period of 40 years from plasma wave receivers built by physicist Don Gurnett, and weave them into music. Willie Williams (light designer for rock group U2) used the NASA archive of space imagery as the basis for the light show.

5 ***Dramatic Enactment***

Narrative: I stayed for the post-concert narrative discussion with the composer and members of the quartet. The quartet, three men and a woman, obviously knew composer Terry Riley well and participated with him in an informal discussion of the work. The rather impish looking man with wire-rimmed glasses and a very long white wavy beard talked about the level of being overwhelmed by the experience when he received the space sound recordings from NASA. He listened to the sounds over and over until he could begin to identify fragments of melody. In the program he had written, '...my thoughts became filled with images stimulated by locales as distant as Jupiter and Uranus. I could almost feel myself propelled through space as one atmosphere gave way to another...' The discussants answered questions from the small audience and made comments about parts they thought important. Still in a daze from the concert, I listened, in awe of the imagination and creativity embodied in the small group on the stage. Respectfully prefacing his question, a young man in the audience addressed the composer, 'Mr. Riley, I am sure you are familiar with both Eastern and Western music forms, and I could hear both in *Sun Rings*. How did you decide on which form to use for the themes you were working on?' Expecting a technical discussion of his process, I was surprised when the composer said, 'I worked from my emotional response to the sounds, and the form fell into place. I had listened to them so much they felt like part of me.' He wrote in the program notes: 'If only we let the stars mirror back to us the big picture of the universe and the tiny precious speck of it we inhabit that we call Earth, maybe we will be given the humility and insight to love and appreciate all life and living forms wherever our journeys take us.'

6 *Meaning*

As the drama of the concert and the discussion played out before me, I was privileged to witness people who had confronted an idea much bigger than any of them. Along with our ancient forebears, they had dared to look for meaning and connection in the infinite reaches of space. The composer and musicians, along with NASA'S technicians, the physicist from Iowa, and the light designer had translated cosmic sound and vision for human enjoyment. The audience became one with the music.

7 *Touchstone Story*

Allow fragments of melody to emerge from the overwhelming mass and adopt them as starting points in discovery.

Conclusion

'Music is everybody's possession. It's only publishers who think that people own it.' (John Lennon)[11] Publishers play an important role in transmitting knowledge of all sorts, including music, but Lennon's point is well taken. Music has been with us forever and continues to be important in all cultures and social groups. It can be shared without knowledge of a particular language, and plays through us at many levels. Music as one of the Expressive Art types, offers opportunity for dramatic expression, psychological understanding and storytelling in almost limitless ways. DPS is useful in understanding musical experiences for which traditional methods are difficult if not impossible.

9
Visual Art

Some of the pictures are truly mysterious to me,
which is why I so often say publicly that
I don't know or don't care what they're really about.
And yet I can also say that the paintings are prayers,
that they have to do with whatever it is that
makes you want more than what daily life affords.
Susan Rothenberg[1]

Making art is deeply personal, whether the form is finger painting or the most remote digitalised work produced through mathematically directed electronic media. Even in shared work, such as mural making or other collective pieces, the individual brings his or her unique vision to the process. The lure of creating form and colour through unbounded involvement predates history and continues into realms unimagined even a decade ago. This personal aspect, the idiosyncratic container each person brings to visual art, whether as viewer or creator, makes this Expressive Art type invaluable in the DPS repertoire.

Describing Visual Art in words, or even writing about creating it, moves the emotional experience into a different realm. Direct emotional experience takes expression through external activity that can be shared over time with other people. Viewers who happen on a child's drawing on the sidewalk stop, look, and may wonder about the child who made the marks. They may reflect on a personal experience evoked by the colour, a shape, the mere fact of the image in that space. Responses might range from feeling irritated or downright angry at intrusion or messiness, to feeling happy, touched because this is wistfully reminiscent of one's own childhood. We are not *tabula rasa*. For one viewer, bright red smears might be rage, for another joy, another blood or fire, another the glory of a vivid sunrise. In its most basic form, painting, drawing or smearing, channel rational and emotional expression from inside to out – from covert to visible. At another level of intention, the artist may be hoping to communicate or evoke responses in the viewer, rather than being mainly self-expressive.

Regardless of the artist's intent, this expression interacts with whatever the viewer brings to the work, creating a particular inter-subjective space that can then become shared material in a DPS session. 'The clay saved my life', Veronica Kyle, a formerly homeless woman enrolled at Sacramento City College is quoted as saying in a *Sacramento Bee* newspaper feature. 'I love clay more than I loved the drugs, the alcohol...There's just me and the clay. I lose myself. I get the feel for the clay. The clay tells me what it wants and I adhere to that.'[2]

As with any Expressive Art type, from the point of view of the artist, expression is part, but not all, of the process. Mastery of the craft, with all that involves, can become absorbing with its challenges, disappointments and thrill of accomplishment. Matisse reportedly said, 'I have always tried to hide my own efforts and wished my works to have the lightness and joyousness of a springtime, which never lets anyone suspect the labours it cost'.[3] Making art is about mechanics and problem solving as well as about expression. Sculptors know a lot about gravity. Discipline and diligence go into gaining skill with media that ultimately allows the artist to achieve desired outcomes. Mixing paint, glazes, choosing painting tools and supports, all the mundane aspects of art, contribute to the impact of the work.

Graphic arts from the world of commerce shape our visual world and impact us from every direction in the urban environments many of us inhabit. Colours and shapes bombard us, moving and speaking on electronic media of all kinds or assuming more stationary form on signs, buildings and vehicles. Digital art has moved into the fine arts through photography, cinema and animation, and appears in every imaginable genre, including the work of painters who move back and forth from computer to canvas. The point is not to judge the genre, but to participate in creating and viewing, allowing Visual Art in whatever form, to speak its piece.

The power of art to connect the individual with inner self as well as with the energy of the artist, of the 'collective' and the 'collective unconscious' speaks to those who are open to taking in the experience. Sharing this experience with others through DPS has the power to unveil feelings and motivation that have been hidden, or barely in the artist's or the participant's awareness. Bringing these feelings into the open not only allows revelations for the individual, but for others who may have a related experience with the work of art or the art-making process.

As mentioned earlier from the work of Stephen J. Newton, when art comes through a flow state, it contains unconscious form, the parts that the artist does not necessarily intend – brush strokes, accidents of form, unintentional colours or objects – in addition to the more obvious aspects of colour, form and content.[4] Although we may not be able to measure it directly, absorbing art that has been produced in this state may awaken similar connection with the unconscious, or even the ineffable, for the viewer. Opening to emotional experience with visual art gives us access to experience we have not been able to articulate verbally.

An **interview with Chris Reding**,[5] a northern California artist, who for the last 13 years has taught art at Sacramento City College, offers some thoughts on both the process of making art and the participation of the viewer.

> **Dramatic** expression in Visual Art reflects that everyone comes from a different place. The first thing we do as babies is respond to shapes and colours. Kids immediately start gesture drawing, there is something about these shapes and forms that connects us. They are expressive; they are memory pieces.
>
> Visual Art is very meditative for me – there is this wonderful kind of quiet thoughtfulness about it, so that it changes everything about your life. In a **Psychological** sense, I think it changes how you think and daydream. It is **storytelling**, a conversation – that is what every artist wants from their viewer: an exchange. You do not just want to have this conversation alone. It's exciting stuff so you want to speak out – it is good because it will let other people have the experience of it and imagine themselves part of it.

Painting is probably the visual art form that comes to mind first for most people, but the art world is always in flux. Although painters continue to explore colour, shape and light, others are moving into media that is more technical, less dependent on the established art world of galleries and museums, taking art to the streets. Performance Art comes in as many forms as there are artists. The pieces mentioned below have significant visual and theatrical aspects.

Ricardo Rivera,[6] San Francisco Bay Area sculptor and video artist, works as artist-in-residence at San Francisco's Exploratorium, where he engages in visual/science and other arcane constructions. One such work is a 'brain' that rotates to follow the viewer from a TV screen, occasionally reflecting the viewer's image on the screen. He frequently references childhood experiences, for example, of riding a bike alone in his hometown, of miscommunications with people, or of discrimination. He then reinterprets these experiences in a struggle with clarity. Along this vein, Ricardo took to the streets of San Francisco with his rendition of bicycle performance art.

The following is an experiential account of this performance, written by Nina Krebs.

1 *Expressive Art experience*

Visual Art (Performance): On *Vente de Noviembre* (November 20, 2004 – the date commemorates the Mexican Revolution of 1910) dark has come to the Mission District of San Francisco. A faint glow fans from the open door on a smattering of waiting people outside the Pond Gallery in the late fall chill. Occasional traffic dots the narrow side street where parked cars fill every inch of curb space. A chain link fence encloses vast darkness across the alley from the gallery.

2 *Element*

Playwright Psychotheatrics: Ideal vehicle to explore the essence of an experience for an individual, couple or small group.

3 *Craft*

Expressive Writing: The following description evolved from rough notes jotted down after the performance and was followed by an interview with the artist/performer, Ricardo Rivera:

Blaring *tamborazo* music arrives before the rider, announcing an occasion of importance. The bicycle's light projects a blue-white beam brighter than the emerging blur of a white-clad human form – a masked ice-cream vendor playing loud Mexican music, ghostly and garish at the same time. The rigged bike looks like a typical 3-wheeled ice cream cart, but this box holds no sweet treats. It contains a generator that stores energy when the rider pedals and runs a projector that throws an image onto any surface he passes.

He slows and halts near the lighted gallery door, awkwardly balancing the unwieldy rig, places a boom box playing the relentless music on the sidewalk, takes a basket of apples from the handle bar and deposits that, too. The rough-carved white mask reveals nothing. Nobody approaches or talks to him, nor does he speak. After a bit he rides off, waits for the light at the corner and doubles back on the other side of the street, projecting the pulsing image – a heart or an apple (?) fabricated with shiny material – on to the brick building there. He pedals his way around the corner and disappears, *tamborazo* still loud on the sidewalk's boom box, drowning out the strains the rider takes with him into the night.

4 *Story Map*

Orientation: Ricardo Rivera told me about the up-coming performance and I went to San Francisco to see it. I was currently taking an independent study art class from him at Sacramento City College and had a strong interest in his work. I had seen some of his work in a gallery and was excited about it, due to its interactive power and intersubjective content.

Complication: I wanted to know more, to gain a better understanding of this new work in particular and performance art in general. The impact on me was strong but left me feeling like I didn't quite get something that I should understand. I was missing out. I had seen a person I know in a situation where he was anonymous and strange, leaving me nonplussed and without my usual way of making contact.

Sequence of events: A first-time visitor at the Pond Gallery, a small *avant garde* venue that features emerging artists and non-traditional work, I felt less than comfortable in the hip, youngish crowd. I knew no one and of course Ricardo wasn't there because he was out riding his rig in the Mission District, an area where strangers are not always welcome and crime is not unusual. The wait went on for over an hour. I wondered about Ricardo's safety and about what kind of response he was getting. I had no idea what the performance was, other than what I gleaned from some people in the gallery I talked with who knew him.

When the rider appeared, I was off balance. The white figure slowly pedaling toward me appeared menacing and did not seem like Ricardo as I know him. The loud music more than filled the space. I took a few photos, but the event happened quickly and I was left feeling that I didn't really see it. I didn't know the meaning of the music, or the significance of the apples or the boom box placed on the sidewalk. A drunken man came from the alley by the gallery and picked up the boom box. I wondered if he was part of the performance, but no, he just wanted the radio. He hung around, talking to people in the group for a while and started to leave with the radio. I paid him $5.00 to get it back. The whole thing was unsettling. I was exhausted and decided to forego the party that would follow and left the gallery before Ricardo returned from his ride. I just wanted supper and the comfort of my hotel.

Resolution: I sent Ricardo the photos and asked if he would have coffee with me to talk about the event. He agreed.

Coda: This event that I had anticipated as enjoyable was unsettling and I wanted to know more about it.

5 *Dramatic Enactment*

Narrative: I kept a journal of my experience of this performance and how it affected me. I also talked to close friends about the performance and its impact. Their views helped me to clarify certain areas. Using *Theatre* would have been enlightening. Directing players to be the rider, the drunken man, the gallery people, and me would offer an opportunity for me to explore some very old feelings of social discomfort and control issues in ambiguous situations, as well as the additional impact of the artwork. It would also give Ricardo an opportunity to see at least one person's reaction to his performance.

6 *Meaning*

I like to think I am open to cross-cultural experience. I have even written a book about it.[7] Ricardo's performance haunted me. I can still visualise him riding out of the dark, music blaring, masked face staring straight ahead, handle bars wobbling uncertainly. If the goal was to push me off center so I could re-examine my comfort zone, it worked. Next time I hope I reach for an apple.

7 *Touchstone Story*

Take more risk with ambiguity and try to stay open for what lies beneath the surface. For the person who has not pursued art as a career or even over a long period, creating and viewing art is a key to new and vastly rewarding life experience.

San Francisco artist Tina Heringer[8] who was preparing a performance piece for delivery to the Oakland Art Gallery, discussed both the street performance and gallery aspects of her work:

> The beauty question in art is part of the **dramatic** and also the **psychological** seduction of wanting to look at something. It's fun to do the drawings that are part of the documentation, the **storytelling**.

Tina discussed the complexity of performance art – the preparation. In addition to her own costume, she was creating a life-size dummy that she would transport from San Francisco, across the Bay to Oakland on public transit – also creating a video. Craft and experience go into each of these parts, and then there is the performance itself that often requires not only aesthetic competence but also courage and stamina.

After several semesters as a (retired psychologist) art student, Nina Krebs[9] had the privilege of creating and hanging a show at the Kondos Gallery on the campus of Sacramento City College. Here the project is outlined in the Dramatic Psycholological Storytelling format to demonstrate the model in this context using Playwright Psychotheatrics.

Visual Art Case Study by Nina Krebs

In February 2003, during my third semester at Sacramento City College, I arranged with my friend, Heather Folsom, and my husband David Krebs, to spend a day at the empty Kondos gallery working on two separate half-day projects. I was the director for the first project which involved hanging several 10 and 12-foot fabric *trees* and some other pieces in the gallery in order to photograph them. The second project was to photograph my performance as Artemisia Gentileschi in the pose she adopted for her self-portrait in the 17th century. The 'Artemisia' photographs were the raw material for a digital composite I wanted to make to represent the spirit of Artemisia, a Renaissance painter who portrayed women realistically rather than as idealised waifs as had been the case up until her time. Heather Folsom was the director for the Artemisia project.

1 *Expressive Art experience*

Visual Art: In this case, the Expressive Art experience is a show, *Portent and Portal: The Soul and Spirit of Everywoman*, at the Gregory Kondos Gallery, Sacramento City College, May 2003.

2 *Element*

Playwright Psychotheatrics: The ideal vehicle to explore the essence of an experience for an individual, couple or small group.

3 *Craft*

Expressive Writing excerpt: When I started 'making art' as they say, a year or so after closing my psychology practice, my goal was to ignore the critic who has governed so much of my life, especially perhaps, my creative efforts. She spoke often and loudly: 'Too messy, too gruesome, not possible.' Although I had explored painting a few times, I had never concentrated on learning about or creating art. Having idealised artists all my life, thinking 'talent' is something possessed by others, it didn't occur to me that I could 'be' an artist. Working through *The Artist's Way*,[10] which involved daily expressive writing, helped me to clarify that devoting time and energy to making art was a priority.

Through the work I did with my first teacher and then at City College, I began to understand that art is much broader than skill at drawing and painting.

Seeing my work hanging in the gallery was a transformational experience. Because the pieces were large, they required uncluttered space, which neither classroom nor home could provide. Until that point, even though I had created them, I hadn't *seen* them. Being able to witness my work in the gallery environment, along with my struggle to embody the form and spirit of Artemisia, allowed me to take in the imagery in a completely different way than I had been able to do while working on it. I became the viewer rather than the artist. No longer 'possessing' the work. The process encouraged me to risk asking the gallery director for a show. He agreed to it. Only later did I discover that *artists*, not students, are *invited* to hang shows in that gallery!

4 *Story Map*

Orientation: During my spring semester 2003 while taking classes at Sacramento City College, without even realising it, I fell into a rabbit hole of sorts and my world turned upside down. I've heard people talk about their creativity being channelled and that is as close as I can come to remembering that time when one thing led to another, and yet another, combined with a compulsion to keep going, with no particular goal in mind other than making the work. I made lots of it.

Complication: The gallery director had agreed to give me a show, but I had no central organising theme. When my mentor, Chris Reding, who thank goodness had agreed to help me, saw my collected work assembled in the gallery ready to be placed, her comment was, 'This is going to be a hard show...' As I followed her gaze, I could see that, even though to me the work was coherent, neither colour and form nor content would hold it together for anyone else. I became painfully aware that I was in over my head.

Sequence of events: Chris asked me to focus on what I was trying to do, and I realised that my goal was to create a mood, a feeling of inclusion for the viewer upon walking into the gallery. I hoped that standing among the somewhat ephemeral sculptural forms, the trees that represented women artists would instil a sense of how we are all connected through an invisible golden chain. Even though I spent as much or more time and energy on each of the pieces that composed the rest of the show, the art on the walls became secondary, creating a context and container for the installation. With helpful editing and assistance in grouping and spacing pieces, a sense of unity began to emerge. The centerpiece of the show was WOMANTREEWOMAN, an installation of six, ten-foot trees representing women artists through the ages, my teachers, my student and myself. I had constructed the first tree in class as part of a self-portrait project. Since the idea came from drawing a tree with a natural 'face' and then superimposing my own features using the computer program Adobe Photoshop, I wanted to build something that had greater resemblance to a real tree. I came up with the idea of using fabric and started experimenting. A friend suggested making 'trees' of people I know. Since the way I was blending tree forms and faces creates disturbing imagery, I decided not to subject my family and friends to such manipulation but moved on to the idea of *women artists through the ages*. Scratching the surface of this idea, I made 'trees' for Artemisia Gentileschi and Eva Hesse – two favorite artists; Tina Heringer and Chris Reding – teachers; Gina deAmicis, student and me. Hanging in the centre of the gallery, the trees made a small forest; a magic circle of feminine art spirits. Lithographs, digital prints – including the Artemisia piece, drawings, paintings, a couple of constructed pieces and some mixed media work completed the show.

My husband Dave and I spent two full days hanging the work, with help from Chris Reding and Chris Daubert, the gallery director. I had worked as hard as I could from February to May preparing, and thought it would be a simple matter to place the work. I had no idea how much time, energy and attention to detail moving it from floor to wall, and ceiling in some cases, would be required. The second night after everything was in place, I practically fell into bed and dreamed:

> I was a therapist...someone came to get me to help a woman in crisis. They took me by the hand and we ran to find the woman. I had been getting dressed but had no clothes on. I was trying to step into my shorts, but they said, 'You don't have time!!! Run! Hurry!'
> On the way to wherever, I grabbed a big shirt – fuchsia silk – that I thought would at least be big enough to wrap around me. As I ran, I clumsily and ineffectively tried to cover myself, but I was exposed. I worried about how I could be very credible as a helper in such a state.

I had been so intent on getting the work together, hanging the show and preparing for the party I was going to have, I was not tracking the shadow side of the experience. It was a big leap for me to expose this whole new, unrefined aspect of my life and I had been in denial about my feelings of vulnerability.

Resolution: At the gallery, walking among the trees, I felt happy and proud – changed by the process of making the work and hanging it. Yes, much more exposed than I ever had been behind the shield of confidentiality as a therapist. Ideas for the imagery and for the show, as well as the audacity to ask for it, came to me from a place I can't describe or defend. The best part eludes description either in words or pictures. It's the fact that *Portent and Portal* happened, especially the 'installation' aspect, which I had not anticipated.

The gallery director's comment, 'This show works because there is no pretense toward coherence' echoed my mentor's earlier concern, and made me laugh because in a way this was correct. In another way, coherence flowed through the spiritual underpinnings of the work; all of it constructed in my attempt at authenticity and willingness to take the next step.

Coda: For the first time in my life I had a profound experience through a project that emerged without a predetermined goal and which developed over time. I didn't start out making work for a show. In February, after I knew the show was going to happen, I became goal-oriented: constructed trees, had a series of digital prints made with pigmented ink on good paper, matted and framed prints, paintings and drawings in order to refine the presentation of those pieces.

5 *Drama Enactment*

Narrative: At the time of this event, it would have been exciting to do an Imaginal Psychotheatrics session with people who attended the show. Not to analyse the art, but to explore the responses evoked, in the viewers as well as the artist and helpers. The Dramatic Enactment that did happen involved people walking around the show, among the trees, creating movement in the forest and adding their shadows to the walls. Some of them shared their comments with me. 'I walk into the gallery and feel my spirit lift', a college staff member told me. A young student said, 'I come in here every day to feel the magic and think about when I can do something like this'. At the local farmers' market two years after the show, I saw a woman I spoke with only briefly at the show and hadn't seen since. She told me she had subsequently been making artwork and that she had wanted to talk with me about the show and about the powerful spiritual experience she had there. Of course, not everyone who saw it thought it was great. Some questioned whether it was art at all.

6 *Meaning*

Taking my inner voice seriously and giving myself permission to do what I really want to do takes me where I want to go. When I began the journey into making art, I vowed I would not do things to please others or to earn praise. I have worked to be open to learning from my teachers, but I have stayed true to ideas as they come to me. Doing so makes me feel grounded and whole.

7 Touchstone Story
There are lots of ways to make a difference. Being an artist is one of them.

Conclusion

Carey Allen and Lucy Milan, theatre/media students from Charles Sturt University in Australia, traveled to Vietnam to interview Suzanne Lecht,[11] Art Director for the Art Vietnam Gallery, whose comments make a fitting summary for this chapter:

> Art is **dramatic** as it has the ability to transport people to another world, a world that is seemingly better, or more relaxing, or just with some idyllic beauty. Maybe that makes people feel better in a **psychological** sense. Personally, I like difficult art because it makes me think and it makes me feel and I want to try to understand, so when I see some kind of complex work of art it's very interesting to me. I think, 'What is going on in the head of this artist?' 'What are they trying to say?' Communication, **storytelling** is everything. Traditionally art has been used in healing, from the understanding that is gained from stories that art reveals. If somebody asked me, just came in, and said: paint what works well in your gallery, what makes it work? I would just think of fields of colour – a certain colour – colours that fit the atmosphere of what I want to feel when I'm here. But it would be interesting to see how everybody depicts their lives – like when you ask children to depict their family. That can be very revealing because children are much more free to express what they feel, not what they think people want to see. People should have more access to art, and by that I mean museums – or galleries. Places *for art* are often times very inaccessible to people who may need it more than others.

10
Dance and Kinaesthetics

Dance (and Kinaesthetics) can empower individuals and communities ... a force that can unite, uplift, teach, build, inspire and heal ... the hidden language of the soul.
Martha Graham

> Our voices belong first to our bodies, only secondly to our native language. We 'voice' our feelings before we have words to frame them in. As we acquire language, is it possible we lose our innate ability to 'voice' our deepest feelings? Before we learn to speak, time is seamless, no verbs and nouns but recognisable sensations – wordlessness means everything, is continuous.[1]

We have a complex inner speech, which works when we act. When we are saturated and totally involved, then our 'ancient literacy' takes over. Dance and Kinaesthetics enable us to access our fundamental (physical) memory, give us the ability to conceive kaleidoscopically and simultaneously, in addition to perceiving in chronological order. Movement in time is now, intrinsically of the present, totally focused and interactive rather than historical contemplation.

Dance and Kinaesthetics are **dramatic** methods to reunite and express the unification of the body, mind and soul. For thousands of years Dance and Kinaesthetics have been considered a way to communicate with the divine. They are an expression of spirituality in cultures and traditions all over the world, representing the sacred life journey, a celebration of the seasons and of the rhythms of our lives. Dance and Kinaesthetics are about connections: with our self, with each other, with our world, a way to re-establish contact with the earth and our fellow beings. This has been the sacred theme of Dance (Kinaesthetics) from the beginning of time. Inner logic, dreams, symbols and intuitive concepts are expressed through Dance and Kinaesthetics.

Dance and Kinaesthetics are **psychological**. Movement is the 'royal route into the psyche', there is a 'primordial level which underlies speech, namely the level of the act and interact...from the point of view of the human race, speech is a fairly late development in the human being'.[2]

Exercise (the active body = Dance and Kinaesthetics) is increasingly being recognised by medical professionals as an effective treatment for chronic diseases like depression, diabetes and osteoporosis.[3]

To feel the power and importance of this Expressive Art type, one need only imagine Dance and Kinaesthetics as passion. Imagine not allowing this movement. No passion, not being able to let things go, no release, constraining everything, good and bad. And then, to move, to express, to create!!!

Storytelling – all cultures recognise the importance of Dance and Kinaesthetics to tell sacred stories. Yet, storytelling does not have to follow chronological and historical formats. Time is relative. Movement is always in the present. It is just that the present is constantly occurring; it is always now. Stories, therefore, can be and are in the present moment; through movement you are in the here and now of the story.

Dance and Kinaesthetics are part of the spiritual essence of cultures throughout the world. For Indigenous Australians it is a way to keep the traditions alive and vibrant. Today, all of us can re-establish our storyline connections to our self, each other and the earth through Dance and Kinaesthetics. Traditional American Indian dances, for example, are essential to the collective psychology, cultural heritage and spiritual practices of the tribes.

Group movement, whether it be dance, yoga or a workout at the gym, creates its own camaraderie and proprioceptive connection. Working out in a group is different from a solo workout. The energy of the group creates wings that support individuals in sustaining activity longer with reduced fatigue. People who otherwise may have little to share conversationally, or may even be combative, can exercise or dance together harmoniously.

Carol Woodruff, academic in Human Movement at Charles Sturt University, highlights the dramatic, psychological and storytelling aspects of Kinaesthetics in the following discusssion:[4]

> From a structured point of view, the human body represents itself in a variety of levels, from the sculptured human anatomy body image

down to everybody else. So the **dramatic** effect can be a visual perception of the human body – how we see it, how we perceive it, how it's used. Human movement is broader than that. It's broader than just the image of the human body, but it's also how the human body allows us to express a persona. Body image is in the way we look, how we feel, how we gesture, ability to perform, whether that is a sport, a recreational activity, or an incidental exercise. All these allow us to express our sense of wellbeing. It's not just a sporting wellbeing but a health wellbeing. There are many levels on which the human body, through movement, can be seen as an expressive form. In a health sense, if you feel good, your body is going to express that. A smile on your face, posture, expression, communication – non-verbal, verbal, with other people, will come through as an expressive form.

Having **psychological** self-efficacy, being comfortable by being active, we feel better about ourselves because we know we can walk up the hill. We know we can walk around the block, either with the dog or with the pram or whatever. Therefore, we feel more willing to do it and by achieving that, it's a reinforcement that: 'Hey, I can manage that. I can manage it as part of my day, my activity, my normal routine, and feel good.' We are more likely, when walking the dog, to say hello to somebody along the way and therefore we gain a sense of belonging: socialisation. Doing that walk, at the same time, will bring contact with similar people: affiliation. The same people doing the same things at the same time and it is a rewarding experience. For example, a hiker may be solitary, or part of a group walk, but if someone comes the other way on the trail, more than likely some acknowledgment will occur. People are still strangers, but the usual barriers soften for a moment.

When you listen to people this is **storytelling**, many memories of their lives will revolve around physical activity. The school sports carnival or the school physical education class. A positive experience or a poor experience will have some meaning and become a topic of conversation. We will say: 'I disliked physical education when I was at school because we had to do this', or 'the teacher made me do that' or 'I fell over' or 'I embarrassed myself'. So there is a story there that can carry on through adult life about something that made a memorable experience. Usually there's an association, or there can be an association. For example: 'The first time I went into a gym', I can remember that and people, again, cement that incident in time. That experience in itself is a story. Listening to the

> comments of clients doing the personal training program here at the university at the moment, for example, a woman this morning said to me: 'This is so good, I am enjoying this!' This is about six weeks or more into the program. She never came into the gym setting before this program started. Now she is coming by herself, willing to bring other people into that setting and she is enjoying it. That is a journey. That is a story that she will relate to many other people in her own sphere of contact: her family, workmates, colleagues, the community. She will express that journey in a positive way which is great, because now that person is comfortable in that setting and is willing to continue. I think everybody has a story or more than one story that revolves around physical activity and physical experience.

An **interview by Rob Allen with Graeme Murphy**, Director of the Sydney Dance Company illustrates our poetic/mythic connections with Dance.[5]

Graeme, please share your views on the contribution that Dance makes in our life and the meaning it holds in our life.

Well, it is a form of communication, above everything, for me. I love the way it communicates. I love the directness – the **dramatic** aspects, of going directly from a physical action seen on stage through the eyes of the spectator and into the brain and then somehow directly into the parts of the brain that seem to deal with emotions. A mark of my success is if I have touched somebody, if I have made them laugh or if I have made them cry. This is particularly rewarding for some reason. You are actually somehow touching somebody in the most indirect way possible. Dance can have that emotional effect. The viewer identifies with the body. I mean it is wonderful to be fabulously emotional in athleticism, which touches us all. But it touches us at a football match too. With Dance you can't just shut your eyes and enjoy it, otherwise you are just listening to music. But, you are not directly reading it as one would a piece of literature, which directs you very much – what you are supposed to be thinking, what you are supposed to be feeling – in much the same way that television gives you so little leeway to think anything except what the television says – it even focuses for you. With dance – you have to make your own focus – you have to make choices!

What ***psychological*** *Meaning does Dance provide in our life?*

When it comes to Dance, most people's point of view is – I love to dance personally, I love the process of losing myself on the disco floor or at a club. You are one and you do not know where the music enters you and where it exits your body and you do not know whether you are the music or whether you are a person. It is that beautiful moment that all religions seek to find, that being in tune with oneself. Yet, very rarely does the general public regard it as a spectator activity. It is really something that you do or you do not; some people never dance. Most people dance at an early age and then, at some point it becomes unfashionable, for young boys especially. Or at some point it just drifts out of their life because we don't feel it's enhancing; there are no role models for it. Others have an absolutely essential need, somewhere within their genetic makeup, no matter what happens. No matter if we have never seen a performance. No matter what happens, we dance.

It seems quite beneficial to actively participate in Dance and Kinaesthetics, however, are there any benefits in being a spectator?

Research has demonstrated that when people watch Dance, certain areas of the brain light up ... the viewer really could almost get a physical feeling of doing it. The brain can actually tune in; probably wish fulfilment. 'That is how it would feel if I were doing it.' Of course their bodies are not trained for formal Dance and that probably adds to the absolute thrill. It is that vicarious thing – of watching something extraordinary happening – and the brain is already aligning with that person on the stage – so it is connecting. Who wants to be passive when you can actually go and do a dance class or do aerobics? But it is not actually just that – it is about connecting – you and a higher power.

If you look back to communities like the Native American Indian and the Indigenous people here in Australia – Dance seems essential to their culture, almost a form of sacred ***storytelling?***

Absolutely, to all cultures. In fact, I think about that a lot too, and I think how we have lost that – how it's been beaten out of us. On the primal aspect of Dance, there is no doubt that movement preceded sound for me. I mean the act of being born is all about movement.

I am appalled that we think that words somehow are the focus of human development because for me, the great emotions are depicted in movement. Afterwards these are talked about, afterwards these are made into literature; afterwards these are glorified by the word. But the deed happens first. If you love somebody – that is a physical act before it is spoken. If you hate somebody it is the same. Words follow after and the deed is talked about but everything we do, can be done without words; it precedes words. The same in terms of the primal picture, words follow to tell about events that happened, but the events happened without words.

Dance Case Study – application by Rob Allen

Description: *Some Rooms*[6] is a metaphor for our life journey. The four rooms are transforming. The Bedroom is first, next the Bathroom, after this the Changing Room and last the Reading Room.
DPS (modified to fit the circumstances of this situation, as it is always.)

1 *Expressive Art type*

Dance: This case study explored the experience of Dance through the production of *Some Rooms* by the Sydney Dance Company, created and directed by Graeme Murphy and performed by a series of solo performers: one performer for each room. Dance complements all the Expressive Arts, yet is very unique. Movement is primal, it takes you to other realms of knowledge, somehow more basic and elemental – whether watching or doing!

2 *Element*

Playwright Psychotheatrics is designed for the individual, couple or very small group. This method creates a vehicle for revealing underlying meanings and themes plus allows for an overall description of the experience.

3 *Craft*

Expressive Writing (Pennebaker 1997)[7] – where the writer explores the relationship between the experience to their own life – you sit alone and just write about your experience, minimum 20 minutes, maximum 30 minutes. The very act of writing allows the thought processes to slow down and actually alters the way the experience is represented and understood in our minds, leading to greater insight and clarity. This was completed after watching the performance of *Some Rooms* and the second Dramatic Enactment (following).

Bedroom is a 'dwelling place of youthful dreams, where the voyager creates his fantasy of idealised love'. The dancer's movements are full of joy, excitement, discovery – gliding with open arms, prancing, jumping, frolicking – almost peacock like!

This took me back to my childhood and adolescence. I do not have many memories of this period as it was not a happy time for me but now I am here again and I do remember wanting to do well at school and the need to be recognised. My fantasy of idealised love was to be included, wanting to be part of this family, to have a girlfriend, to be somebody.

Bathroom is a 'harsh sophisticated world, a place of cleansing and ritual'. The Dancer now very different with jerky movements, scrubbing laboured, awkward, moping, sad, almost like a lost dog.

This is where I learned to conform or be punished. Before, I always won awards at school and was in the gifted children's program, but now I am in a youth reformatory for *incorrigible* behaviour and having to survive a six-month sentence at the age of 14. I am forced to clean the bathroom as punishment for being new here, my introduction to this institution. I remember thinking that I was under the thumb of the authorities who were crushing me. The pain would get much worse if I did not obey and follow the rules, as in *Beneath the Wheel* by Herman Hesse.

Changing Room 'a place of confusion, of questioning, where sexuality and identity conflict'.

The Dancer first goes to one side of the stage skipping, then slowly back, almost bewildered, then frantic movements, panic attacks, then relaxing, finally sitting on the floor in a comfortable position, resolved.

This came late for me, not until my thirties and after I was married and a father and living in different countries. All about change, so much change. I felt I was on an adventure, but a very dangerous one, like climbing a very steep mountain. Yes this is exactly what this period was like. Easily I could lose my footing and fall – so far below, but it is all so exhilarating and the views are so beautiful; this sense of challenge is so real and so very perilous!

Reading Room is 'the last place, a place of introspection, calm and learning, as the physical gives way to the spiritual'.

Now the Dancer moves comfortably to the chair, looks at items, photos, books, then getting up, stretches very comfortably. There is peace here.

How did I end up in this place? Sometimes I pinch myself as it could have been so very different. Then I remember that I did make this happen. I feel lucky to be here, feel blessed to be a father, my most important role. Such wonder and so little did I realise what a fantastic gift this would be. Thank you Carey. My wife Roslyn is my partner. We are such good friends and soul mates. Old friends, Tom and Nina, are still with me. My work is a joy. How did this happen? I find such connection, such inclusion, affiliation, actualisation. I am so fortunate!

4 *Story Map*

Orientation: Set design is of four distinct rooms, reflecting stages of life that we all must journey through. First the bedroom is simple. Just a bed and wardrobe and nightstand. The lighting is pleasant and the dancer is enthusiastic, seems excited and happy. The music is enchanting. The next room – the bathroom is stark. The lighting seems cold: a toilet, bathtub, washbasin. The dancer moves slowly, cleansing with a washcloth, ponderous, oppressive. This is a bleak room. The Changing Room is a wardrobe with lots of clothes, shoes, hats and bright pictures. The dancer is frantic, trying this on and that on, fast paced. The Reading Room is the last room, filled with books, a nice comfortable chair, a lovely glowing fireplace and the dancer is relaxed, stretching, contemplative. So relaxed but so graceful and beautiful to watch. The Dancer is me! It is my journey! At first it was just a dance, fantastic art yes, but then, I somehow realised 'it is me'. Then, once again, back to the stream of just happening: my journey.

Complication: Each room has different aspects that need to be dealt with in some way. How these are experienced and the choices we then make help to shape our character.

Sequence of events: A life journey depicted through the four rooms. If older, then we have gone through these four rooms and can reflect on these, re-create them and actually change our perceptions. What if you are younger? Possibly a time to think of these major arenas we must all enter at some time: our seasons. There is wisdom in this realisation also.

Resolution: We never resolve our life. We just live as well as we can. We try not to have major regrets or we endeavour to come to terms with these. Finally we need to have *integrity* and not *despair* at our most vulnerable time, the 'hour of the wolf'. The hour just before dawn. The coldest and darkest time. This, then, is followed by the light of the day: realisation, clarity, hope and affiliation.

Coda: It is not the destination but the journey that counts. (Not original, but true)

5 *Dramatic Enactment*

(Using the 7 Expressive Arts). This happened twice: Narrative – after the performance, discussing this with the two lovely women who attended with me, my wife, Roslyn Medaris and my sister-in-law, Trish Ludgate; Narrative – after the Story Map and Craft steps and *before* Meaning, when I again discussed this with my wife.

6 *Meaning*

The journey of the dancer is about affiliation. If dancing alone, then despair, but if the rooms are filled with others that matter, then there is integrity. It means something. This is the richness, the joy in living and sharing with others.

7 *Touchstone Story*

Reminds me of so many fairytales. Those tales of wisdom. They speak of fighting dragons but even if we win, if we are alone, then we are still hollow, sterile. To have the real treasure is about being with others. This is fertility: to have a creative life, *you reap what you sow*!

Dance and Kinaesthetics: in Dramatic Psychological Storytelling

Whether one is the dancer or the viewer, the athlete or the audience, dedicated movement, Kinaesthetics, happens now, always in the present. Although movement can be captured on film, the effect is very different from the immediate experience that comes alive with its particular joy, pain, smell, touch and sound. Nonverbal communication, through movement, originates and is received differently by the brain than are words, thus having a very different impact. It is liberating for someone highly verbal to undertake this Expressive Art type, as a way of pushing beyond their comfort zone into new experience and perhaps new insights.

11
Ritual and Epic

The function of ritual, as I understand it, is to give form to human life, not in the way of a mere surface arrangement, but in depth. In ancient times, every social occasion was ritually structured and the sense of depth was rendered through the maintenance of a religious tone. Today, on the other hand, the religious tone is reserved for exceptional, very special 'sacred', occasions. And yet even in the patterns of our secular life, ritual survives. It can be recognized, for example, not only in the decorum of courts and regulation of military life, but also in the manner of people sitting down to the table together.

Campbell, Joseph[1]

Ritual and Epic have a profound impact on us personally, interpersonally and collectively. Rituals help establish our identity and influence with whom we identify. In another way, Epics transform us; these are events that we live through, either directly or vicariously, that we will always remember.

Ritual is a ceremony, performance, rite, observance, protocol, custom or tradition; it is a prescribed order of performing. Epic is a saga, monumental and vast, grand or heroic, a blockbuster.[2] An Epic is a critical incident that is overwhelming, remarkable and consequential – it can fragment or bring individuals, groups or societies together.

A Ritual is a set form of rites; a container for life transitions. Weddings, funerals, baptisms – or, on a broader, secular note, tailgate parties at sports events. These all provide form and make note of a life event for an individual or a group. Traditional religious services of all kinds are Ritual based, and participants know what to expect as the service progresses. Families and groups of all kinds create Rituals for special events or transitions as each member plays his or her part to carry on traditions that have evolved over time. Whether Rituals are invented as oases of certainty in contemporary life, or have been handed down through cultures from antiquity, they provide form, predictability and a sense of belonging to those who participate.

Rituals assist in the ability to gain perspectives on changes, offer relatedness, tradition, a greater sense of balance and help us all to weather difficulties. Frequently transitions are destabilising, resulting from a form of crisis, an emotionally significant event, a radical change of status and require a stabilising force such as that which Ritual brings. Ritual has always been used to honour cultural and personal traditions and turning points. Rituals provide a way to reinforce connections among people.

Ritual and Epic are both **dramatic**, due to the unique manner in which they are expressed. Ritual has an order. There is a prescribed manner in its performance. The expression is established through custom, designed for transformation and is known to all involved. Epic is overwhelming, an all encompassing, life-changing experience – for instance a tsunami, earthquake or a significant personal or group tragedy or triumph.

Psychological qualities include transformation, emotionally, cognitively and behaviourally. Ritual and Epic can either reinforce our identity or be so challenging as to forever change us. 'One dimension of mental illness may arise because an increasing number of individuals are forced to accomplish their transitions alone and with private symbols.'[3] 'We have the opportunity to introduce additional stability points and rituals into our society, such as new holidays, pageants, ceremonies and games. Such mechanisms could not only provide a backdrop of continuity into everyday life, but serve to integrate societies and cushion them somewhat from the fragmenting impact of super-industrialism.'[4]

Storytelling is an important part of Ritual and Epic. Ritual tells a much-defined collective story that frames its performance; this is based on custom and tradition and is part of a particular 'culture'. From viewing or participating in this ritual, we then have our own personal story, as it relates to the collective: explaining how participating in the ritual affected us. Then specific group stories, tailored to the group itself and created by the group, in relation to their experience of the Ritual, emerge as part of the shared experience.

Epic is the opposite. At first improvisational stories emerge, individuals trying to make personal sense of the event. Then specific group stories created through interpersonal interaction begin to coalesce, and only much later is there a collective story.

The following **interview by Rob Allen with Rev. Margaret Voerman**[5] explores the dramatic, psychological and storytelling characteristics of Ritual using the Anglican Church as a vehicle for our investigation.

Please describe how Ritual is dramatic, how it is psychological and how it is storytelling?

When Ritual is well carried out, designed well, things don't just happen accidentally, they happen because they have reason behind them. Design is an important part of Ritual that makes it **dramatic.** For instance, the way things are laid out, the way people move and are placed. These are the things that make each occasion special and dramatic. You can have disorganised liturgy where people are getting up one after another and wandering around, not ready to carry out their role, or you can have Ritual that is well designed, where people know their roles. Most Rituals have a high point, for example the Baptism high point is when you are pouring the water and you are actually blessing the child. This is symbolic cleansing and renewal.

Is it dramatic because of the way it is being expressed, in that people have certain roles?

Yes, and they are robed in different ways to distinguish what they do. There is pageantry and symbolism like in the colours that we wear at different times. It is very powerful. There are a lot of requirements. The gospel always happens on the right hand side and the readings on the left. The preaching is always from the right. Good Ritual enfolds people, they can relax into it, and they can shed responsibilities and go deeply into their own spiritual world. When Ritual is carried out ineptly, people can not really relax into it and they may feel uneasy. People have different roles in Ritual. To carry on with the Baptism, for example, certain people hold the child, candles are lit, and they hold the light for the child. These elements draw people into the whole ceremony.

What psychological aspects of Ritual are important?

When Ritual is unsatisfactorily performed and poorly carried out, you lose out in a **psychological** sense, very much as you would lose the audience of a play if somebody is hesitant about their part. People become conscious that it is only a play and then the emotional draw-card is missing. People choose different religions, unless they are born into something that is very strong, that suit them emotionally. The Rituals attract that person. The choice of what you say, the music you use, appeals to that person and so you get that individuality.

While Ritual does serve the individual who likes things to be done in a particular way and wants it to be very set, it is also dealing with the collective. For example, with suicide, family and friends need to psychologically go on, to continue to cope with their lives at that emotional level. Such a tragedy makes everybody insecure and worried about the meaning of life. They need reassurance at that time. The whole tone of the Ritual is going to reflect this.

Funerals are really not so much for the dead as for the living, to meet the needs of the living and for various reasons people's funerals are designed differently. Unless you have written specifications of what you want said and done at your funeral, very often the family have their own ideas about what they are looking for at that time. All life-changing transitions have prescribed rituals.

To be encouraged and to experience hope, that is what ritual is for. Styles of worship are psychological too: formal or informal. How people choose things that they can respond to and even the place where a ritual happens can reflect the individual and the collective. For instance, in choosing the setting of the place, some people are comfortable with enclosed and small spaces and others are looking for an open space. Very often in a cathedral, because it is big, people take up positions in the building and Sunday-by-Sunday they are in the same position. There are no place cards specifying who should sit where, but you know that certain people are going to be sitting over there and others are going to be over here and even a kind of separation of social layers becomes apparent in that way, which is interesting.

Does Ritual tell a story?

Ritual includes **storytelling**. For instance, baptisms usually include a prayer which reflects the history of the people of God through time; Moses leading the people through the waters of the Red Sea, or Christ in the deep waters of death and resurrection, are both related to the sacrament of baptism and the pouring of the water.

When we talk about a communion of saints, we are talking about everybody that has gone before us, so that we are this enormous collective: the human race. We join in the stream of history, when we enact

Ritual. There is a big initiative in Australia, 'Beyond Blue' targeting depression. For some odd reason everything that we are talking about suddenly brought me to the realisation that if people are not part of the story, if they do not have meaning in their lives, which Ritual gives them, then they may be lost ... in other words, they do not feel like they are part of this deeper 'collective' story any longer.

A lot of people are drifting, you have this search for meaning, young people who cannot see the point of what they do or cannot see a future for themselves that has any impact. Whereas being part of this huge collective is something to hang onto. What is happening to us in our lives has happened to others before and this is how they dealt with it. That is why for some people, and for me, I know, that Ritual is very important.

End of Interview

Labyrinth – Ritual Case Study[6]

DPS (modified to fit the circumstances of this situation, as it is always.) This case study outlines Rob Allen's engagement with a specific Ritual form.

1 *Expressive Art type*
Ritual and Epic: This case study explored the experience of the Labyrinth, an archetypal, ancient sacred space.

2 *Element*
Playwright Psychotheatrics: Playwright is designed for the individual, couple or very small group. This method creates a vehicle for revealing underlying Meaning and themes plus allows for an overall description of the experience.

3 *Craft*
Expressive Writing:[7] Where the writer explores the relationship between the experience to his or her life – by sitting alone, to write about what happened for not less than 20 minutes or more than 30. The act of writing allows the thought processes to slow down and actually alters the way the experience is represented and understood in our minds, leading to greater insight and clarity. This was completed after experiencing the Labyrinth walk.

Purgation: Walking to the centre of the Labyrinth – *images* of my mother, brother Rick, sister Renee (deceased), niece Katherine, wife Roslyn, son Carey and friends Tom and Nina. Setting: visiting my homeland, family conflicts arising, coming to terms – issues of grief and loss, guilt, responsibilities, penance but feeling settled. (America is my homeland, yes, but my home is now in Australia); Missing my wife, Roslyn and son, Carey.

Illumination: In the centre of the Labyrinth – abandonment, so many desertions – my mother grew up as a foster child; my life as the 'other' child ruled by a step-father; my sister dead of a heroin overdose, her children left behind; I break away from my roots for survival; creating distance by moving to Australia; the present: a rewarding and healthy life, by establishing new roots, especially with my own family, wife, Roslyn and son, Carey. My work and friendships flourish.

Union: Walking from the centre to the end of the Labyrinth. I like where I am in my life. I am happy with my choices. I have created a healthy, more nourishing life. Memories surface of my past life in America. The smothering enmeshment, yet family ties and responsibilities remain. I have to remember the toxicity and keep my distance; I cannot become entangled in all these family dynamics. Feeling blessed to have a new life, which is nourishing and creative. Valuing the ones I love: my friends, my family and my work – my second chance.

4 ***Story Map***

Orientation: Indoor Labyrinth – on the floor of Grace Cathedral in San Francisco. No one else is present. I am alone.

Complication: Feeling apprehensive. I have never experienced the Labyrinth before, although I read several books on sacred spaces and on labyrinths. I'm not sure if I am going to do it 'right'. During and after the experience I found this quite foolish as the experience just flowed. It is 'right' just to do it.

Sequence of events: The experience was described in detail in Craft through Expressive Writing. The walk consisted of three distinct stages of the Labyrinth. The first part, *Purgation:* I started to blend into the walk, become one with it, thoughts start to flow and patterns set. When I reached the centre, *Illumination:* just stayed and opened myself to the experience until I was ready to leave. I found *Union:* the walk out of the Labyrinth completed the experience for me, bringing a sense of tranquillity.

Resolution: I had concerns about what I was undertaking, however, I found actually doing the experience very natural and effortless.

Coda: in the end what really counts is passion and compassion.

5 ***Dramatic Enactment***

(*Using the 7 Expressive Arts*): This ritual walk happened on two levels: The first, *Kinaesthetic* – Labyrinth Walk: Consisted of three stages – 1) Purgation: walking to the centre, 2) Illumination: in the centre, and 3) Union: leaving the centre to complete the journey. I was unaware of time during the experience. I noted start and finish times, however, and the journey lasted 38 minutes. This was a very moving and liberating experience. The act of walking in this sacred space, eyes on the path and letting myself go in a meditative sense, transported me to another dimension. Thoughts and images flooded in, then took form. The second, *Visual Art*: the setting of the Labyrinth on the floor of Grace Cathedral is visually spectacular, although the Labyrinth design itself is moving, no matter where it might be located. Later I purchased a Labyrinth design on fabric that can be easily folded up. I found tracing the Labyrinth with my index finger brought back vivid images of my journey.

6 *Meaning*
It is good to be where I am now and to be passionate about where I am.

7 *Touchstone Story*
The classic mythological journey kept playing over and over again in my mind. *Birth* – leaving the womb, being on my own: independence. *Dragon* – guilt, regrets, what ifs? This path leads back to the womb: enmeshment and oblivion. Or, go forward; keep my independence and sense of self. *Treasure* – wealth is the wisdom to understand the journey. Yes, bittersweet, but this is part of the price. Accept this and be passionate about where you are right now. My destiny is in my hands: my choices. *Kingdom:* creating a realm is being fertile. Having a son is not just biological but it means really 'being' a Dad, just as having a marriage means really being there for my wife and being a partner in the true sense. My life will be fertile or barren depending on my relationships; I will reap what I sow in this life.

Sacred place

> *A sacred space can be defined as such because it emanates an influence which goes beyond its physical form. It influences the psyche of man, his surroundings and sometimes even his nature.*[8]

After walking the Labyrinth, **Rob Allen** had the opportunity to **interview The Reverend Dr Lauren Artress**[9] regarding the concept of sacred space, an area in which she is an internationally recognised authority. The opportunity to speak with her directly helped to shape his experience of the Labyrinth, using information she shared:

The Labyrinth is both Apopathic and Katopathic. Each is **dramatic** as they are expressive paths, a blueprint for transformation. The Apopathic path is the path of silence. Christian traditions talk about ridding the mind of all images. It is expressed as mindfulness in Buddhism and in different methods around the world. People who are trained, for instance, in centering prayer in the Christian tradition are taught to use a sacred phrase, because if you are going to quiet the mind, it is like a dog with a bone, you have to give it something to do. The sacred phrase quiets the mind, it does not mean thought does not go through it, but you are not attached to the thought. That is one pathway through the Labyrinth. The Katopathic path is really the path that is less recognised. It is truncated in the Christian tradition because people are frightened of the imagination. Visualisation is scary and you can imagine anything and if you can do that, that's where the 'devil is going to play' ...

The fear of imagination?

There is a lot of repression around the world: I mean look at the Taliban, you look at some of the ways of instilling fear in people and controlling them – it is controlling the imagination. What people are afraid of is the power of symbols, however you are using them. Carl Jung talks about the *I Ching*. You drop these coins and there is a moment where they all land and that moment is like a snapshot in time. Then you take that snapshot and you compare it against your own psyche and spiritual nature at that moment – a very intuitive process, it speaks directly. Symbols speak directly to the intuition and that is what we are afraid of. Again, the imagination, the **psychological**, the intuitive, the feminine, the earth!

The Labyrinth is a symbolic path, it is a beautiful combination of where the literal is figurative and the figurative is literal. When the psyche perceives sacredness, there is no boundary between the inner and the outer world. Good symbology is layered, somebody can walk in the Labyrinth and see one thing. They can be fascinated with the turns and then they'll realise 'My God, I'm at a turn in my life right now. No wonder I'm fascinated by it'.

Are there particular uses for the Labyrinth?

Labyrinths are great any time people are in transition. Any time people are hurting or looking for healing. The Labyrinth is an archetypal form. Not only is it sacred space, it generates a feeling of sacredness. A lot of hospitals are using it because it is such a holistic vision. You walk into the Labyrinth; you go into another world, the integration of mind, body and spirit for people. Cancer survivors or people who are working with stress, can use it as an insight tool and/or a supportive tool and people can find solace in the Labyrinth.

Would you please comment on the views of scientists like David Suzuki, in 'Sacred Balance',[10] *stating that scientific positivism reduces us and we need sacredness and meaning for us to grow, to be nourished.*

I think that spiritual hunger has a lot to do with losing the symbolic world, the aliveness, the freshness and seeing the beauty in things. We have embraced Descartes, and then extended this through Darwin, that we live in a dead world and that is what we are going to get; we are going to get a dead world. Jane Goodall, Professor at Stanford University, comes to Grace Cathedral every year for seminars. She was almost cast out of her field because she named the chimpanzees that she was working with in Africa. She did not name them number '23'; instead she gave them personal names like 'Blackbeard'. There was an outcry, 'My God, you can not personalise these animals; you can not have personal feelings here.' What we miss by that is we miss the poetry of the soul. That is where there is this hunger; this is where we have lost our meaning. The rational has remained: The right way, the sole way and at a great cost to our interior world. What about soul? What about imagination, what about intuition? What about the receptive: you can think about the receptive archetype as the feminine archetype and we are bankrupt on that level. That is why people are searching. The searching is far more extensive than the churches can handle, because they are caught, too, they are caught in their own outdated thinking. Even though it may be somewhat rational and somewhat intuitive, it is still compartmentalised. For instance, 'God the Father'. We still use that language here. In the name of the Father, the Son, the Holy Spirit. If they would just say Mother/Father... The container is so stiff, so rigid, even trying to capture the poetry of the mythology of the legend in Christianity; it is not working because it does not allow the intuitive, the mytho-poetic to find its place.

Knowing by discovering?

Yes, discovery – what do our dreams mean, what does this mean? What happened to me, what does that mean? Discovery facilitates **storytelling**, my story, your story, our story. This involves changing from the 'me' to the 'we' perspective. The Labyrinth is 'our' story, it is an archetype, a sacred space, it is by its very nature interactional, as we live our story, discover about you, me and we. The Labyrinth is about discovery, the more open you are, the more interactional you are. The Labyrinth is used in rituals, like rites of passage, acknowledgment, recognition, forgiveness, healing, and birth celebrations – or in ceremonies. It is sacred space and being in a place where people feel safe, people feel open. It is an area of enormous creativity; it is a new paradigm ritual.

Rob Allen's wife, Roslyn Medaris, also walked the Labyrinth at the Grace Cathedral in San Francisco on a subsequent visit, and recorded her very personal experience. DPS could be applied to her experience, in the same way that it was applied to Rob's. She relates her experience, walking the labyrinth, as follows:

> I will try and explain the Labyrinth walk as best I can, in retrospect. It is not a maze, as you may know but rather a path you follow. A symbolic representation of one's own path in life perhaps! You start at a certain point and the path meanders considerably before you reach the centre. The path prior to the centre is representative of where you've been, of your past, or it was for me. The centre is the point where you can pause and let go of any burdens you may be carrying along the way. Beyond this centre point was for me, representative of walking forward, into the present or where you are in your life right now. This depends on the person making the walk no doubt, but this is what it felt like for me.
>
> I didn't have any prior expectations really. I just wanted to walk the Labyrinth at the Grace Cathedral having read quite a lot about it. So, here I was in San Francisco and, of course, I was not going to miss out on this opportunity. I walked fairly slowly from the starting point. I wasn't really thinking of anything and I didn't quite know what to expect. Because the path tends to meander a fair bit, it takes a while to reach the centre. I started to think about my life but nothing major came into my mind to start with, other than thoughts of my family; my daughter Melissa, husband, Rob and his son Carey.
>
> I don't think I was in a meditative state at the beginning. Strangely, when I reached the centre, I was struck by an overwhelming sensation that Tim was there (I lost my son in 1986 when he was only 16). I said 'I love you Tim' several times, although not out loud, and felt very peaceful and happy to be there with him at that

moment. When I walked out of the centre, I was aware that my husband, Rob, had caught up with me at some point. I felt overwhelmed by sorrow after leaving the centre point, and every step I took felt like I was walking further away from Tim, leaving him behind. I knew I couldn't turn around and go back. I had to keep moving forward. Every now and again I felt my grief consuming me and I had to stop and take control of my emotions. I could have broken down completely and it may have been very therapeutic for me if I had done so. I was aware, however, of some students sitting drawing off to the side of the Labyrinth, of Rob just behind me somewhere and of another man walking the Labyrinth at the same time. I kept stopping and wiping my eyes, blowing my nose, thinking about my life and about where I was right now. At one stage, Rob and I were on a parallel path and he accidentally brushed against me. I thought it was appropriate that he was there at that point, if this was indeed representative of my life and that he would catch up with me at the end, which he did.

Towards the end of the labyrinth walk, I began thinking about my beautiful daughter, Melissa and her partner Paul and I thought about how lucky I was to be going home to my extended family in Australia. It seems I contemplated my life in a very short space of time, in actual fact, and at some stage, when I was alone in that sacred space, I was with my son again.

Epic

Epic differs from Ritual in that Ritual provides formal behaviour, often with involved symbolism, costume and objects, to which the individual or group relates. Epic involves powerful experience to which the individual or group attempts to apply some form of understanding.

The following case study, from the perspective of author Rob Allen, involves just such an experience, an Epic event, the Kelso High School fire, that was life-changing for many people in the community of Bathurst, NSW, Australia.

A Case Study by Rob Allen – Kelso High School Fire[11]

DPS (modified to fit the circumstances of this situation, as it is always.)

1 *Expressive Art form*

Ritual and Epic: This case study explored the use of Ritual and Epic through a tragic event that affected our entire community.[12]

2 *Element*

Combination of *Playwright and Imaginal Psychotheatrics*. Playwright is designed for the individual, couple or very small group. Imaginal is designed for specific groups that share certain characteristics in common. Both these methods create a vehicle for revealing underlying Meanings and themes, plus they allow for an overall description of the experience.

3 *Craft*

Expressive Writing:[13] Where the writer explores the relationship between the experiences to his or her life. Sitting alone, just write about what has happened, not less than 20 minutes or more than 30. The act of writing allows the thought processes to slow down and actually alters the way the experience is represented and understood in our minds, leading to greater insight and clarity. This was completed after experiencing the tragic event of the burning of Kelso High School.

Rhetorical Reality Analysis:[14] Where the experience/story is a series of added links by those involved either directly or indirectly through discussion. This soon develops into a strong 'chain' reflecting a group story. In this situation, my impression of the experience occurred first (formalised through *Expressive Writing* – 'Kelso High Burns' below) and then is reflected to others, who also add to this by sharing their impressions of the experience. The story now starts to be 'chained' out and transforms into a group reality.

Playwright Psychotheatrics: *Kelso High School Burns* – All you could see were blackened ruins with the fire still smouldering. It looked like a war zone. Just like photos I have seen in books about World War II, Dresden or Stalingrad. Just like those cities, except this was in a suburban community where we live: my wife Roslyn, son Carey and I. Our little suburb of Kelso, in Bathurst, our local community's High School, where Roslyn's children had attended some years before. Our place, a war zone? This makes no sense to me! Possibly it was accidental, maybe an electrical fire? We hope so. The tragedy, then, would be somehow more comprehensible. If it were deliberately started, however, what repercussions for our community? We are talking about an entire school burned down, not just one building; a High School, a place of learning for hundreds of students; a part of their community; their hopes, dreams, all their precious work, gone up in flames. It crosses my mind that if someone did this deliberately, then they have attacked these students, they have attacked us, our community. They have spoilt it for so many. It would be like a knife to the heart of our community. It means that 'monsters' walk among us. This is quite an unsettling thought. We all hope it is an accident, otherwise it becomes unimaginable.

Roslyn and I are in our car. It is Saturday morning. Kelso High School burned to the ground during the night. My son Carey saw a newsflash and he and his girlfriend Lucy went up to witness it. They said it was like a fireball, with flames thirty feet high or more. We see groups all huddled together at the front of what was once Kelso High School. It is winter but it is more than just the cold they are experiencing. This scene is chilling, numbing. Some are crying; their bodies and faces are twisted in pain. A war zone, we hope and pray it is an accident.*

Imaginal Psychotheatrics – group story themes: My wife, Roslyn, shared a sense of loss and shock with so many others in our community. The following is a brief account of her recollection:

> I did not learn about the Kelso High School fire until the next morning. I was terribly upset and had to drive up to the site and see the smouldering buildings for myself. People were standing around looking shocked. I saw some familiar faces. Teachers who had been there since the school first opened. Pupils stood with their arms around each other, commiserating together. There was a strong sense of a community coming together to share a common tragedy. This was not a tragedy on a grand scale, but for the Kelso Community, that day, we felt a keen sense of loss. My children had been through the school many years before. My youngest child was now 31. Even so, I found myself wiping tears from my eyes.

4 *Story Map*

Orientation: Kelso High School, Bathurst, NSW Australia.

Complication: Destruction by fire of our local high school.

Sequence of events: Sirens screaming in the night. News flashes on TV with a warning to stay away from the scene, so as not to impede assistance. Next day we drive up to see what remains of the school. Shocked and overwhelmed, people are milling about, some still in night clothes. It is early morning. The day has just started but many from the local community are present at the site.

---

* Forensic evidence later determined the cause of the fire was electrical and later found that the warning detection alarms were outdated and inadequate.

Resolution: To find out what really happened. We all want to try to make it right: to assist the high school students and their parents. Charles Sturt University offers assistance by making the university available to the students and teachers until the high school is rebuilt. There is a sense of relief that we are helping.

Coda: The school is at the very heart of our community.

5 *Dramatic Enactment*

This happened many times. Following are some of the key Dramatic Enactments: *Visual Art* – newspapers publishing photographs that documented the event – reviewing these later brings all the memories back and is a focal point for discussion with others. *Narrative* immediately after the event, discussing this with my wife, Roslyn and son Carey and his girlfriend, Lucy. They also experienced the event but separately from me. Talking with others in our local community, who also shared this event. *Film* – extensive coverage on television so that this event became an on-going dramatic enactment and served as a Facilitator for narrative experiences.

6 *Meaning*

Something wonderful came out of the Kelso High School fire. We all discovered what that school really meant to us. It gave us a new sense of belonging, of being part of something. It brought the community together in many ways, especially the school community.

7 *Touchstone Story*

Sense of bewilderment and confusion, a numbing, aching feeling, a surreal sense, followed by fear and anger. How did this happen? Why? Realisation of how much this school meant to us and to our community. This is our children's sacred place. This is the heart of our community.

Applications of DPS using the Expressive Arts: with Imaginal, Playwright and Montage Psychotheatrics

Regardless of our chosen paths, events that are important to us, or to those around us, impact and change us. We often have strong feelings about such experience and yet find difficulty in expressing our feelings or grasping the essence of what has occurred. Ritual and Epic, as Expressive Art types in DPS contain opportunities for clarifying life experience.

The special qualities of Ritual, whether it is old or newly created are dramatic and ripe for exploration through DPS. The power of Epic is readily accessible, often experienced by many in different ways, which lends depth to exploration through DPS, as illustrated through the examples in this chapter.

The DPS process assists in enhancing internal *locus of control*, the expectancy that your outcomes are contingent more on your own efforts than on outside forces such as luck, fate or the power of others. 'The opportunity to make this shift from victim to having dominion over one's own life is the key. When people have an internal locus of control, they feel that by their acts they have some control and some power in their lives.'[15] Working with life events through Ritual and Epic, may not change the outcome of events that have occurred, but it has the capacity to change perceptions and provide a sense of wellbeing, which empowers us in life's journey.

Part III

Psychotheatrics

12
Imaginal Psychotheatrics

Men are not worried by things,
but by their ideas about things.
When we meet with difficulties,
become anxious or troubled,
let us not blame others,
but rather ourselves,
that is, our ideas about things.
Epictetus

The term *imaginal*, from the Latin *imago*, relates to the *imagination* and using rhetorical figures in discourse. Its use with Psychotheatrics describes a group process that nourishes and explores shared experience and imagery that may be viewed, created, or both. Imaginal Psychotheatrics is designed for people who hold an important characteristic in common. In a group setting, people with similar experiences explore a situation related to that shared experience. As they engage with the experience, they create an energy system that combines two complex dynamics: 1) the message of the Expressive Arts rendition and their experience of it, with 2) their relationship with each other and/or their common experience.

Although this magic mirror reflects each individual on a unique basis, in an Imaginal Psychotheatrics group there is a process that utilises artistic creativity to illuminate shared issues because the group contains a common characteristic. Many will gain when just one of its members looks into the mirror.

Group members using Imaginal Psychotheatrics, may work in the same department or profession, share a struggle like alcohol dependence, be going through divorce or be involved in a mutual interest like an educational objective – e.g. for police officers understanding domestic violence situations, or human resource concerns such as team development. They may be friends or associates who want to delve into a particular topic or project. It is not necessary that people in the group be in agreement with each other. In fact, Imaginal Psychotheatrics is a powerful tool for conflict management. It is necessary that group members be willing to meet with each other, respect the vulnerabilities of others, and bring their honest participation to the process. As with Playwright and Montage Psychotheatrics, Imaginal action is preceded by the Biography and Discussion phase and followed by Coalescence. Imaginal Psychotheatrics may be used in Clinical and Counselling, Human Resources and Education and Awareness settings.

Biography and Discussion

In the Imaginal Psychotheatrics process the Biography and Discussion phase has two steps: the first before the group is formed and the second in the initial development of the group process.

Imaginal Psychotheatrics is designed for people with an important shared common characteristic. In creating groundwork for participation, ask those who will take part to familiarize themselves with the 7 Expressive Art types prior to the workshop session, and select personally relevant works in as many categories as possible that relate to common group issues. This preview provides a ready frame of reference for selecting Expressive Art for the Drama Enactment. Forethought will create an energy system that combines the message of the art and group members' experience of it in relationship with each other. In Education the common focus may be the particular content to be learned. In Clinical and Counselling this could be a common issue or problem: like alcoholism, or obesity, or struggles with parenthood, or other concerns. In Human Resources it could be a training and development issue or human factors concern.

Minimal guidelines for participation in an Imaginal Psychotheatrics group:

- Individuals chosen should have a common identifiable characteristic, which is the focus of interest or desired behaviour change for all members in that group.
- Individuals need to have sufficient interpersonal controls to allow participation in a group process, and
- Individuals should have the potential to benefit from an on-going group.

If a group is considering the use of the Imaginal Psychotheatrics process or if people are being referred to an Imaginal group, it is important that each one knows what the identified focus of the group is and consents to involvement in working on that focus. Lack of clarity and consent can cloud issues of responsibility as they arise in the group process. Topic focus and consent to be involved are the main issues for this Biography and Discussion phase. How these issues are clarified will depend on the application and the skills of the Facilitator.

The Imaginal Psychotheatrics process can be useful as a one-time experience for a group of people sharing a common variable. However, in order to benefit from the richness of group feedback and shared experience, an on-going commitment is desirable.

After the group is formed, the Biography and Discussion step continues. This is designed so that group members will become knowledgeable about each other. It is important that this step be accomplished in such a way that people in the group gain enough trust to begin to share feelings with each other. The process is often rewarding in itself and it is important. As soon as group members can feel somewhat comfortable with each other, the action phase can begin.

A simple and powerful technique for beginning an Imaginal Psychotheatrics group is a short personal history exercise, giving each person up to ten minutes to share 'who I am'. This provides the group with information about each person and makes apparent the similarities and differences of people in the group. To learn more about each other makes self-disclosure less daunting. Facilitators may use other getting-acquainted exercises of their choice.

The size of the group may vary according to the needs of the situation and the application in which it is being used. Fewer than six people in a group tends to limit the action flexibility in the group and can lead to less-balanced input in the discussion phase. Imaginal Psychotheatrics can be used with very large groups, using a sample group 'in front' or in the centre of a circle with everyone in the audience vicariously sharing the experience. Here again serious limitations are placed on discussion. However, if each member debriefs the experience with a Facilitator, or other group member, the value is enhanced. Six to 12 participants is the ideal group size, allowing for personal interaction and discussion.

Without having to be so detailed that it restricts exploration, clarity about desired outcomes will help the group maintain focus. It is useful to brainstorm desired outcomes and be clear about who is responsible for follow up. In some situations, each individual is responsible for his or her own learning process. In Human Resource settings, a manager or leader may be responsible for facilitating outcomes in the organisation at large. Any change process happens in a system, so preparing both group members and the system to support that change is an essential step.

Coalescence follows the 7 Step action stage of DPS. You will find more detail at the end of this chapter.

7 Step action stage

In Imaginal Psychotheatrics the focus is on the targeted group and change, with the clients (students, staff members or participants) in charge, directly assisted and challenged by the Facilitator. Now is the time to activate the 7 Step action stage of DPS. The outline here is intended as a guide for the Facilitator and the group. It may work out that these particular steps make sense in this sequence, but sometimes another sequence may work better. Steps may be repeated or deleted, as necessary.

After welcome and introductions, the Facilitator first outlines the basic steps in the model to prepare the group for the DPS process. The group shares a common characteristic (eg for Clinical and Counselling 'alcohol dependence' or, for Education, a learning objective such as 'what it is like to be a refugee').

1 *Expressive Art type*

Ask the client to list examples in as many of 7 categories as possible for later storytelling possibilities.

Narrative – oral, informal writing, book, poem, news article
Film – cinema, television, video
Theatre – formal play, performance, or a scenario
Music – song, concert, composition
Visual Art – painting, drawing, sculpture, collage, installation, performance
Dance and Kinaesthetics – choreographed or informal; designed movement, sport, viewing performance
Ritual and Epic – ceremony (birth, marriage); spectacle, happening (Olympics), organisational ritual

The Expressive Art type is chosen to reflect the story theme of the group (characteristic held in common) this can be through either an individual story that reflects this theme or by just starting with the general theme. The Facilitator can choose one of the Expressive Art types reflecting the general characteristic/theme of the group to start the reflection process necessary to express the story. Or group members may have an Expressive Art type that reflects their story as well as the group theme. For example, the group may view a film that has a theme related to the core group issue, or a member may share a favorite piece of music that illustrates the concern. Good examples are given in the previous Expressive Arts chapters utilising different types to illustrate Imaginal Psychotheatrics group stories.

2 *Element*

Imaginal Psychotheatrics is the Element of choice here. However, as DPS unfolds, one of the other two Psychotheatrics Elements may prove useful. Playwright may assist in exploring a particular relationship, and Montage might work well for future executive or leadership development, for instance.

3 *Craft*

Rhetorical Reality Analysis: In transient organisations where history is not shared, telling a story and linking it to the stories of others creates a context. This can be done in an environment where only a modicum of trust exists. Ernst Bormann[1] has found that groups use 'fantasy chains' to develop a common culture. A 'fantasy chain' is the story that is often repeated in a group (work, family, etc.) as it is passed from one group member to another, or as it is being told to a new group member or stranger. 'The content consists of characters, real or fictitious, playing out a dramatic situation in a setting removed in time and space from the here and now transactions of the group. The fantasies picked up and chained out by the group not only reflected the members common preoccupations but served to make those commonalties public.'[2]

When group members respond emotionally to the dramatic situation, they publicly proclaim some commitment to an attitude. Indeed, improvising in a spontaneous group dramatisation is a powerful force for attitude change. Dramas also imply motives. By chaining into the group 'reality' the members gain motivation. Organised effective action emerges from shared meaning.

DPS uses Rhetorical Reality Analysis (adapted from Bormann's work) as a method for dramatic communication. The reality chain is a technique to take the original story and carry it forward by having each member in the group add his or her experience or interpretation 'link' to the story. As group members add to the chain, they repeat a piece of the original story and add their unique link to it so the story keeps its essence. It is transformed by this 'chaining' into a dynamic group story. This process allows group members to respond rationally and emotionally, whereby an attitudinal commitment is made toward a new reality.

Each Rhetorical Reality Analysis link in the chain must relate to the original story revealed through one of the 7 Expressive Arts in Step 1 of DPS. This is then further developed by group members, link by link into a group story. As each link is added to this developing story, it grows stronger and more powerful. Each chain segment should only be a short scenario of a personal experience that relates closely to the original story or previous links; otherwise the energy field dissipates. The Facilitator has an important role to facilitate this step in the process by assisting the clients to stay on track and keep their contributions manageably brief. This group story is then further developed through the Story Map in the next step of DPS.

The Facilitator's group process skills help the group stay on track here.

- A brief summary of the original story is given by a group member through one of the 7 Expressive Arts in Step 1 of DPS, or by the Facilitator if necessary.
- Each group member adds his or her link to chain the story forward.
- This link is the member's perspective on the developing group story, adding information or a different interpretation, but maintaining connection with the original story and/or previous links.
- The Facilitator may help the group member make the connection with the original story and/or previous links.
- When members diverge from the original story and/or previous links, the Facilitator helps them reconnect and maintain focus. At this point, the Facilitator needs to remember that too many details impede the process. The story that reflects a central concern will do the necessary work.

This group story, as it has been elaborated through the chaining process, is the basis for the next step, Story Map and then actualised in the Dramatic Enactment later.

4 *Story Map*

The Story Map provides the opportunity for the group to mould the links developed in Rhetorical Reality Analysis into a 'group story' reality. The Facilitator serves as a guide, noting main points and ideas and working with the group to complete the Story Map. Here are some guidelines for using the Story Map:

- It is better to keep the number of **characters** small. Try to have no more than four at any one time as a maximum; three or fewer works best if possible. A good way to decide on who is going to be in the story is to list all the characters possible, then rank their importance at the time (this can change later for many reasons – new insights, different time perspective). After ranking the level of importance, choose the top five maximum, better four, best three or less. This is the first run through. Later this can change; you can add or remove characters.
- **When** is the story happening? This is the time perspective and directly affects who will be in the group story and their importance. The time needs to directly relate to the Orientation of your story – past, present or future. If in the past, why? If you are going to be an archaeologist and dig up the past, then this particular time must be very important or possibly you are just exploring? (This is OK too)! If in the present, then this may be a good way to create a new perspective on the existential NOW. If the setting is the future, then you are looking at this process determining possibilities. Actually by doing this you may influence the future.
- **Where** it is happening? This is the location – at home or the office or at a restaurant or where? It may help to actually set the scenario, describe the setting, what does it look like? What items are there? If you can paint a mental picture of the location this will assist the story immensely. In fact why not just get a pencil and some paper and draw the setting!
- **What** is going on? What are the issues of concern here? It is better to have ONE major issue with a few minor issues. The issue(s) do not have to be problems or negatives; They can be positive and affirmative.

The Story Map assists in organising complex dynamics so that all group members have created and are in agreement with this group story. If disagreements occur in the process of creating the Story Map, it will be necessary to try to resolve these in order to proceed. Normally this is not an issue of concern.

Story Map:

	Rhetorical Reality Analysis links	**Group story**
Title List title or succinctly describe the story.		
Orientation Who is in the story? When is it happening? What is going on? How does the story start? What is the first sentence? Where is it happening? What does the setting look like? What words will be used to describe the setting and how can this help paint a mind picture?		
Initiating Event What specific event(s) inspired this story?		
Characters Who are the most important characters in the story? What are they like? What do they look like? What sort of personalities do they have? How do they talk in the story?		
Complication What challenge(s) does the main character need to overcome?		
Sequence of Events What events happen first, next, last? What does the main character do? Does he/she act or react in a believable way?		

	Rhetorical Reality Analysis links	Group story
Resolution How will things work out? What issues need to be confronted? How will this story end?		
Coda The message or moral of the story.		

5 ***Dramatic Enactment***

This is the actualisation of the group story from the Story Map. Any one, or more, of the 7 Expressive Arts is appropriate to utilise for the Dramatic Enactment in order to reflect and highlight the group story. These can be utilised immediately, or the next time the group meets. If immediately, then group members will be encouraged by the Facilitator to contribute examples that reflect the group story. If later, the 'homework' for each group member can be to bring in an example from one of the 7 Expressive Arts or possibly several ideas from the 7 Expressive Arts.

The full description in the Story Map may be too complex. If so, choose a representative slice, a scenario. Try to capture the essence of what just occurred; if missed, don't worry, review with the group and try again. Choose a part of the story that 'best' reflects the group story. Later, other segments can be enacted if desirable.

Narrative – a poem, or a newspaper article, a book, journal notes, or just a group discussion of the Story Map, or anything read or written can be used for this purpose.

Film – a movie, television episode, photograph or the like. The group could even 'create a video' to represent the experience. This can be at a 'home movie' level, however the significance will still be quite profound. This 'home movie' can then be discussed and altered later, depending on the circumstances.

Theatre – a formal performance that highlights the Story Map, or alternatively the group may want to perform an informal but planned story and then revise and change as necessary.

Music – an existing song, composition or melody, or one that the group creates?

Visual Art – an existing sketch, drawing, painting, sculpture, or one the group creates?

Dance and Kinaesthetics – formal choreographed performance or some significant movement/activity. The body is the focus here. The group or members may create a dance to signify the group story or design a kinaesthetic activity that reflects their story.

Ritual and Epic – ceremony, rite, or a very significant event/happening, or special occasion? The possibilities for group creation of a ritual or a happening/event that highlights and reflects the group story are endless.

The Dramatic Enactment differentiates Imaginal Psychotheatrics from other group processes. The clients produce and direct a brief, informal Dramatic Enactment based on the material gathered through Rhetorical Reality Analysis and the Story Map. The clients are involved but always as a witness to ensure objectivity and rationality.

Actually, the 7 Steps of DPS are designed especially to promote this witness/objective approach. The Dramatic Enactment is the most intensive example of this process.

The witness approach is critical to ensure rational objectivity/catharsis in utilising the 7 Expressive Arts for the Dramatic Enactment. The very act of creation and certainly the act of utilising any of the 7 Expressive Arts almost automatically creates a witness or observer position. The only exception sometimes is Theatre and therefore it is imperative never to act in a role portraying self. This may be overwhelming and leads to vulnerability through subjectivity and possible manipulation, as in psychodrama. The other 6 Expressive Arts by the act of creation, or utilisation, ensure an artifact that may be related to, but is still separate and distinct from the self, thus ensuring the witness perspective necessary for objectivity and rationality.

Experiencing the Biography and Discussion stage, completing the Rhetorical Reality Analysis, Story Map and then Dramatic Enactment gives group members heightened awareness of personal and group dynamics. The action phase is the opportunity to translate these from verbalisations, to actions, and to view them experientially.

The Dramatic Enactment presentation includes not only the original story as chained out in Rhetorical Reality Analysis and then further developed in the Story Map, but also expanded parts of it and new options. It is important that the clients not spend time with excessive explanations, but really see the situation and then expand parts and options through action. In this way, 'truth' will be maintained. Discussion is the last step.

Since this process is a powerful one, it is important that it be used with proper safeguards and never in a capricious way. The individual's right to terminate participation or to stop the action at any point must be respected if the process is to be compatible with the individual responsibility values underlying DPS.

Remember also that the number of times the Dramatic Enactment is utilised depends on the needs and goals of the group.

6 *Meaning*

After the Dramatic Enactment the group has an opportunity to review what has happened and sift through all the material that has unfolded in the previous steps. What is the *meaning* in all this? Also look for signposts in what values and attitudes were expressed. This stage is all about exploring what the original story represented in Step 1, through an Expressive Art type and then developed by the group through Step 3: Craft – Rhetorical Reality Analysis and then further refined in Step 4: the Story Map.

It is now time to test the previous steps and challenge what has occurred. You are then able to discover and legitimise the Meaning of the story that has now been developed and illustrated through the Dramatic Enactment. As the group begins to work on the outcomes, it is helpful to have members contribute what they have learned through a brainstorming process. As this evolves, the group and the Facilitator can create categories of new learning for future decision making and action.

Frequently, people see things about themselves they had not known before, or the way through an impasse may be revealed. The Facilitator can be helpful here in pointing out observations made throughout the action or by being supportive to group members as they grapple with material that may be painful or surprising.

Understanding a situation can often be enough. From this point, the clients can make whatever decisions are necessary, based on a fresh view of the material.

Sometimes, though, insight may increase frustration. Group members may complain, 'I can see what I need to do, but I don't know how', or 'I don't think I can do it'. Or, 'We can't do any more until (a particular situation or conflict) is resolved'. At this point, the group and the Facilitator determine what their next steps will be. This could include another Dramatic Enactment, or some form of conflict management, team building, coaching, or other change process.

7 *Touchstone Story*

Once the original story is illustrated in the Expressive Art type and transformed through Rhetorical Reality Analysis and the Story Map, a transcendence of new meanings has occurred. This tapestry is the Touchstone Story. The group, using the Facilitator as a guide, defines the **essence** of learning that has emerged through the process. This may differ for various group members, but to the extent that the group can arrive at a phrase, a headline, a title, a poem, or a representative symbol or object, each can take from the experience a reminder of the magic of the process.

Coalescence

Coalescence depends on the conditions of the Imaginal group, the needs of the individuals and the style of the Facilitator. The emphasis is on the clients actualising the goals that the action stage has set in motion. The energy here that has been derived from the cathartic effect of the DPS 7 Step action stage now has to be channelled to reach the desired conclusion. The on-going support of the group can be a powerful force in the process of behaviour change for an individual and for the group. Coalescence is the process through which the group, and individuals, integrate new learning and go on to translate selected facets into new behaviour. Depending on the situation, varying degrees of this process may occur in the group or outside the group.

The on-going group process that follows the DPS 7 Step action stage is essential to support the new learning and new directions that have unfolded. Change within a system is difficult, and maintaining support and intention relies on the commitment of those involved to carry it forward in order to bring about lasting change.

13
Playwright Psychotheatrics

Everywhere man blames nature and fate,
yet his fate is mostly but the echo
of his character and passions,
his mistakes and weaknesses.
Democritus

The term 'playwright' describes not only one who writes a play, but one who 'crafts' a 'drama'. A *wright* is a maker, a creator – one who constructs something. In *Dramatic Psychological Storytelling* (DPS), we focus on *dramatis*, meaning 'to express' the story, 'your story'/'our story' by reflecting on an incident, crisis, adventure, circumstance or disturbance.

Playwright Psychotheatrics is designed to work with individuals, dyads or very small groups. As with Imaginal and Montage Psychotheatrics, the 7 Step action stage of Playwright Psychotheatrics is preceded by the Biography and Discussion phase and followed by Coalescence. Playwright Psychotheatrics may be used in all three DPS areas: Clinical and Counselling, Human Resources and Education/Awareness.

Playwright Psychotheatrics is a process designed to help individuals, couples/dyads or very small groups view their behaviour, introduce new options, experiment with those options and move forward. When working with couples, the Facilitator may decide whether to treat each person as an individual and work with parallel experiences, or to treat their story as one.

In Playwright Psychotheatrics the focus is on *change*, with the client in charge but directly assisted and challenged by the Facilitator.

Biography and Discussion

Biography and Discussion provide an opportunity to understand the individual, couple/dyad or very small group's psychological foundations, goals and expectations for the 7 Step DPS action stage. It is important during this time to focus on a specific area for development. Depending on the applications, Clinical and Counselling, Human Resources or Education and Awareness, in which the 7 Step DPS action phase is being developed, a Facilitator such as a therapist, teacher, or human resource professional will assist. Regardless of the area, the 7 Step DPS action stage is essentially the same.

In preparation for undertaking 7 Step DPS, the client(s) and Facilitator work together to clarify underpinnings of their work. Asking the client to review the 7 Expressive Arts and select personally relevant works in as many categories as possible, sets the stage for beginning the Playwright Psychotheatrics process. Attention here is on the process, since the content will emerged in the Expressive Writing and Story Map phases.

- The optimal situation involves an area that is vital to the client. Otherwise the impact of the process is diluted.
- The situation may be past-reality (what actually happened), past-rewrite (to change what happened), present or future.
- 'The story' expression may be designed to release energy that has been blocked for some reason or other; or it may be used to amplify good feelings or positive images.
- The story expression must be truthful (real) to the person.

Now the Biography and Discussion stage is complete.

Planning for Coalescence

Without having to be so detailed that it restricts exploration, clarity about desired outcomes will help the client maintain focus. It is useful to brainstorm desired outcomes and be clear about who is responsible for follow up. In some situations, each individual is responsible for his or her own learning process. In human resource settings, a manager or leader may be responsible for facilitating outcomes in the organisation at large. Any change process happens in a system, so preparing both group members and the system to support that change is an essential step. Coalescence follows the 7 Step action stage of DPS. There is more detail at the end of this chapter.

Playwright Psychotheatrics – 7 Step Action Model

1 *Expressive Art type*

The 'story' is the objective, the central point and purpose – e.g. in therapy panic attacks; in education, indigenous and cross-cultural issues; and in human resources workplace motivation; all developed through the story. An Expressive Art type can assist in reflecting and expressing this story, which later can then be refined and developed specifically to meet the special needs and requirements of the particular population. The story can be reflected and expressed using one or more of the following:

Narrative – oral, informal writing, book, poem, news article
Film – cinema, television, video
Theatre – formal play, performance, or a scenario
Music – song, concert, composition, group practice
Visual Art – painting, drawing, sculpture, collage, installation, performance
Dance and Kinaesthetics – choreographed or informal; designed movement, sport, viewing performance
Ritual and Epic – ceremony (birth, marriage); spectacle, happening (Olympics), organisational ritual

The Expressive Art type is chosen to reflect the story objectives. The Facilitator may choose one of the Expressive Art types that handles the subject matter well. Or the client(s) may have an Expressive Art type that reflects the story objectives. Good examples are given in the previous Expressive Arts chapters, utilising different Expressive Art types to illustrate Playwright Psychotheatrics stories.

2 *Element*

Playwright Psychotheatrics is the Element of choice here. However, as DPS unfolds, it may be useful to use one of the other two Psychotheatrics Elements. Imaginal could be useful in exploring a particular characteristic that the client(s) and others share and Montage might work well if an extremely intensive focus is needed.

3 *Craft*

Expressive Writing

> What would it mean to live
> in a city whose people were changing despair into hope?
> You yourself must change it.
> What would it feel like to know your country was changing?
> You yourself must change it.

Though your life felt arduous, new and unmapped
what would it mean to stand on the first page of the end of despair?
Dreams Before Waking, Adrienne Rich[1]

In Playwright Psychotheatrics, the client(s), individual, dyad or very small group engages in the technique of Expressive Writing to convey their experience. This is the objective or focus of this application as reflected through the particular Expressive Art type and helps to further develop the story.

Writing a situation can be a powerful cathartic experience. Words on the page open doors of healing and hope, even – maybe, especially – if no one reads them but the writer. In *The Artist's Way*,[2] Julia Cameron recommends 'morning pages', 'three pages of long-hand writing, strictly stream-of-consciousness...' every day. Follow Natalie Goldberg's advice when you begin to question yourself about taking time out to write: '...just dive into the page, be full of answers, but don't justify yourself'.[3]

Expressive writing, as exercise or meditative practice, even if you never go back and read a word of it, relieves stress. The trick is to turn off the censor, all those critics intruding from the past, and let the writing flow. No one will check spelling, grammar, or content. The closer the writing holds to unmonitored thought processes the better for clarifying the true self. Nowhere else in life do we have permission and privacy for this level of reflection, confession and exploration of dreams, thoughts, feelings and motives. If the writer does choose to revisit the page, the information will be processed differently than if heard or spoken. Writing objectifies information; optical nerves receive and process it so that a fresh perspective may be unveiled.

James Pennebaker's work, *Opening Up: The Healing Power of Expressing Emotions*,[4] carries these ideas forward and demonstrates that inhibition negatively affects the immune system. Through physiological research he shows that writing about trauma or 'confessing' one's secrets, lowers blood pressure and other stress indicators. Expressive writing can improve physical as well as mental health.

Expressive writing creates the groundwork for the Dramatic Enactment step. Directions that the Facilitator offers for an Expressive Writing session might include something like: 'Spend the next twenty or thirty minutes writing something important to you that comes to mind. Try not to censor or judge. Don't worry about grammar, punctuation, spelling, sequence, or relevance. Simply write what comes to your mind with no worry about form.'

As the client, find a comfortable, harmonious place where you will be uninterrupted for a twenty to thirty-minute session of expressive writing. These guidelines help:

- Put yourself in a private, permeable bubble alone with your thoughts and feelings.
- Try to avoid censoring. Say to internal critics, 'Yes, I hear you, but I am doing it this way...'
- Sentence structure, spelling and grammar are unimportant here.
- Let words flow from the deepest part of you onto the page.
- Try writing without lifting your hand. Just keep going.
- Later is time enough to decide what you will share.

When the writing session is complete, the client reviews the work silently and privately, searching for key words and themes. On a separate piece of paper, note the selected words and phrases for discussion with the Facilitator. Use these cues as guides to explore further in the Dramatic Enactment. Depending on the situation, the Facilitator may be more or less involved in this part of the process.

4 *Story Map*

Now it will be useful to fill in the Story Map. Avoid getting carried away with details and 'correctness'. The goal is to include just enough information to further develop the story that represents the situation/objective.

Title Succinctly describe your story.	
Orientation Who is in the story? When is it happening? What is going on? How will you start your story? What will your first sentence be? Where is it happening? What will the setting look like? What words will you use to describe the setting and how can you help paint a mind picture?	
Initiating Event What specific event inspired you to create this story?	

Complication What challenge(s) does the main character need to overcome?	
Sequence of Events What events happen first, next, last? What does the main character do? Does he/she act and react in a believable way?	
Resolution How will things work out? What issues need to be confronted? How will your story end?	
Coda The message or moral of the story.	

When working with couples – it may help to work with each individually up to the Story Map. Having them create one story together that becomes the content for the Dramatic Enactment may assist in clarifying particular areas that would benefit from a shared vision/illustration. This would be particularly effective for problem solving.

5 *Dramatic Enactment*

Focusing on an area of concern, writing about it, and then bringing it to life is an experience different from any other. Because of this difference, newness and unfamiliarity, resistance to the process is likely to rise along the way. Here, the Facilitator's skill in supporting the client through that natural defence makes the difference between taking the journey experience further or just giving up and avoiding this as too difficult to work through.

This is the actualisation of the story from the Expressive Writing and Story Map steps. Any one or more of the 7 Expressive Arts is appropriate to utilise for the Dramatic Enactment – to reflect and highlight the developing story. These can be utilised immediately or the next time there is a session. If immediately, then the client(s) will be encouraged by the Facilitator to contribute examples that reflect the developing story. If later, the 'homework' for the client(s) can be to continue collecting examples of various Expressive Art forms that are particularly meaningful.

Possibly the full description in the Story Map may be too complex. If so, choose a representative slice, a scenario. Try to capture the essence of what just occurred; if missed, don't worry, review and try again. Simply choose a part of the story that 'best' reflects the story under discussion. Later, other segments can be enacted if desirable.

Narrative – possibly a poem, or a newspaper article, a book, journal notes, or just a discussion of the Story Map, or something else that has been written or read.
Film – possibly a movie, television episode, photograph or video. The client could even create a video to represent the experience. This can be at a home movie level, however, the significance will still be quite profound. This home movie can then be changed later, depending on the circumstances.
Theatre – possibly to attend a formal performance that highlights the *Story Map* or the client(s) and Facilitator may act out a scenario and then revise and change as necessary.
Music – possibly a song, composition or melody, or one that the client(s) creates?
Visual Art – possibly a sketch, drawing, painting, sculpture, or one the client(s) devises?
Dance and Kinaesthetics – refer to a formal choreographed performance or some significant movement/activity. The body is the focus here. The client(s) may design a dance to signify the story or design a kinaesthetic activity that reflects this.
Ritual and Epic – ceremony, rite, or a very significant event/happening, or special occasion. The possibilities for creation of a Ritual or a happening/event that highlights and reflects the story are endless.

The Dramatic Enactment is another example that differentiates Playwright Psychotheatrics from other processes. The client(s) produces and directs a brief, informal Dramatic Enactment based on the material gathered through Expressive Writing and the Story Map. The client(s) is involved but always as a witness to ensure objectivity and rationality. The Dramatic Enactment creates a 'magic mirror' that enhances the discovery of options and new styles of thinking, feeling and behaving!

The 7 Expressive Arts chapters give numerous examples of how easily Playwright Psychotheatrics is utilised with a particular Expressive Art type to first convey the story in Step 1 and then later for the Dramatic Enactment. The Facilitator may either be directly involved or at least serve as an adviser.

For example using Film: the client(s) has several options for the Dramatic Enactment:

1 A particular movie or video is specially selected to reflect the story at this point in time – later this would be followed by discussion (Narrative) or another Expressive Art type to review and highlight important aspects with the Facilitator. A video has advantages as particular key parts can be replayed for emphasis or review, where as attending a movie at a cinema would not afford this feature. Both a movie or video can certainly explore the relevance as it relates to the developing story.
2 Create a 'story movie' with the Facilitator involved (directly or indirectly) – the client(s) helps to produce and direct the scenarios and can be in it but only portraying others – this ensures objectivity and rational catharsis. It would be necessary to have access to a video camera and possibly some simple movie editing software that is readily available. Overall the film Dramatic Enactment would follow these procedures:

   - An important aspect or key area of the Story Map is then summarised into a brief film scenario, with the help of the Facilitator.
   - The client(s) is the director and producer of the film scenario reflecting the story, with the Facilitator assisting as an adviser.
   - During the production of the film, the client(s) reviews this with the Facilitator until the final product has been achieved.

3 The client(s) may prefer to design a 'photo story' – it would be necessary to have access to a camera, preferably digital for ease of review and design effects. The client(s) and Facilitator would follow the same format as the story movie but this time using photos as the vehicle of expression.

After the client(s) produces and directs the situation, he or she can 'see' it, live through it and change it. As the client's projection is in 3-D form, as producer-director, the ownership of the behaviour and the responsibility rests with them. This 3-D form of the client's projection takes it beyond mere verbalisation and transforms it into the unification of physical and psychological processes. In this psychophysical synthesis, catharsis can occur and lead to cognitive behavioural analysis and change.

The other Expressive Art types can follow this same format in the Dramatic Enactment step. Experiencing the Biography and Discussion stage, completing the Expressive Writing, Story Map and then Enactment gives the client heightened awareness of personal and group dynamics. The action phase is the opportunity to translate these from verbalisations to actions and to view them experientially. The Dramatic Enactment produces a three-dimensional image that illuminates the 'story'.

- The Dramatic Enactment presentation includes not only the original story as illustrated in Expressive Writing and then further developed in the Story Map, but also expanded parts of it and new options. It is important that the client(s) not spend time with excessive explanations, but rather expand parts and options through action. In this way, *truthfulness* will be maintained.
- Discussion is the last step:
  a. The client(s) outlines insights or new learning.
  b. New options may be identified with an outline of planned behaviour changes or goals.

The number of times that Dramatic Enactment is utilised depends on the needs and goals of the client(s). Since this process is a powerful one, it is important that it be used with proper safeguards and never in a capricious way. The individual's right to terminate participation or to stop the action at any point must be respected if the process is to be compatible with the individual responsibility values underlying DPS.

6 *Meaning*

After the Dramatic Enactment, pause to review what has taken place in the developing story. What is the Meaning in all this? Also look for signposts in what values and attitudes were expressed. This stage is about discovery of what the original story is really about, as reflected in Step 1 Expressive Art experience and then illustrated in Step 3 Expressive Writing and further developed in Step 4 Story Map.

It is now time to examine the previous steps and challenge what has occurred. You can then discover and legitimatise the meaning of the story that has now been developed and illustrated through the Dramatic Enactment. After this has been completed we have the essence for the foundation of the Touchstone Story.

Frequently, people see things about themselves they had not known before, or the way through an impasse is revealed. The Facilitator can be helpful here in pointing out observations made throughout the action or by being supportive to the client(s) as they grapple with material that may be painful or surprising.

Understanding a situation can often be enough. From this point, the client(s) can make whatever decisions are necessary, based on a fresh view of the situation. Sometimes, though, insight may increase frustration. The client(s) may need further assistance expressing, 'I can see what I need to do, but I don't know how', or 'I don't think I can do it'. Here another Playwright Psychotheatrics experience may be helpful, or Coalescence at the end of 7 Step DPS may be used as a time to design an incremental plan for behaviour change.

7 *Touchstone Story*

Clarification of learning from the action phase occurs here. Is there a way to symbolise the key learning(s) with a word, title, headline or object? Once an original story is transformed a transcendence of new meanings has occurred – this tapestry is the Touchstone Story. It is expected that there will ultimately be several Touchstones.

Coalescence

On completing the 7 Step action stages of the DPS process, newly discovered learning can be underscored and new steps outlined to enhance these cognitive behavioural changes.

The model in which the action has occurred, Clinical and Counselling, Human Resources or Education and Awareness and the person using the process, determines the techniques used during the coalescence stage. A therapist, human resources professional or teacher may work with the client(s) through coalescence, using approaches that the Facilitator would generally use in working for cognitive behavioural changes.

Since the Playwright Psychotheatrics process is designed to emphasise the client(s) responsibility for his or her actions and decisions, it would be consistent with this point of view if the coalescence process maintains this position. The period of coalescence varies from a quick debriefing to on-going involvement, depending on the individuals and the change that has been developed and actualised.

Conclusion

Playwright Psychotheatrics offers a unique opportunity for translating thoughts and words into action for the purpose of understanding oneself and significant others. By translating thoughts and words into dramatic expression, even for a moment, the client(s) gains perspectives that far outweigh the time and energy invested. Working through resistance and proceeding with Playwright Psychotheatrics opens possibilities for cognitive behavioural changes that are enhanced through illustrative action. The concept of taking the raw material of Expressive Writing, then developing this material through the Story Map and working and refining it further to construct a Dramatic Enactment, underlies the Playwright Psychotheatrics Element.

14
Montage Psychotheatrics

Montage, a special effect that fast forwards, rearranges and transforms, appeared early in film-making to elevate movies from documentation to magic. A scene appears, dissolves and reappears transformed. A variation on this theme can happen in real life.

The action phase of Montage Psychotheatrics consists of the individual residing for a period of time, from several hours to a week, in an environment structured to assist the client in two ways: 1) to provide support for the **Transformation Personality Role** (TPR) by providing activities and social reinforcement, and 2) to remove him or her from the surroundings and people that reinforce the usual behaviours, in order to enhance experimentation with new ways of being.

As with Imaginal and Playwright Psychotheatrics, Montage Psychotheatrics action is preceded by the Biography and Discussion phase and followed by the Coalescence phase. Montage Psychotheatrics may be used in all three Dramatic Psychological Storytelling (DPS) applications: Clinical and Counselling, Human Resources and Education.

The central theme of all the Psychotheatrics Elements, Imaginal, Playwright and Montage is that the essential nature of a person is to recreate him or herself. Furthermore, truth exists for a particular individual only as he or she produces it in intersubjective action; in essence, the person becomes producer-director of his or her own life. The locus of control is internal; responsibility, psychological ownership and destiny are within the person. The extension of this premise is that a person may create a transformed personality, which is the fundamental principle of Montage Psychotheatrics.

Biography and Discussion

The Biography and Discussion stage for Montage Psychotheatrics must be accomplished with great care. If this stage is not completed adequately Montage Psychotheatrics will either be less effective or possibly quite problematic.

Whether Montage Psychotheatrics is to be used for therapy, education or in an organisational setting for coaching or leadership training, the criteria upon which the Facilitator should base the use of the Montage Psychotheatrics action stage with a particular client must include **all** of the following:

- Clients who choose this approach should be attempting significant life-style changes;
- Clients should be able to identify specific behaviours that they wish to change and integrate into their normal functioning;
- Clients should have sufficient contact with reality to deal with their own personality changes;
- Clients should understand and be willing to risk upsetting the homeostasis of the social units to which they belong.

If this Element is to be used for therapy, these criteria are particularly important. In typical psychotherapeutic approaches there is usually opportunity for the client to adjust to personality changes as these changes evolve over a period of time. In Montage Psychotheatrics, the changes occur in a short time span (action stage) and the Facilitator and client must take this fully into consideration. These criteria must be followed, whether applied to therapy, education or human resources because the personality change that takes place after the action stage can be very significant to the client and those around him or her. We must consider also the intense energy of the action stage, which can be overpowering for some people.

During the Biography and Discussion stage the client develops the TPR (Transformation Personality Role). This process is designed to translate the individual's goals for change into behaviours that he or she will focus on during the Craft step, using Method of Physical Action to actualise the TPR. Identifying desirable new behaviours is the first step toward dramatising those behaviours in the Montage Psychotheatrics process. A fuzzy image of how the person would like to change is not enough. The Facilitator can assist the client in developing an in-depth biography of the personality (mental, verbal and physical processes) that the person wants to assume.

People have a tendency to lock themselves into a fixed situation, which in turn can lead to a fixed definition of themselves. Fixed definitions must be rejected before the person can create a TPR based on what he or she wants to be and become. It is necessary that the changes the person is to undertake are within realistic grasp of that person. Far-fetched goals can lead to feelings of frustration and inadequacy that add to the individual's struggles. Concerning this premise, there are two types of fantasy: 1) fantasy that has the potential to become reality, and 2) fantasy that has very low probability of ever becoming reality. The concentration in Montage Psychotheatrics is on the fantasy – TPR – that is possible for the client.

The Facilitator should emphasise the question, 'What kind of person do you want to be?' After preparation of the TPR is complete, the Dramatic Enactment can begin, wherein the TPR can be actualised. After the TPR is well developed, the individual knows what changes he or she will focus on. The next step is for that individual, with the assistance of the Facilitator, to design activities for the Dramatic Enactment in order to provide the person with an opportunity to operationalise the behaviours. The more specific the planning is, for both experimentation and reinforcement of new behaviours, the better.

Warning and applications

Montage Psychotheatrics is an extremely powerful process which should only be used under highly restricted conditions and only with the guidance of trained professionals in Clinical and Counselling, Human Resources and Education. In all circumstances, the TPR must always be positive and the client must have a clear grounding in reality. To use this process with a fragile personality could be quite destructive.

This approach could be applied in the following situations and circumstances:

- Human Resources: especially for training and development purposes. See Chapter 16 for a detailed case study example using leadership skills.
- Clinical and Counselling: positive aspects of the Five Factor Model of personality[1] are ideal to work with. Each of the five major personality traits is made up of facets that have clear emotional, cognitive and behavioural components to work with and actualise.

- Education: for example to 'be in someone else's shoes' as part of a school bullying program. The Montage Psychotheatrics action step would need to be modified here so it would not be so involved or intense.

Planning for Coalescence

The client and Facilitator will invest significant time, thought and energy into the action stage of Montage Psychotheatrics, especially the TPR. Plans for coalescence are important, too. Social systems have a way of snapping back into place, crushing new growth before it has a chance to mature. What safeguards can the client put in place to welcome transformation? Returning to the situation that created the need for change without consciously preparing substantial support is self-defeating. Are there people, environmental arrangements or other aspects that can help create a receptive transition into the TPR? Planning for re-entry is as important as creating the TPR.

7 Step action stage – Montage Psychotheatrics

Seven Step DPS used in Montage Psychotheatrics shares similarities but is also quite different from Imaginal Psychotheatrics and Playwright Psychotheatrics. Montage Psychotheatrics has been specially created for individual personality and character transformation in a collective setting. All three types of Psychotheatrics are about *change*, with the client (staff member, student, or participant) in charge but directly assisted and challenged by the Facilitator.

We have adapted the Method of Physical Action, created by Konstantin Stanislavski and later modified by Jean Benedetti[2] for the TPR. CAUTION: this process is extremely powerful and is designed for character transformation. It is essential that the Method of Physical Action be used under proper guidance. For an example of a detailed case study using Montage Psychotheatrics, please see Chapter 16: Human Resources, Case Study: Leadership Skills Profile (pp. 188–92).

1 *Expressive Art type*

Story: What Expressive Art type is the inspiration for the story or reflects and illustrates the story? This will assist in developing the foundation of the story, which will later be modified and changed but originates here.

Narrative – oral, informal writing, book, poem, news article
Film – cinema, television, video
Theatre – formal play, performance, or a scenario
Music – song, concert, composition, group practice

Visual Art – painting, drawing, sculpture, collage, installation, performance
Dance and Kinaesthetics – choreographed or informal; designed movement, sport, viewing performance
Ritual and Epic – ceremony (birth, marriage); spectacle, happening (Olympics), or an organisational ritual

2 *Element*

Montage Psychotheatrics involves individual change in a collective setting. With the help and support of the Facilitator, the client will work out the TPR that they will practice in a Dramatic Enactment.

3 *Craft*

Method of Physical Action. In order to actualise the Method of Physical Action, in the TPR that you have chosen, please consider the following 5 phases:

Phase I: The Way We Behave

The REAL I: the need to keep an imprint of your real personality by listing and describing memorable experiences; what these meant to you and how it shaped you. This provides protection of the true self, the REAL I, which is critical in order to keep you grounded.

Necessity: the recognition that all behaviour is purposeful and is goal directed. Please list goals and then specific objectives that you have for your REAL I and now for your new TPR.

Feelings: the emotions resulting from interaction with others and the environment. Please describe and list examples of your important feelings in specific circumstances for both your REAL I and your TPR for the following emotions:[3] *love* (fondness, infatuation), *joy* (bliss, pride, contentment), *anger* (annoyance, contempt, hostility, jealousy), *sadness* (agony, guilt, grief, loneliness), *fear* (horror, worry).

Organic Actions: these are habitual actions you perform with their own logic and sequence (like getting dressed in the morning before going out). List and describe several of these actions, with examples for both your REAL I and for the new TPR you are creating.

Phase II: Created Behaviour

The TPR is based on a specific character you are creating. First outline your TPR according to possibilities that you hope to achieve. How close is your REAL I to what you want for your TPR? The gap between your REAL I and TPR is the focus of your work here. Include in your description of this 'gap', what you will need to achieve in cognitive, emotional and behavioural terms, with specific examples.

REAL I to your new TPR: You need to create your new TPR from your REAL I. In order to do this you will need to: (a) first understand and be able to follow the story you will create in the Story Map (this is completed in the next step) and describe the situations and demands you will be encountering. (b) After you complete the Story Map, it will help you to be conscious of, and then have imaginative manipulation of, your natural responses – in an harmonious relationship between the elements of your REAL I and the TPR you hope to achieve.

At this point it is necessary to move to the Story Map step of DPS and complete these phases, then return here to the *Craft* to complete the following aspects in relation to your TPR. There will be considerable movement between this point in the Craft – Method of Physical Action step and the Story Map steps. After this, please complete Phases I through to III below:

Phase III: improvisation and written journal

Creative Goal: describe how the experience of becoming the TPR would be for you, after first thoroughly reviewing and understanding the Story Map.

Given Circumstances: this is the Story Map you created and will be the foundation for your new TPR. Now please extend this into other life circumstances, interactions with others and other life events for your new TPR.

Past, Present and Future: in this phase you are creating a 3-dimensional TPR that will start to come to life by imagining and then actually preparing a very brief biography of your past and future TPR. You are already involved in the present.

Supertask: these are the main themes, the intrinsic nature, the substance, the reality, the significance of the TPR that need to be described.

Cognition: specific examples need to be developed describing thoughts and inner monologue that are consistent with and expressive of the developing Transformation Personality Role.

Emotion Memory: list and describe feelings from your REAL I that will be helpful with your new TPR, concerning the change you want to achieve.

Phase IV: Cognitive, physical and emotional integration.

Creative Goal: the essence and distinctive features of the Story Map and TPR need to be identified and linked to behaviour through actions.

External Characterisation: describe and clarify your new TPR code of conduct, values and ideas. Next illustrate these by linking with specific examples and explain how these would be actualised through external behaviour and appearance.

Staging: How will the new TPR be actualised? You need to be specific on the venue, interaction with others and situations that are necessary for the actualisation of the TPR to occur.

Phase V: The actualisation of cognitive, physical and emotional integration of TPR.

Creative Goal: your new TPR now needs to be actualised, however it is necessary to keep your REAL I solid for safety and grounding.

Given Circumstances: use the Story Map you created as it will provide a clear sense of direction.

Supertask: focus on the main themes, the intrinsic nature, the substance, the reality, the significance of your TPR for actualisation and reflect this through specific cognition, behaviour and feelings.

	REAL I	**TPR**
Essence personality/character		
Given circumstances Who is in your life? What is the time frame? What is going on? Where is it happening? What does the setting look like? What events are important?		
Events What specific events are important? Link to desire for change resulting in TPR.		
Emotions What feelings are important to you? Link to desire for change resulting in TPR.		
Complication What challenge(s) do you need to overcome?		
Inner monologue and mental images Give examples of pictures in your head and thoughts that recur.		

Method of Physical Action

4 *Story Map*

The Story Map will assist in creating the TPR. The goal is to include just enough information to further develop the *story* that represents the TPR.

	REAL I	TPR
Title List title or succinctly describe the TPR.		
Orientation for TPR Who is in the story? When is it happening? What is going on? How does the story start? What is the first sentence? Where is it happening? What does the setting look like? What words will you use to describe the setting and how can you help paint a mind picture?		
Initiating Events What specific events inspired this story/TPR?		
Characters Describe the most important characters that will assist in the TPR. What are they like? What do they look like? What sort of personalities do they have? How do they act, think and feel in the story?		
Complication What challenge(s) does the main character/TPR need to overcome?		
Sequence of Events What events happen first, next, last? What does the main character/TPR do? How does the TPR act and react in a believable way?		

	REAL I	TPR
Resolution How will things work out? What issues need to be confronted? How will the story end?		
Coda The message or moral of the story/TPR.		

5 *Dramatic Enactment*

This is the dramatic performance of the Story Map and the actualisation of the Craft: Method of Physical Action. This is very different than Imaginal and Playwright Psychotheatrics. Instead of a short scenario, the Dramatic Enactment involves performance of the TPR over several hours to several days. This is truly living and becoming, transforming into the TPR of the Story Map as actualised through the Craft: Method of Physical Action. Montage Psychotheatrics is extremely powerful. This transformation can blur the boundaries of self and TPR and lead to *possession*. However, this may be exactly what is required and hoped for!

The Dramatic Enactment is designed to enhance the possibilities of becoming the TPR. Ideally this should occur at a facility provided for that purpose. All participants in the process will have been through the Biography and Discussion stage and are at the point of trying to actualise their TPRs. All 7 Expressive Art types from Step 1 can be used here to reflect and enhance the TPR however the use of Theatre will be essential.

During the session the participants interact with each other and go about their activities in their TPR. It is necessary to provide adequate psychological safeguards for people participating in this process. It is good practice to have a professional Facilitator either in the setting or on call in the event that the stress of engaging in the TPR, without the usual environmental controls that exist for all of us, proves to be too great for a participant.

Staging the Dramatic Enactment

(i) Dramatic Enactment should last at least one hour and no longer than three days.

(ii) To assume the TPR the client must be consciously truthful to it verbally, mentally and physically. The client must be conscious of how he or she should speak at all times. In speaking, the client must be aware of his or her intonations, word selection and meaning. Physically, the client must act the TPR. This involves movement, dress, gestures and other major personal characteristics. Mentally, the client must learn to think like the TPR. This can be achieved by the client setting forth the issues, problems, events and situations of the TPR and reacting to them. This will enhance the TPR, make it become active and working and will create solidification. The TPR should be seen in terms of actions that are guided by the main traits of the new character. At different times the client will merge (verbally, physically and mentally) with the TPR in spontaneous action or thought. It is vital for the client to be consciously truthful (verbally, physically and mentally) to the TPR, or spontaneous synthesis will not occur and the TPR will not be realised. Often, the client will feel 'artificial' at first because he or she is aware of the willpower required to become the TPR. When the client merges with the TPR they will look up and notice that they have *been* the TPR for a length of time. The shock is profound when this realisation occurs. Now the client knows that it can happen and that it has happened. As time proceeds, the spontaneous synthesis will become more and more frequent until the client has become the TPR.

(iii) Clients should not disclose the role-acting process (TPR) to other clients at the Environmental Adaptation Session and should not challenge another client about his or her TPR.

(iv) It is best but not vital if the clients do not know each another. The objective of the EAS (Environmental Adaptation Session) is for the client to actualise his or her TPR and this may be more difficult to do around people with whom one is familiar. They would see the client as he or she was and not as what he or she wants to become and will probably hold the client back. There will be situations where these concerns are not as relevant and it may even be desirable for familiarity with others.

(v) If possible, the Environmental Adaptation Facility (EAF) can be extended for reality focus so that the clients can interact with the 'outside world'. This exercise will help test and solidify the TPR, by the clients relating to everyday life. This extension can be time spent in a bowling alley, a restaurant or wherever people congregate. The Facilitator should assist in deciding where and when the reality focus will be utilised.

(vi) The compatibility factor will be a consideration of the Facilitator in the screening process for selecting clients for the EAS. It is very important that clients interact with each other in such a manner as to lead to the growth and actualisation of everyone's TPR.

(vii) The Facilitator will carefully structure the time before and during the EAS. Action sheets should be given to each client, and they should agree to implement them. This procedure will enable the Facilitator to create situations to help the clients achieve their TPRs. Each client's action sheet will be worked out individually by the Facilitator so as to meet his or her unique requirements.

(viii) Interaction props should be provided (materials such as games, a pool table, etc.) that will enhance interaction among clients.

(ix) The goal of the EAS is to have the clients actualise their TPRs. The EAS should not be an encounter group; in fact, nothing could be more destructive. Even if a client merges with his or her TPR for only a few minutes, it has happened and is a reality. The client knows that this merger has taken place, that it is no longer a fantasy. The client knows that a real change has taken place. The door is now open.

(x) A Facilitator, as regulator, should always be present during the EAS. He or she will enhance interaction among the clients, help them to merge with their TPRs and provide stability and safeguards if necessary.

An individual has merged with his or her TPR when new actions are interwoven with thoughts and he or she is so accustomed to them that it is not apparent where the 'real' personality ends and that of the TPR begins.

As with Imaginal Psychotheatrics and Playwright Psychotheatrics, the client is involved but still has the witness perspective to ensure objectivity and rationality. For Montage Psychotheatrics however, the witness is very different as the client becomes the TPR, so this may seem contradictory. In actuality, the witness perspective is ensured by the detailed planning of the TPR by the client, who is objectively and rationally in charge of this process.

6 *Meaning*

Following the Dramatic Enactment is an ideal time to reflect on the experience. What is the Meaning in all this? Is this what was wanted? If not, then the TPR should be revised and actualised again. It probably is not necessary at this point for a full Dramatic Enactment to take place, rather just a rehearsal until the client feels that the TPR is happening. Then a short Dramatic Enactment can take place to actualise the TPR.

It is now time to review the previous stages and challenge what has occurred and then discover and legitimatise the Meaning of the experience that has emerged. Given the complexity of Montage Psychotheatrics, sifting through revelations, new learning and practice with the TPR will follow for some time to come.

7 *Touchstone Story*

The successful TPR is the Touchstone Story actualised.

Coalescence

The coalescence stage involves the solidification of the process. While in the coalescence stage, the Facilitator and client must determine whether or not the goals have been realised. The emphasis here is on the client merging with the TPR that the action stage has created. Energy is present from the cathartic effect of the action stage; it should now be channelled to reach the desired goals. Obviously, the TPR overlaps both the action and the coalescence stages, but the coalescence stage is utilised to solidify the TPR. If this has already taken place in the action stage, then the coalescence stage will be brief. The time involved in coalescence depends on the individual, the Facilitator and on the desired TPR.

Variations of Montage Psychotheatrics

There are several variations of Montage Psychotheatrics that may prove useful:

Adjunct: If a client and Facilitator believe that this process would be useful with other models (for example Cognitive Behaviour Therapy) it can be used as an adjunctive process.

People Who Know Each Other: A general rule is not to have people together in the EAS who are familiar with each other, as this normally would tend to inhibit each other's TPR actualisation. However, where deemed appropriate, people who are familiar (friends, married couples, or others) could benefit from sharing the EAS. The sharing of the EAS by people who are close may enable them to actualise the TPRs together. This could very well have positive benefits in a relationship, as both would be mutually supportive and not faced with the situation of a partner having to adapt to this without proper reference points.

Inpatient Facility: The regular process can be modified for use in an inpatient facility Instead of the person being a 'patient', the person would be a 'client'. An inpatient facility will be much more effective if it were designed for creative and positive growth than for the treatment of 'illness'. In this variation, concentration would not be fixed on 'dysfunction' and 'illness' but on the creative and positive aspects of the TPR, which would be beneficial to the person.

The Halfway House: Montage Psychotheatrics (and the Environmental Adaptation Facility) can be used in residences for people undergoing a major life-style transition (with individuals who have substance abuse problems, for instance). The goals for this variation are the same as for an inpatient facility.

Conclusion

The Human Resources chapter gives a detailed example of the application of Montage Psychotheatrics. Montage Psychotheatrics is a tool for complex change in a controlled collective environment. It is ideal for human resources for coaching, leadership development, or situations where people want to change clearly identifiable behaviours or characteristics. It is also very well suited for therapy and education applications as significant change is possible with this method when the client is fully involved and all support systems are in place. Montage Psychotheatrics needs to be carefully implemented under the guidance of a professional Facilitator such as a human resource professional, therapist or educator.

Part IV
Applications

15
Clinical and Counselling

In Greek, the word for 'soul' is psyche.
It also means 'breath' or 'life'.
This ancient word carries the wisdom that
we are more than our genetic makeup.
More than our life histories,
more than our cultural lineage.
Carol Gilligan, *The Birth of Pleasure*[1]

Psychotherapy involves far more than fixing what is wrong in a person's life. Whether in analytically oriented personal psychotherapy or in drug and alcohol counselling, a shift to personal responsibility creates the possibility for significant change. The client finds something of value in her or his life, something bigger than the **self**, which warrants the work and sacrifice required for gaining higher ground. The *Dramatic Psychological Storytelling* (DPS) model is about 'detecting' that Meaning, as Victor Frankl[2] stated. From Freud's earliest efforts and use of the word psyche/soul, at least one stream of the Clinical and Counselling world has centered on a search for Meaning. The introduction of Frankl's logotherapy in the 1950's, along with the work of Rollo May[3] and others brought that focus forward.

Today the search for the true self – emphasis on self-esteem and self-actualisation – persists, despite heavy emphasis on medication instead of, or in conjunction with, brief therapy. The arduous process of uncovering and embracing one's true self with its flaws as well as strengths, builds an essential foundation for authenticity. That process is a step, but not a completion. Relationships with others and the cosmos are important too. Promoting **I** and diminishing **thou** leads to the depletion of both and the loss of overarching values.

Thanks to the work of people like James Hillman, Jean Houston, John Robinson, Donald Sandner, Alice Miller, Marion Woodman and others, the art of soul making moves beyond the medical model and traditional psychotherapy to explore the individual's connection, not only with self, but with the numerous possibilities of larger connections.

Although DPS is firmly based on phenomenological intersubjective 'meaning and experience', it is easily used with behaviouristic or humanistic methods. **Meaning**, the sixth step in the model, is designed to sift the client's learning experience at whatever level he or she chooses to pursue it. The authors' perspective is that connection with something bigger than self is key to the healing process: that sacred psychology has ancient roots that connect us all.

Marion Woodman, in *Addiction to Perfection*,[4] reaches for this cosmic connection in a feminine context outside traditional religion: 'The wisdom of Sophia...is the Wisdom of the unknowable. It is non-rational, nonrepeatable, and nonconsistent. It belongs to the here-and-now, the immediate moment.' Woodman's next comment has a patriarchal religious tint, but the powerful imagery is quotable: 'William Blake describes it as the moment in each day that Satan cannot find, as short as the pulsation of an artery. It is the moment in which life is conceived not in some repeatable fashion, for it is unique and particular to the moment.'[5] That moment of immediacy, when the true self connects with cosmic wisdom, allows for awareness and choice informed by more than an individual's past, cultural lineage or social context.

From time to time, just such a moment is the treasure revealed by the DPS process. That is not a promise, of course. Usually the treasure is a mere nugget, but useful. DPS transports the client's dynamics from behind defences to the dramatic 'seeing place', making them accessible to both client and therapist/Facilitator for understanding, exploration and creative change. As part of an active process, the client contributes the content and selects story slices for illumination. Using the model, part of the power of this process is that, following a brief scenario, it tends to shine light on more than the specific drama under consideration.

This chapter is designed to assist clinicians who will serve as Facilitators for implementing DPS in therapeutic settings with individuals, couples or groups. The authors assume that those who will be guiding the process are knowledgeable about ethics and standards of practice in their fields and are skilled at facilitating interventions. The chapter's examples provide overviews for working through DPS and are intended to be illustrative, not definitive or limiting.

Skills for facilitating DPS in a clinical setting

Chapter 18 *Facilitator Skills*, deals specifically with skills necessary for working through DPS and outlines procedures that are useful. Before attempting the process, review that chapter and be clear about what is needed so attention can be on the client's work rather than on determining what the next procedure should be.

In her work as a psychologist at Bathurst Community Health Centre's Drug and Alcohol Service, in NSW, Australia, Roslyn Medaris conducted a six week Relapse Prevention Program. From the beginning, she was looking for a dynamic way to 'wrap up' the experience for the participants. She chose to use DPS, facilitated by her husband, Rob Allen, for the sixth session. Following is Roslyn's summary of the first six-week program in which she utilised DPS in the final session.

Project description: Changing Scenarios, Changing Lives!

This project explored the use of DPS in groupwork with clients who have serious drug and alcohol problems. Storytelling is an effective form of communication for the construction of a collective sense and combined with drama can become a powerful visual connection for deep meaning. In particular, the DPS format creates a visual phenomenological framework depicting challenges, strategies and outcomes that develop into a dynamic storybook. My goal was to help participants finish the program, feeling not only motivated to achieve the goals that they had set for themselves, but also confident that they now had the skills needed to be able to put all this into practice once they were faced with the reality of their life and their situation back in the 'real' world. It was about this time that my husband began working on DPS. While involved with him in the initial planning for the new publication, I became aware of how useful this model could be, if we were to incorporate it into my existing Relapse Prevention Program. I asked Rob if he would consider co-facilitating the final session of my six-week program, using DPS, and he agreed.

1 *Expressive Art Experience*

Narrative, Oral Style: In this situation we used the Narrative (oral story) as the Expressive Art type of choice. However, any of the other six Expressive Art forms could easily have been used as the experience. For example, the film *Little Fish*, starring Cate Blanchett; music such as Johnny Cash singing *Folsom Prison Blues* or a graphic photo of a substance abuse related event could have been utilised also.

2 *Element*

Imaginal Psychotheatrics is the choice in this case, given that the participants all share a common concern. It is a group of drug and alcohol dependent clients, the majority of whom are 'involuntary' or 'coerced' clients, often referred by the courts.

3 *Craft*

Rhetorical Reality Analysis: We begin by asking for a volunteer to briefly relate to us the 'story' of the last time they had a 'lapse' or a 'relapse', or found themselves making a 'seemingly irrelevant decision' which ultimately led to such a lapse. After a brief personal story by one of the participants, we then asked the other participants to build onto this original story. Using *Rhetorical Reality Analysis* (modified from Ernst Bormann's work[6]), group members added brief examples, or links, to the story from their individual experiences. These story links soon became a powerful chain binding the group and transformed the original story into something that the whole group now owned and to which they could all relate. This ultimately became the *Group Story: Arnie's Story*.

4 *Story Map*

Orientation: An acquaintance, Gary, asked Arnie for a lift to a house out of town saying he wanted to get some 'pot'.

Complication: He came out of the house and said 'Hey, they've got some "pure" stuff!' (Amphetamines or 'speed', which happened to be Arnie's drug of choice!)

Sequence of Events: Arnie bought drugs and 'shot up' immediately (intravenous use).

Resolution: Arnie realised he had been set up. He could have gone back the next day for more but did not, although he had the money. He recognised that it was a lapse and not a full-blown relapse.

5 *Dramatic Enactment*

Theatre: Any of the seven Expressive Art types could be used here, either singly or in combination, for the Dramatic Enactment. We chose to use theatre to play out part of the story to highlight key aspects. The enactment of this part of the story has participants becoming both Director and Producer of a story that they themselves now own. The story can then be re-enacted with the participants being encouraged to describe to the Facilitators who are the 'actors' in this scenario, how they can avoid a lapse or a relapse in this situation. For example, the Facilitator, who is now the actor in this scenario, might say, 'What would I be thinking right now, if I were to avoid this lapse?' 'How would I be feeling?' 'What would be happening around me right now?'

'What am I doing now?' 'How am I behaving?' 'What would I be thinking if I were in this situation?' 'OK then, so what happens next?'

The scene was first enacted with a client as Director of 'Arnie' and with the Facilitator portraying Arnie and a group member portraying Gary, the acquaintance to whom he gave the lift. Later this same scene was re-enacted with Arnie now avoiding the lapse.

6 *Meaning*

Participants are able to recognise the difference between a lapse and a relapse. By re-enacting the original scenario, and giving it a 'preferred scenario' ending, the group is able to see how a more positive outcome could be achieved both in this instance and in the future. Arnie and the group are now able to recognise the difference between a lapse and a relapse. Also the Dramatic Enactment, by illustrating preferred possibilities, enabled the group to see how a more positive outcome could be achieved in their own real life scenarios.

7 *Touchstone Story*

The essense of this group story, or the Touchstone Story, is: *The ability to resist using the drug when it is offered to me.*

The group sees in a very dynamic way, which is both visual and auditory, how to avoid what we refer to as a High Risk Situation. This model can be used around any High Risk Situation that has been identified by a member of the group. In most cases all members of the group can relate to these situations or have experienced similar setbacks in their own attempts to avoid drug and alcohol use. During the course of the telling and re-telling of this story, the main themes can be pulled out and explored further by the therapists, in consultation with the group, either now or at a later date.

Trial results to date

It is useful to write down all of the themes that are identified in both the original story and the group story, as each member of the group adds a link to the chain. Themes are also identified from the Touchstone Story, once it is transformed into a different reality. Some of these themes included such things as *avoiding impulsivity, your circle of friends, peer pressure, negative thinking* or *'stinkin thinkin'* (to coin my own expression) and the impact that this has on how we feel and subsequently behave. Support networks and the importance of having someone who you can turn to for support were seen to be important. Support groups such as Alcoholics Anonymous and Narcotics Anonymous were seen as good examples of such networks. All of these themes, once identified, can be further explored with the groups concerned and more so in particular settings. Used within a drug rehabilitation facility, for example, a different theme, once identified by the group, could be discussed each time the group came together, with strategies developed to overcome the negatives and maintain the positives of each of these themes. Each contains important aspects for maintaining abstinence and taking control of one's life.

Themes (**Note:** The main themes were extracted from group therapy sessions using DPS. Quotes used are composite examples and also reflect comments by drug and alcohol clients in general. In order to protect confidentiality, no real clients have been used for the purpose of this illustrative example.)

Circle of Friends:
'The big thing, I reckon though, is who you're knocking around with. Fair dinkum, that's the big one!'

'I've got no friends left. The people I use with, they're not real friends. They don't want to know you when you're straight.'

'I've tried to make new friends but they find out about me and that's it. It's all over!'

'I'd chosen the drug over all my friends that I'd valued so much and that really scarred me up.'

Peer Pressure:
'I'm trying to get off the "pot" and where I live, they all use it. They'll say: "Come on man", and I say, "No thanks, I'm trying to give that shit up". But they keep on going with the pressure, you know, peer pressure. They make it hard for you to say No.'

Escape:
'Things just seemed to get on top of me – it was an escape I suppose and it just made me forget, you know, all the pain!'

Losing Control:
'I lost control. I looked for support in every area that I could and I'd sort of come up against the proverbial brick wall. I guess you feel like you're drowning really – and you need a lifeline.'

'I think that feeling of helplessness and that loss of control is something everyone here has gone through.'

Impulsivity:
'If the stuff's there, I'm gone! I have to do it. Next minute its hanging out me arm.'

Lapse/Relapse:
'Each time I relapsed, I was starting to get over the physical pain, starting to feel good and then, with monotonous regularity – I just had "shit happen", so I just kept on using (cannabis) for the pain.'

Recognising the difference between a lapse and relapse:
'I was in two minds. I knew I'd be pissed off, in fact, I was severely pissed off – with myself for using and with the bloke who took me there and offered it to me. Then at the end of it, I thought: "Well that was good in a way because it tested me. I had a lapse, but then I could have gone and got more money the next day, but I didn't, I stayed away from the stuff". I felt good about that!'

Insight:
'When you're on it – you feel positive and you feel like you can do anything – and talk to anyone and accomplish anything – and you sort of can, but not really – you're fooling yourself. Like – the drug's fooling you!' 'I don't know why I used – it's insane. You're just hurting yourself, killing yourself!'

On DPS:
'You've got more out of us today in this session than the last five sessions put together.'

Benefits – innovative approach

The benefit of this approach is that it complements the Relapse Prevention activities that the group has been involved in up to this point and also fits within a harm minimisation framework. It is designed for illustrative 3-D action and is, therefore, an effective adjunct to the Cognitive Behaviour Therapy principles that have been incorporated into the programme. It illustrates, in a very dynamic way, the concept that by changing the way we think about a situation, it is possible to alter the way we feel and in turn change our behaviour. It also allows for inarticulate clients to participate actively as spectators and does not require that they are active participants in order for them to benefit by observational learning. More articulate group members can participate more actively and thus assist other group members who prefer not to be outspoken or directive. It has surprised me, however, how DPS tends to bring out the extrovert in most of our participants, even those who normally take a back seat. In this particular situation we used the Expressive Art type of Theatre for the Dramatic Enactment. The fact that the participants do not have to role-play, or become actors in their own personal story, appears to make them more enthusiastic about becoming involved in the process. By becoming the Director of this group story, and telling someone else what to do and how to think and feel about a situation, they are suddenly able to step outside themselves, and the skills they have not always practiced in the real life situation will be brought forward here. In addition, playing others but never themselves of course, enables objectivity and also allows true experiential learning, allowing them to 'be in the others' shoes'. Finally the participants as spectators experienced observational learning related directly to their lives. Obviously, those who are more confident and more skilled at meeting such challenges will be more directive, with the others tending to follow suit as they recall what they have learned up to this point, thus enabling them to become more and more involved in the Touchstone Story as it unfolds.

Finally, the DPS model appears to accelerate the therapeutic process, and for the purpose of the groups that I run in Bathurst NSW Australia, it helps to bring all those threads together in the final session, allowing participants to view and understand the full tapestry.

DPS and therapy

Working through DPS involves direct focus on personal material, thus carrying a high degree of meaning for the participant. The clients place part of their inner lives on view to be turned and examined, reshaped and then re-internalised, initiating a response that may range from humility to awe. In her example, Roslyn Medaris points to the power of having the client serve as director or spectator rather than role-playing. In the Dramatic Enactment the client can mould the action into accurate reflections of experience, conflict, confusion, triumph or desire. Unconscious actions or motivations may become apparent, inviting awareness and choice regarding possible outcomes. Consciously inventing and absorbing imagery that is different from life experience opens new options for the client.

Beginning with an Expressive Art form as entry into psychologically relevant material offers an alternatives approach, indirect access to areas that might otherwise feel too threatening. For instance, choosing a song or movie scene that embodies feeling about the issue of concern, then writing truthfully using James Pennebaker's (1997)[7] approach to deepen experience, followed by story creation which evolves into a short drama brings personal dynamics on stage for the client as witness. The Facilitator guide supports the client through the process and is available to help maintain focus and search for Meaning, while the client maintains control and direction. A fresh array of information opens for exploration, along with a sense of connection with others who have faced similar concerns.

DPS, can be described in terms of cognitive behavioural principles, role theory, Gestalt therapy and other action-oriented approaches. Since publication of *Psychotheatrics: The New Art of Self-Transformation* in 1979,[8] the healing qualities of narrative and story telling have acquired prominence in communications studies. Missing links that explain the effectiveness of Psychotheatrics slipped into place as the authors became familiar with clinical theories that existed at the time, but were not popularised until the 1980s: self-psychology, object relations and research on small group communication for instance.

During early experimentation and writing about Psychotheatrics, the authors emphasised the difference between Psychotheatrics and Psychodrama, the technique that Jacob Moreno had popularised as part of the humanistic psychology movement. The prime difference in psychotheatrics is that the client produces and directs the drama rather than acting in it, as is the case in psychodrama. At face value, this difference may not seem profound, but differing results are observable. Narrative Therapy, Cognitive Behavioural Therapy and Schema Therapy highlight the applications possible when combined with DPS and support this objective witness approach. Subsequent understanding of object relations theory and the use of intersubjective space illuminate the difference of the power potential from those perspectives.

If you are familiar with concepts such as observational learning, cognitive behavioural principles, object relations, self-psychology, ego psychology, Narrative Therapy, or intersubjective space, the feasibility of DPS becomes apparent. These points of view offer contexts for understanding the power of DPS. In particular they lend credence to the Dramatic Enactment because of its heightened capacity for objectifying even the most confusing, painful or intimate conflicts. Creating the story through dramatic action (Psychotheatrics) using the 7 Expressive Arts, in order to observe at some distance, gives the event, conflict or uncertainty an identity of its own: personifies it in a way. The client can then reorganise this material and process it in a different form. The new drama can become a healthy. self-regulating other, to replace the old imagery.

You need not be familiar with the above-named approaches to use the DPS model, which is useful in conjunction with change processes from the least directive to the most structured. The concepts mentioned above, however, help explain dynamically some of what is apparent behaviourally. James F. Masterson's 1985[9] work in object relations, followed by many others, centers on the way we take in and internalise parts of the people who are important in our lives, either positively or negatively, and use those parts in our own psychological make up. Seeing one's 'self-object', whole or in parts, displayed through the DPS process, offers the opportunity to incorporate those parts in new ways. The parts, 'objects', on view become palpable. We get to see ourselves differently and thus can choose to work at containing or diminishing negative parts as well as enhancing or adding positive ones.

Intersubjective space is another psychological concept with high relevance for the DPS process, especially the Dramatic Enactment, but for all the other steps as well. When two people engage in heartfelt conversation and relationship, something happens that is bigger than both of them. The relationship itself becomes an entity, a 'third' as psychologist Jessica Benjamin (1998)[10] refers to it, that has a life of its own. This entity, the relationship, is palpable and identifiable. A woman's relationship with her husband, for example, is different from her relationship with her daughter, which is different again from her relationship with her son. Each has identifiable characteristics, holding patterns, history and boundaries. Each is a container of sorts.

A path of predictability develops in a relationship that offers enrichment and a cushion of support (or the opposite, as noted in Roslyn Medaris's example above). After a while, however, it may become quite binding and difficult to change. The container quality of a relationship allows things to happen that could not happen outside the relationship.

The Dramatic Enactment, using one or more of the seven Expressive Art types, is able to provide this container, serving as the processor in which change can happen. The intersubjective space is between the individual or organisation and the material that is at issue. The client is like one person in a conversation and the material on stage is the other. As the invisible third, the DPS process holds that space and provides a safety net for the work in progress.

Both the cushion of support and the binding qualities of this invisible third force are relevant to DPS work. In storytelling, or the creation of dramatic action by using the seven Expressive Arts types, the individual becomes part of something bigger than *self*. When the DPS process becomes a 'third' in the relationship between client and his or her material, the possibility to take in new imagery and attempt new ways of being expands exponentially.

Concretisation is a term that describes at least one process for carrying forward the gains made through using the DPS model. In order for behaviour to be carried forward, the individual must experience ownership and 'organisation' of that feeling or behaviour. This is the work of coalescence in DPS.

Atwood and Stolorow (1984)[11] suggest pathways of concretisation. They propose that the need to maintain the organisation of experience is a central motive in the patterning of human action. In fact, it is the 'supra-ordinate' principle of motivation. This idea emphasises how important it is for us to be able to discern patterns in behaviour, whether they are positive or negative. Having the opportunity to see and reorganise one's feelings, wishes, and behaviour allows the client to clarify the patterning necessary for change to occur. In the coalescence stage the work of internalising new findings is consistent with this concept from the field of self-psychology. Of particular relevance to DPS are Cognitive Behavioural Therapy, Schema Therapy and Narrative Therapy due to their compatibility and their practical applications. DPS can be used by practitioners in conjunction with all three of these models, in a seamless manner.

Cognitive Behavioural Therapy postulates that the way an individual structures and interprets experience determines mood and subsequent behaviour. Judith Beck (Director – Beck Institute for Cognitive Therapy and Research), has stated that the way we perceive a situation influences how we feel emotionally and how we behave. (Beck, 1995).[12] Our beliefs determine our feelings and actions; the important task is to identify distorted thinking and to modify these dysfunctional beliefs, which will change the way we relate to others and also change our behaviour. It is not the situation itself that affects how a person feels and behaves but the particular belief concerning the situation in relation to self and to others. DPS allows for the creation of a safe objective/subjective environment to 'see' situations through implicit (story) and explicit (dramatic) enactment. This provides an opportunity to challenge distorted thinking and dysfunctional beliefs and to replace these with more appropriate cognitions, through actualising new options by rehearsal of possibilities; this re-enactment reinforces the self-efficacy required to achieve these goals.

Schema Therapy expands the traditional definition of a schema in the context of psychology and psychotherapy, as an organising principle that makes sense of one's life. The traditional definition of a schema is a cognitive mental plan that serves as a guide for action, interpreting information and solving problems: A general framework that emphasises overall relationships and downplays details. Schema Therapy developed by Jeffrey Young also recognises the emotional component of a schema and provides a more comprehensive definition: 'broad, pervasive theme or pattern; comprised of memories, emotions and bodily sensations; regarding oneself and one's relationships; developed during childhood or adolescence; elaborated throughout one's lifetime'.[13]

The research of LeDoux (1996)[14] provides strong support for emotional memory. His research has found traumatic events are stored in different parts of the brain: 'conscious memories involve the hippocampus and related cortical areas and unconscious memories are established by fear based conditioning mechanisms through an amygdala-based system'. DPS highlights the affective components of a schema and allows for these to be revealed through the Craft and Story Map of DPS and then illustrated by the Dramatic Enactment.

Through action methods, DPS is able not only to reveal the affective components of a schema but then to replace these with more functional aspects through implicit (story) and explicit enactment (dramatic action) using any one or more of the 7 Expressive Art types. Furthermore, DPS uses the rational cathartic method of Augusto Boal's *Rainbow of Desire*[15] and Bertold Brecht's Epic Theatre model[16] rather than the Aristolean emotional cathartic method used by Sigmund Freud. The difference in these two approaches is significant. The DPS model allows for the revealing of subjective/affective components, while the client is detached as an objective witness. This distance provides rational control.

In Narrative Therapy, meaning is developed in self and relationships by 'storying' experience, thus interacting with others. A person is active in the 'performance' of these stories that shape the self and our relationships with others. The 'problem' is not with the person but with the 'dominant story'. It helps to externalise this story and to map how this dominant story has influenced life and relationships. In terms of psychopathology, Michael White and David Epston (1990)[17] emphasise 'alternative stories' instead of a dysfunctional dominant story. These alternative stories are possible but just not recognised or actualised; they usually have been experienced but neglected in favour of the dominant story. By being an audience to the 'performance' of these alternative stories, a person gains self-efficacy and agency. The enhancement of an alternative or even a new story can be further achieved through the 'performance' to an external audience; they also act as witnesses to the performance and contribute to its meaning. The DPS model is firmly based in storytelling and is enhanced through performance using any one or more of the 7 Expressive Art types and externalisation, with the client as witness. All of these aspects complement the Narrative Therapy model.

Moving from theory to practice, the following is an abbreviated description of a professional development workshop for seven therapists – four women, three men – conducted by the authors. Therapists attended this workshop with very little preconceived idea of what would happen. All knew the therapist hosting the workshop, but they didn't all know each other or the Facilitators. They had expressed interest in the DPS model and agreed to meet for four hours to explore this method. After a brief explanation of Imaginal Psychotheatrics, but not of the 7 Step model for which discussion was promised later, the action began, as follows:

1 *Expressive Art type*

Narrative: Oral Story – After introductions, some discussion of the schedule and general expectations for the day, Facilitator (Rob Allen) asks the group to suggest some work-related topics about which they feel passionate. The items noted on the white board during a brainstorming session included:

- Authenticity while working as a therapist
- Bearing the client's pain
- Accurate empathy/Detachment
- Play – how we play in therapy – forms of play
- Limit to what you know/don't know
- I don't know this person – openness – excitement
- Learn the client's stories
- How to stay open to ourselves and others
- On the edge – excitement

2 *Element*

Since this is a group with shared interest and background, Imaginal Psychotheatrics is the Element of choice. The Facilitator briefly explains how the process works.

3 *Craft*

Rhetorical Reality Analysis

Facilitator: 'Does anyone have a story that embodies some of the ideas we just brainstormed?' 'Who would like to start?' Silence. The therapists who are probably more comfortable than most people with silence and waiting, sit still in their chairs. Before too long a woman speaks:

Jenna: 'I had the experience a few months ago, of working with someone who was making good progress with some of her life issues – her relationship, her job. Things seemed to be going better for her and I was thinking our work together was finished. I found myself somewhat bored during our sessions and wasn't sure whether she should be staying in therapy. As this thought was running through my mind, I saw her take a deep breath. She looked at me and said: "There is something I have never told anyone..." That moment of openness that comes once in a while in working with clients, is the one where I feel on the edge. I saw the client "move up" above the chatter of her everyday issues.'

Facilitator encourages conversation in the room about whether Jenna's scenario is one everyone in the group can relate to. Agreement comes after just a bit more discussion about the danger and the opportunity in such a moment including some shared experiences.

Others follow Jenna's lead until most, if not all, have contributed a comment or a story (links developed through Rhetorical Reality Analysis).

Rhetorical Reality Analysis: At this point the story is chained around the room, with other therapists adding in similar experiences, including their feelings at the moment of truth or similar moments. Both successes and empathic failures are offered. Words like excitement, fear, shadow, abyss, come into the conversation. It is clear that everyone knows what Jenna is talking about and relates to the story. Co-Facilitator, Nina listening to this, has a concern (unexpressed) that the scenario is so tiny it will not produce much in the way of dramatic action. The energy in the room is high however, and all the members of the group are involved. The Facilitator suggests dramatising the scenario.

4 *Story Map*

Orientation: Two players/actors will be needed: client and therapist. The action occurs in the therapist's office.

Complication: The therapist's feelings of anticipation, anxiety, fear and desire to handle the situation delicately when a client begins to open a deep wound.

Sequence of Events: In the therapist's office during a session, the client shifts from relatively ordinary conversation to the statement, 'There is something I have never told anyone...'

The therapist leans forward, her eyes widen slightly, as she looks directly at the client. She knows this is the moment that the therapy will deepen or the client will shut off, depending on how safe the client feels.

Resolution: The therapist handles the moment well with the client revealing what it is that burdens her.

Coda: The therapist can create and sustain a safe environment for the client.

5 *Dramatic Enactment*

Expressive Art type: Theatre – The Facilitator chooses actors/players to fill the roles of the client and the therapist. The Facilitator directs the player representing the client, while Jenna directs the player acting as the therapist 'Anne'. They situate themselves appropriately and the scenario begins. Client begins rambling about her relationship with her husband being better, feeling better...

Therapist (Anne) is attending, but not intent. Therapist reflects the thought: 'You're feeling better...' A pause follows. 'Yes', the client says, and stops. She takes a deep breath and says: 'There is something I have never told anyone...'

At this point, the Facilitator stops the action and turns to Jenna. 'Is this the way it happened?' The two of them discuss the action and then make some corrections in the way the actors/players are seated. Facilitator then asks Jenna, 'What was going on in your mind at this point?'

Jenna: 'I know this is an important moment, and I want to do a good job...'

Facilitator: 'Tell Anne what your thoughts were as much as you can so she can act them for you.'

Jenna gives the actor, who is playing the therapist, directions.

Client repeats line: 'There is something I have never told anyone.'

Therapist: responds, non-verbally, moving forward. Her eyes widen slightly.
Her face softens.

Client: 'When I was a teenager, I used to clean the parish hall at St. Bartholomew's. Father Ralph was not a very nice man.'

Facilitator: 'Jenna, what was going on in your mind at that moment?'

Jenna: 'I felt like – this was great – the reason I was there – the real reason she was in therapy. I also felt very sad for her. And, then I thought, "Oh No, this is dangerous! This is going to be about molestation or something really painful. I'm going to have to get the authorities involved." Since I grew up in the same faith, the molester might even be someone I know. I have to keep my attention on her (the client) or she will withdraw.'

Facilitator to therapist actor: 'Anne, you're a therapist, too. Did some of these thoughts come to you while you were playing the role?'

Anne: 'No. I was only thinking about the client, hoping that I could hold the space and not frighten her away. I suddenly felt very sad.'

Facilitator: 'What are other people feeling at this point?'

Several people share stories about similar situations. Jenna, touched by the way 'Anne' played the role, says that it was a peak moment for her. She feels affirmed in her decision to be a therapist. Others validate this point. Discussion about the therapist's legal responsibilities and how they complicate the relationship with the client flows, with most people making several contributions.

Facilitator: 'My sense is that we have finished this part of the process. Shall we take a break and come back for the next step?'

Group members glance around at each other.

Co-Facilitator: 'Just a second. I suggest we do another Dramatic Enactment and focus on the conflict going on in Jenna's head. I think it would be useful to deal with the "Oh No, issue".' Discussion. Participants agree and bring up related experiences. Jenna adds another twist. 'Just as I was thinking about the reporting issue, the client said, as if she were reading my mind, *"He's dead!"*.'

Facilitator sets up the Dramatic Enactment and asks co-Facilitator to play role of therapist, focused on administrative/legal issues. 'Anne' continues in client-centered therapist role.

Therapist Player Anne: 'I feel sad but encouraged that the client has dropped into this moment of truth. I hope I can be here for her in a way that she feels safe enough to go on...'

Therapist Player (Nina): 'Oh, bother. Now I'm going to have to tell the client about her legal rights and responsibilities, notify the authorities. Maybe I should remind her of the agreement she signed when she entered therapy that this kind of matter must be reported...'

This dialogue continues for a few rounds. Both actors are becoming less certain of their positions.

Facilitator: 'Jenna, are they on the right track?' She nods.

Facilitator to the players: 'What is it like for each of you to be in these roles?'

Anne: 'I'm getting deeply in touch with the whole reason for being a therapist. And, I am very touched to be here doing this because Nina was my mentor.'

Nina: 'This reminds me of how much I loved being a therapist and of why I chose that path.'

Anne: 'I can see in a whole new way how the legal issues of being a therapist are an important part of the therapy. For the first time, it feels like an important part of my job.'

Facilitator to 'Anne': 'Can you hold Nina's hand?' 'Anne' reaches across the small table between them to hold Nina's hand. Both are teary. This move signifies the two roles coming together. Silence.

Jenna: 'This is so powerful for me. They have really played both sides of my feelings, which are much more together now. I can see how I can deal with the complexity of a critical moment without having to be scared. I feel like I am getting so much out of this. I can feel more secure putting myself on the line. It's important to be able to do that, a rational and emotional commitment to take that kind of risk. It's exhausting and uplifting.'

Group discussion about how the scenario was really about the therapist's internal process, not so much what was going on with the client. The second Dramatic Enactment deepened the Meaning as the scenario moved into less acceptable feelings that Jenna had the courage to express.

6 ***Meaning***

During a working lunch, the discussion continued, with Facilitator indirectly eliciting comments about the meaning of the experience for all involved. Everyone had something to add. Several people said they had a whole new view of the relationship between the purely therapeutic and the more administrative aspects of their work. The therapists who played the roles, deepened their real relationships with their colleagues through this process. Jenna, the producer, felt more connection with the actors/players than with others in the room. Several people mentioned they would be much more relaxed in a 'moment of truth' situation next time. One person mentioned that this is an emotive, intuitive process, but it can be done in a systematic way. Another added that it is also cognitive because it lets people have a distance so they can process their own material and not be overwhelmed. Two people in the 'audience' felt they were missing out by not being actors/players. Given more time, this issue, which is a common human concern whether one is a therapist or not, could be the subject of another Dramatic Enactment, but in this situation it would have been useful to talk about how to benefit from vicarious experience.

7 Touchstone Story

Co-Facilitator asked the group to brainstorm some of the words that came to mind in thinking of the day's work. Their comments form this unpolished poem.

Risk, layers, grit
Abyss, cliff
Competence, connection, grace
Flow
Sacred space, empathy, excitement
Moment of truth
Opening, polarity, we
Integration, hold the polarity
Gratitude

The group members felt that although the ideas represented were similar to the first brainstorm of the day, they were now distilled and potent. Several expressed amazement at how much had happened in a very short time.

Even though this work was not therapy, the issue involved is a familiar one to therapists. The brief scenario was rich enough to produce plenty of dramatic action and, like any other brief excerpt that has authenticity, expanded easily enough. More scenarios could be enacted and would eventually include everyone who wanted to be directly involved by following emerging themes:

- the moment of truth for one therapist
- therapists' conflicted thoughts and feelings at that critical moment

- issues of exclusion brought up by audience members
- or any of the items listed in the *Touchstone Story* section above

Viktor Frankl's statement that meaning is not invented, it is detected, was affirmed in this workshop. The same is true when a therapist employs 7 Step DPS with an individual or couple in therapy. An environment of trust creates the context for work that opens new avenues for exploration. By outlining the client's story and proceeding through the steps that bring it to life, both therapist and client gain access to material that take much longer to otherwise unfold. Then, using the process, they can work together to initiate necessary changes, solutions or meaningful goals.

Conclusion

DPS in a clinical setting has the capacity to uncover material that will be the subject for much future work. In therapeutic treatment sessions or professional workshop settings, information comes forward that provides material for understanding individual and group dynamics. Just as with all therapeutic processes, consideration for the privacy and wellbeing of the client is critical. By turning thoughts and words into observable behaviour, supported by the Expressive Art types, the Facilitator and client gain access to a broad array of information that might never have come forward through traditional therapeutic methods. This heightening of the process can be an important adjunct to work in progress, or serve as a method for accomplishing specific short-term goals.

16
Human Resources

No institution can possibly survive if it needs geniuses or supermen to manage it. It must be organized in such a way as to be able to get along under a leadership composed of average human beings.
Peter F. Drucker[1]

In all our humanness we love, hate, resist and create organisations. We live in them, work in them, play in them and we like or dislike our colleagues within them. Often, organisations are the blessing and bane of our waking hours, even our dreams, shaping the fabric of our life stories. It follows that the stories we tell others and ourselves about life at school, on the job, in religious, sports and recreational organisations are the stories of our own lives. Clarifying and acknowledging shared stories in the organisations where we spend our time can improve life in those social entities, and the lives of their inhabitants in the process.

Organisational culture can be defined as 'the way things are done around here'. It also includes the mindsets, emotional status and motivational roots which belong to the people in a particular organisation. Negative effects and entrenched attitudes of a disruptive culture are difficult to shift. As time passes, organisational stories that may have described one stage of development become outmoded and outlive their usefulness.

An organisation's culture provides a means of speaking about the traditions, unspoken rules and expectations, mythical story line, triumphs and tragedies and the skeletons in the closet that give the organisation its uniqueness. When an organisation's stories do not match the reality of life in that place, the people who work there suffer. Ralph Waldo Emerson believed that 'the organisation is the lengthened shadow of one (person)'.[2] That shadow colours the culture throughout, determining optimism, pessimism and accessibility to change. In particular, understanding the importance of organisational culture has transformed the approach to organisational development and change. Before you can alter work-related practices and procedures, the underlying value systems that support these behaviours must shift.[3] Organisational transformation is likely to include shining light into shadowy corners and perhaps, also addressing issues so sensitive no one will speak them aloud.

Much has been written about family and organisational systems and how difficult change is within them. When one part is altered, all the others rigidify around it to prevent any lasting change. Old ways become even more entrenched with an added layer of 'see I told you nothing new could happen around here'. Looking at the unexpressed values in an organisation is difficult; let alone changing them. *Dramatic Psychological Storytelling* (DPS) in the hands of a skilled Facilitator brings to the organisational setting a way to get behind this armor. Tapping into shared stories, finding Touchstone Stories, and activating the power within them, allows us to slip behind the defensive shield which rises to greet threats of change. DPS, because it is a non-linear, artistic approach that invites and empowers people to step forward with their truth, enables organisational dynamics to be revealed and become available for re-evaluation and change.

Whether it is a one-time intervention or part of an on-going process, the human resources professional makes a decision about the value of using DPS in a particular setting. Support by senior management and staff must exist at least at the level of willingness to make an attempt. The sequence of the process must be managed and adjusted to fit the needs of the organisation. The steps will not all necessarily be carried out in the order presented in DPS. Because decisions and choices need to be made at each step, excellent group skills must be part of the Facilitator's repertoire. The DPS process is flexible and allows significant and relevant content to be incorporated. In order to achieve this, the Facilitator is sifting and guiding, thereby keeping participants on track. Even though organisational examples are present throughout the book, this chapter includes three that illustrate the process.

This chapter is designed to assist human resource professionals who will then be able to serve as Facilitators for implementing DPS in organisational settings, either as a member of that organisation or as external consultants. The authors assume that those who will be directing the process are knowledgeable about the organisation involved and skilled at facilitating interventions. The chapter's examples provide overviews for working through DPS and are intended to be illustrative, not definitive or limiting.

Facilitator responsibilities

The first step, of course, is self preparation. Be sure that you know DPS well enough so that you can be centered as you explain it to the decision makers with whom you will be working. They may not need to know all the steps of the model, but they need assurance that you do. Read Chapter 18: *Facilitator Skills*, carefully and map out your planned intervention, not that you will necessarily disclose it at this point, or even follow it later. Your outline will be a work in progress that may shift as the work unfolds. It will not be rigid. It is important for you to be clear about the steps and have working hypotheses about how they will unfold and the implications for change.

People who participate with you, whether they are decision makers, team members or staff members, need to know that their contributions will be valued and that safeguards are in place for them. If they are to be forthright about their concerns, ideas and needs, they must know the information will not be used against them. DPS is no more effective than any other process, if the circumstances and safeguards are not truly genuine. The Facilitator not only facilitates the process, but serves as the safety net for those involved.

Biography and Discussion and planning for Coalescence

Given the complexity of organisational dynamics, any change intervention must be regarded as part of a process, not an entity unto itself. Careful consideration about the potential impact and how outcomes will meld with the on-going process is essential. It is worth spending whatever time is necessary, to assure that all the stakeholders are informed and consenting to the work that will take place. In order for people to voice observations and concerns authentically, they need to know they will not be punished for their honesty. It is also important for participants to know that the work they do as part of a change process will be valued and utilised. Pilot projects that demonstrate these principles are useful in establishing credibility.

Consent and support by senior management is essential

Change, even if it is beneficial, cannot last if senior management does not support it. The Facilitator must be sensitive to the organisation's culture and be willing either to work within it, or have consent and support to work toward change. When those conditions are met, the process gains credibility.

Imaginal Psychotheatrics in organisations: two cases

A brief example introduces the 7 Step DPS, Imaginal Psychotheatrics experience, in a company where the interest was in exploring the 'purpose' of the company's mission statement in order to see how it currently fits with the organisational culture which is in place. Tandi Pickard and Rob Allen conducted a three-hour session, at FINCO, a financial organisation. Tandi's summary follows:

> When we arrived we stepped into an informal and friendly atmosphere at this enterprise. All the participants introduced themselves and we stood in the kitchen drinking coffee and chatting. The staff of the organisation seemed comfortable with each other, like old friends, fond of each other and concerned about each other's interests at work and at home. This organisational culture seems to involve a shared idea of the business and image of the organisation for which the people work, which is strengthened by sharing successes and failures and each person thinking of him/herself as part of the organisation. People tell stories to one another about things they have in common and these stories tell a lot about the organisational culture. One member of the group who had been the founding Chief Executive Officer and now Chair of the Board of Directors of the organisation told the story of chatting to a friend at a barbeque and discovering that the man (who was a mechanic) was having financial problems which were standing in the way of him developing his business.

The participant who told this story was an older man with a very friendly, down-to-earth manner. He asked how anyone was supposed to make a realistic financial success of a business without a bit of help. He told about how he had chatted to the bank manager on his friend's behalf and helped him in a number of other ways to get a loan and get his business moving. That man eventually repaid his debts and became very successful. The story was warmly received and as the conversation in the workshop proceeded, it was suggested that this story contained the essential elements that defined the purpose of this organisation and made it successful in helping others. After several other staff members also described some of their experiences, including stories of failure, this story was chosen as the original story.

1 *Expressive Art type*

Narrative: The original story told by the founder of the organisation and now Chair of the Board of Directors: 'Older man helps his friend, a proprietor of a local automotive service centre, by finding a way of helping him out of his financial dilemma.'

2 *Element*

Imaginal Psychotheatrics: All members share a common characteristic of belonging to the same organisation, the focus of this intervention.

3 *Craft*

Rhetorical Reality Analysis: Through adding 'links' to the original story, triggers of other stories with elements in common were apparent. This soon became a strong group reality 'chain' blending the first story that began with the founder of the organisation at a barbeque hearing about the possible loss of the life savings of a family business venture due to lack of financial expertise and awareness. He believed the tragedy could be alleviated with the help of an organisation dedicated to assisting small business enterprises to achieve. The community would prosper as well. Group members then added links to this story which continued and helped to build a powerful chain of common elements that then became the group story.

Narrative storytelling, facilitated in this workshop by Rob Allen, allowed this group of employees to articulate a shared rhetorical vision of the organisation. This rhetorical vision integrated the common themes from the stories told by each individual employee related to the original story into a powerful group story.

4 *Story Map*

Orientation:

Who is in the story? An employee of the organisation and a small business owner visibly upset.

When is it happening? The story happened thirty years ago, but is timeless as the themes are repeated constantly within the organisation.

Where is it happening? At a barbeque.

What is going on? The man is upset and almost in tears as he tells a staff member of FINCO that he is in danger of losing his family's life savings in a business venture. The staff member listens and assures the man that this does not have to occur with proper consultation and sharing of expertise.

Complication: The complication in this story was the possible devastating loss of the family life savings and the need for this not to happen. There was also the need to ensure that this does not happen to others in the future.

Sequence of Events: All the characters in our story react to the complication with renewed determination. Although the man may be demoralised at the beginning of the process, by seeking help he demonstrates a willingness to find solutions and overcome obstacles. Similarly, the staff member of FINCO, once engaged, applies all his skills and imagination to the problem. Since the organisation exists to assist customers with their businesses, its employees are knowledgeable and in touch with influential community leaders.

Together the customer and the employee identify the problems the customer is having with the business, develop a list of possible solutions and then work through them until each problem is resolved.

The customer and the employee then make a plan for the future and the customer leaves. The customer forges ahead with the plan and the employee keeps in touch, offering financial advice and moral support if necessary.

Resolution: Resolution comes when the immediate problems are solved and the customer can move forward with the project alone, knowing that he can call on the organisation again if necessary but also feeling that he has what it takes to succeed in this venture.

Coda: A theme in the workshop was the determination of the organisation, as embodied in its employees, to overcome complications. Employees saw setbacks as challenges which served to strengthen their commitment.

A determined person can make a dream come true with hard work and a little practical help.

5 *Dramatic Enactment*

Using *Theatre*: In this workshop the Dramatic Enactment came after the original story had been told by the founder at the barbeque. Then later there was another Dramatic Enactment using Theatre, after the story was chained out by the group and then further developed through the Story Map. Workshop participants agreed on the important elements of the story to be enacted.

Rob Allen guided the group to identify the main elements of the stories they were telling. Two members of the group volunteered to perform the story – which combined these roles: the customer and the employee.

Two participants were Players acting out the story with other group members as Directors and the rest of the group as Spectators. The customer was prevented from rising to his feet by the constraints pressing down on him. Now he was assisted by the staff member, with a 'helping hand'. The customer was then able to shake off the constraints and rise to the challenge of pursuing his business.

6 *Meaning*

There was a great feeling of achievement and wellbeing. We discussed the significance of what we had done and people said that they felt the Dramatic Enactment had portrayed and clarified their ideas and feelings about the purpose of their organisation.

7 *Touchstone Story*

A person with a commercial idea and a degree of determination can be helped by an organisation in which there is a strong culture of mutual support and a belief that everyone deserves help to succeed. The meaning affirms the faith we have in ourselves and others and the ability to take setbacks as challenges which only strengthen the determination to succeed.

Even though from the beginning FINCO appeared to be an organisation in which cooperation and support was valued, working through the DPS model clarified the purpose of the organisation founded on these values. This brief intervention enriched and affirmed the working relationships that already existed in a high-functioning organisation.

A more challenging situation is demonstrated as Amanda Rouhliadeff facilitated the DPS approach at an international marketing firm: MARTEK.

1 *Expressive Art* type

Narrative: MARTEK is a company that has hired a consultant to help deal with complaints about slowly dispensed, low quality work in the advertising campaigns they create for their clients. One member of the MARTEK group identified the problem as one that will sound familiar to many consultants, managers and workers. The marketing department is expected to work in teams. Only one or two team members end up carrying the workload for the entire team. Morale is low. Customer satisfaction is taking a dive.

2 *Element*

The marketing department is a small enough group with a common concern to work well using Imaginal Psychotheatrics. This Element has the potential to get conflicts and concerns into the open in a safe, workable context. According to Bales (1970),[4] dramatic communication creates social reality for groups of people and is a way to examine messages or insights into the group's culture, motivation, emotional style and cohesion. Anderson and Anderson (1997)[5] describe the dramatisation as portraying human experience through quest, sometimes in order to make social comment.

3 *Craft*

Rhetorical Reality Analysis is unique to Imaginal Psychotheatrics in the DPS Model. This activity requires the Facilitator to have excellent group skills. The role of the Facilitator is similar to the role of the guide that Jean Houston[6] described in sacred psychology:

- Must be thoroughly familiar with the material
- Committed to what they are doing and believe in its worth
- Attentive to the timing of the group
- Respectful to everyone's experience

Since DPS is a creative process, it is the Facilitator's responsibility to track both process and content and assure that relevant themes are selected for the Meaning and Touchstone Story steps.

Rhetorical Reality Analysis proceeds in this case through the use of a series of 'links' that each member adds from their experience, directly relating to the original story. This creates a powerful 'chain' that links stories in order to clarify common concerns. In so doing the DPS Imaginal Psychotheatrics process then:

- Carries the original story forward
- Allows group members one by one to add their own experiences or concepts that are similar enough for the story to keep its essence
- Transforms the themes by this chaining to a dynamic group story
- Consists of a dramatic event, past, present or future
- Establishes characters, real or fictitious

Ideally, members respond emotionally and an attitudinal commitment is made as reflected through the dramatisation. The Rhetorical Reality Analysis dramatisation discovers common ground symbolically through an original story that not only reflects the unique culture of the group but also creates a new group reality. According to Bormann,[7] theme analysis is a method of rhetorical criticism underpinned by a general theory of communication called symbolic convergence theory, which attempts to account for the creation, raising and maintenance of group consciousness through communication.

The chained stories revealed MARTEK marketing staff members' perceptions of two team members who they felt were holding up the entire team. As is demonstrated, these offerings may be how they feel in such a situation, how it affects them, the group and their work or environment.

Sample comments that came out of the process reveal the level of demoralisation the group felt. It is important, not only for its content, but also because it reflects employees' willingness to speak up. A thread of common concern becomes only too apparent: *feel helpless; have to do it by self to get it right; others get credit for your work; everyone too busy – hard to set meetings; no sense of ownership of the product – hence no sense of responsibility; management gets obsessed with the latest fad.*

4 *Story Map*

Orientation: All staff members perceived to be involved in the situation are seated in the same room. From here, the Orientation is developed. The narrator is the group member who identified the complication being investigated and with the help of the group, identifies:

Who is in the story? In this case, the whole group as they all have to work in teams
When is it happening? Regularly, as new campaigns constantly need to be developed for different clients, which are all done in teams,
Where is it happening? At MARTEK, in the campaign development teams, and
What is going on? Clients are becoming increasingly dissatisfied with the mundane nature of the end product and the lack of dispatch with which it is delivered. The 'what' is the bigger picture that comes as a result of one of perhaps many complications, which has now become more focused.

The *Complication,* once told, reveals something that will begin a chain of events. These events will affect one or more of the group members or characters. The complication, in this case ineffective teamwork, is the trigger.

The narrator in this session is the person directing the story. This person provides the *Sequence of Events,* and tells how the characters react to the complication, including their feelings and what they do. The purpose of the narrative is to construct a view of the world that informs the group.[8] The events can be told in chronological order or with flashbacks with the narrator's point of view.

This ends with a *Resolution* where the *Complication* is sorted out or the problem is solved. See below for a scenario of the Dramatic Enactment that unfolded at MARTEK Marketing.

The *Coda* is the message or moral learned from the story. This identification may assist in turning a conflict, which may be negative, into something positive.

5 *Dramatic Enactment*

Using *Theatre*: This step may come at any time that is appropriate. For example, after the original story illustrated through the Expressive Art type, again after the Craft step creating a group story and then again after the Story Map fully develops the group story. In the case of MARTEK, the best time to use Dramatic Enactment was after the Story Map.

Members of the group are requested to play parts in the identified *complication* – a few team members representing the group as if it were a scene in a play. Players include:

- Narrator
- client for whom the campaign is being designed
- manager responsible for ensuring the team arrives efficiently at a dynamic and client-appropriate product, on time every time
- team members who design the campaign

The following excerpts demonstrate parts of the Dramatic Enactment at MARTEK:

Client: [speaking to MARTEK marketing manager] 'I'm really not impressed with the campaign your people have developed. Not only was it completed the day after I wanted to launch the campaign; the campaign itself was very average. I do not consider it eye-catching. It appears remarkably similar to several other campaigns circulating at the moment. How is mine supposed to stand out? What am I paying you for?'

Later, the manager confronts the team that devised the campaign for the disgruntled client:

Manager: [slams fist onto table] 'What is going on? We are an advertising company and we need to be dynamic, unique! Why is the campaign you've just the developed the same as every other one you've produced lately? We need to have different ideas – not the same ones recycled! I have clients breathing down my neck – they're not happy – a refund or new campaign is not going to compensate for the campaign flop they've just experienced!'

Team member 1: 'Yes, well, at 2 o'clock in the morning, team member 2 and I ran out of ideas whilst the rest of the team is asleep in bed. When it's just the two of us knocking our heads together, no wonder we keep on coming up with the same stuff! And it's not like we get any credit for doing all this extra work and being stuck with the difficult jobs either.'

Team member 3: 'Well, you can't expect me to be up at 2 am when I'm doing the Henderson account as well! Look, teamwork is the latest fad in business – it's really not working for us...'

Team member 4: 'My little girl has been sick at home – someone has to take care of her – she's only 7! There are so many meetings, and they go on forever – missing a couple should hardly matter when we never accomplish anything in these meetings anyway!'

Team member 1: 'But team member 4 is trained in the legal aspects of the job, so team member 2 and I never know what adventurous things we're actually allowed to do, so we play it safe rather than have a legal suit on our hands...'

Team member 5: 'I always give ideas, but team members 1 and 2 never accept them – they may as well be doing the whole thing themselves!'

Team member 2: 'You are never here to follow it through! To just give an idea and have us work it is not enough – you need to be here to add direction.'

Team member 6: 'It's not like we're doing Joe Burger ad campaigns or anything... Besides, I do my share...'

6 *Meaning*

Once an original story is transformed through the Craft step by the Rhetorical Reality Analysis links building a powerful chain group story and then actualised by the Dramatic Enactment a transcendence of shared and new meanings has occurred. The story is living and dynamic. Stories exist to be changed and are the currency of human growth. Stories conjugate – in the exchange both you and the story change. Stories need to be told and retold, heard and reheard to reveal their meaning. We go to therapists to reveal and heal our stories, to remember them, to dig into their deeper meaning; we check in with our friends to share stories, and work together to reveal the significant aspects of the story, to call forth its illumination.[9]

7 ***Touchstone Story***

- expresses collective sense
- identifies dynamics
- allows agreement on shared meaning
- reveals culture

This analysis looks for patterns and shared meaning, identification of the 'sacred' and 'profane' as manifest through the content of the stories. According to Boyce (1995)[10] the challenge of identifying a Touchstone Story is creating a story that contains all the essential elements and/or dynamics as reflected in the original story and then developed into a group story through links by Rhetorical Reality Analysis, chained into and then further developed by the Story Map and the Dramatic Enactment. A very simple method is to review the procedure with the group and create a Touchstone Story through agreement.

The group from MARTEK identified that organisational structure, accountability and learning to work together were the major themes that made up their Touchstone Story. Thus, all MARTEK group members related collectively to the fact that: 'using the "I" for the "We" without organised, fair structure involving flexibility results in breakdown of the effective team'.

- Learn to work together to create structure and efficiency
- Agree that team success should be rewarded.

Individuals create and are part of an action scenario that is reviewed and performed related to the common experience(s) group members share. This in turn creates a Rhetorical Reality that combines the meaning of the scenario with their possible relationship with each other. At this point MARTEK has 'ownership' and support by team members who have identified the problem and have agreement on shared dynamics of the situation. This work provides a solid platform upon which the manager and team can regroup for more effective performance.

The Resolution, which was a working hypothesis when stated at the onset of the Story Map, may need revision at this point. The Craft identified group story links and then created the powerful group chain.

Later this story was developed further into a group story through the Story Map. And then this was further illustrated through the Dramatic Enactment. Finally the Meaning and a Touchstone Story were revealed and group members were now in a better frame of mind to develop resolutions to the conflict. This DPS process can be a powerful tool assisting individuals or groups to look at their lives, acknowledging the pressures that they are under and devising and testing for themselves potentially more positive ways of responding to those pressures.[11]

Looking at group dynamics in this way can provoke honest and profound discussions around a variety of issues. Working with a character created by the group makes the focus of the session both representative of the group's experience and distanced enough to create a safe witness context for examining issues.

Using Montage Psychotheatrics in an organisational setting

Organisations are environments designed for the purpose of providing goods or services. As we work in them, however, we need interpersonal skills in addition to the technical ones required to ostensibly do the work. The more one ascends the organisational hierarchy, the more complex these interpersonal skills need to be, and it becomes increasingly clear that being a good doctor, engineer, or teacher, does not necessarily make one a good manager or leader. With work and intention, engineers and teachers can learn these skills, which are not usually part of technical or professional curricula, and can become increasingly competent at motivating, managing and leading effectively. The following case study demonstrates a project where people in the financial field, engage in the process of becoming more effective managers/leaders.

Because of its unique capacity to deal with individual behaviour change in a group setting, Montage Psychotheatrics is a tool for helping individuals address complex and diverse goals. Each person can work on different issues in the context of the work group, without colleagues being aware of anyone's specific content. The Transformation Personality Role is the focus, not what was deficient in the old. Used as a coaching tool, DPS, using Montage Psychotheatrics offers a format for exploring and refining needed management and leadership skills.

Case Study – Leadership Skills Profile[12]

Description: The Chief Executive Officer, through the Human Resources Manager, of a large international financial organisation requested in-depth Leadership Skills training for nine executives who had been newly promoted to senior management positions.[13] Each of these nine would soon be in charge of the management of this company's operations in an overseas country. Author, Rob Allen, the Facilitator (consultant) met with the HR manager and CEO for the establishment of key measurable objectives, and then created a detailed **Leadership Skills Profile** program, which was implemented over the course of one month. The Facilitator conducted several meetings for orientation and planning with the nine clients, followed by in depth experiential training. The leadership objectives were established by the CEO and HR manager in consultation with the nine clients and the Facilitator, who then designed the outline of desirable leadership traits that would be the basis for training, using the following research-based guidelines:

Leader Motive Profile (LMP):[14] describes three broad categories of needs necessary for leadership – power, affiliation and achievement. Each of these can be rated on a continuum. *Power* – includes influencing people, seeking positions of authority, controlling conversations and meetings. *Affiliation* – includes warmth, friendliness, the desire to build positive relations. High Affiliation means that one is often reluctant to use discipline, does not act assertively, avoids conflict, is indecisive, may be seen by others as less fair in distributing resources and as partisan. *Achievement*: includes setting positive and challenging goals; also, ambitious, competitive, focused on completing tasks.

Conscientiousness:[15] closely related to achievement – refers to high attention to detail and tendency to be very disciplined, reliable and responsible. This is one of the overall best predictors of performance for a wide range of jobs and professions.

Energy:[16] great leaders are known for high energy, able to complete more work and their energy seems to be highly infectious.

Internal Locus of Control:[17] effective leaders have a high internal locus of control and believe they control their own fates and can influence the world around them.

Self-Monitoring:[18] high self-monitors are sensitive to interpersonal and situational clues, demonstrating behavioural flexibility.

Self-Confidence:[19] people with high self-confidence are more successful as leaders, show greater persistence and intensity when pursuing goals and are more resilient when faced with obstacles and difficulties.

Big Five Personality Factors:[20] Conscientiousness – internal locus of control and need for achievement. Extraversion – has energy and demonstrates reward sensitivity for activities. Openness – networking behaviour, the diversity of people with whom the individual interacts and builds relationships. Neuroticism – demonstrates emotional stability and self-confidence. Agreeableness – affiliation. Effective leaders: high Conscientiousness, high Extraversion, high Openness, low to moderate Neuroticism and low to moderate Agreeableness.

Skills:[21] Three categories of skills related to leaders – technical, conceptual and interpersonal. Technical – expertise in operational procedures, knowledge of field. Conceptual – ability to observe patterns, solve problems and analyse complex situations. This is related to general ability or global intelligence factor. Interpersonal – ability to persuade, build relationships and play politics.

7 Step DPS (modified to fit the circumstances of this situation, as it is always)

1 *Expressive Art type*

The nine clients were requested to select an example from each of the 7 Expressive Arts; (a) relate to the established leadership training objectives and how each was relevant as well as (b) *how* each had personal and professional *connections*. A full afternoon session was devoted to reviewing each of the 7 Expressive Art types in turn, by each of the clients. In order of review – Narrative, Film, Theatre, Music, Visual Art, Dance and Kinaesthetics and Ritual and Epic. This session provided depth to the training objectives for each individual as well as increasing understanding through vicarious learning.

2 *Element*

Montage Psychotheatrics is designed for the individual in a collective setting.

3 *Craft*

Method of Physical Action:[22] In order to actualise the new leadership role desired through the Method of Physical Action, all nine of the clients completed the following steps separately and without consultation, except with the Facilitator.

4 *Story Map*

All nine clients developed a very detailed written graphic representation for their Transformation Personality Role. After this was completed, the Facilitator reviewed these with each client separately and made modifications after mutual agreement. None of the clients were involved with each other in the development of this phase.

Title: Clearly describe the Transformation Personality Role (TPR).

Orientation: Who is in the story? When is it happening? What is going on?

How did the story start? Where is it happening? What does the setting look like? What words will you use to describe the setting and how can you help paint a mind picture?

Complication: What challenge(s) does your TPR need to overcome?

Sequence of events: What events happen first, next, last? What does the TPR do? Explain how the TPR acts and reacts in a believable way?

Resolution: How will things work out? What issues need to be confronted? How will this story end?

Coda: The message or moral of the story?

5 *Dramatic Enactment*

(*Using the 7 Expressive Art types*)

Story Map to Dramatic Enactment: from invention and speculation to actualisation. The key factor was the belief that the TPR can be actualised by creating this 'reality'.

The Facilitator met with each of the nine clients separately to plan the Dramatic Enactment sessions. The objective was to develop and actualise the TPR. The Dramatic Enactments occurred several times, in between other DPS steps. None of the clients were aware of the others' dynamics concerning this stage, although some did participate with each other in activities. All 7 of the Expressive Arts were utilised but not by all clients.

For example:

Narrative – many wrote poems and entered into discussions and commentary in the community.

Film – several watched portrayals that related to their TPR. Some even created photographic representations reflecting their TPR.

Theatre – all rehearsed and performed their TPR several times. Two engaged theatre/media students from a local university to create scenarios that highlighted their TPR.

Music – all selected music that highlighted and added to their TPR. Several even created musical pieces using the guitar and piano.

Visual Art – all sketched TPR interactions, some created pieces reflecting their TPR.

Dance and Kinaesthetics – several went out for the evening and at some point danced; this not only reflected their TPR but also helped to actualise it. All nine participated in extensive kinaesthetic activities

reflecting and actualising their TPR through movement, for example going to the gym, or taking a walk.
Ritual and Epic – all nine either participated in a Ritual that reflected their TPR or created their own Ritual. None used Epic, although this could easily have been done by simply picking a major event that fits.

Since Montage is about the individual in a collective setting, the Facilitator met with each of the nine to refine and polish their individual TPRs, in order to create the maximum effect from interactions with the others and outside situations.

6 *Meaning*

All nine described in detail the meaning of their TPR experience. Afterwards this was discussed as a group.

7 *Touchstone Story*

All nine separately developed a Touchstone Story of their TPR experience.

Conclusion

Organisations are complex entities with interweaving dynamics related to power, entitlement, influence, privilege and economics. The clearer these dynamics become, the more possibility there is to manage and lead them effectively. When an organisation decides to use any intervention, including DPS, it is essential that the process be seen as part of the on-going workflow. Adequate planning and safeguards, clarity about use of results and the competence of the Facilitator are of utmost importance.

If organisations, work groups or departments are willing to invest in exploring this process using the DPS model, this method has the potential to trigger change in an organisation's culture. This multimodal approach goes beyond the facts and touches the psychological essence in people. By slipping behind defensive shields, it has the potential to overcome the obstacles of pride, stubbornness and closed mindedness by shining a little light into the shadow, inducing the 'renaissance' spirit in people and paving the way for change. Or, as in Tandi Pickard's example, a group that is functioning well, gains clarity and affirmation about the values that underlie their organisation's mission.

17
Education and Awareness

I believe that all education proceeds by the participation of the individual in the social consciousness of the race.
I believe that education ... is a process of living and not a preparation for future living.
John Dewey[1]

Education

John Dewey has much more to say that supports the relevance of *Dramatic Psychological Storytelling* (DPS) in educational settings, but these salient points are enough for a beginning. Participating in the social consciousness of the race implies connection beyond 'me'. People remember and learn from their experience more than from passive reception of information. Images and actions are more powerful than the words which are a necessary refinement that, as Dewey says, 'devolve' from action.

Subject matter is an essential part of what we learn at school, but the popularity of a book such as *All I Really Need to Know I Learned in Kindergarten*,[2] speaks to the importance of social learning as well. The massacre at Columbine High School, April 20 1999 and similar tragedies, speak to the failure of our educational institutions to work effectively in that regard. Eric Harris and Dylan Klebold had no shortage of intellect or skill at subject matter. They (and the system that surrounded them) were failures at participating in the intersubjective consciousness of the human race.[3]

Fifty years ago, at the time of John Dewey's death, people studying to become teachers were inundated by his philosophy, which at that time was considered progressive. The active classroom dominated curriculum development; passivity was out. As a student teacher in history at a high school near the university, however, Nina Krebs was surprised that almost all of World History was presented through lecture. Her attempts at creating lesson plans using small groups or other active devices collapsed under student and teacher resistance.

If you imagine yourself back in fifth grade, what do you remember best?

- Playing or fighting with __________
- Content from social studies
- Science project
- Field trip to _________
- Performing in school assembly or class play or watching same
- __________ sitting next to you
- Content from language arts

If you work in a school, how many of the day's activities are likely to involve students actively participating? Nina Krebs' wager is that the higher the participation level of students with each other and teachers, the higher the morale and productivity of all concerned. Participation involves social learning as well as grappling with subject matter. Isolation is one of the most significant issues of our day, and the school can either contribute to it or be a powerful antidote.

Much is known about how we learn, and the process rarely fits a linear model. We learn kinaesthetically, actively, through different senses and at varied speeds. Much of learning is counter-intuitive. A small slice of history, a scenario from the life of a villager during the French Revolution, for instance, examined through Rhetorical Reality Analysis and illustrated through Dramatic Enactment has greater potential for lasting impact than the same scene included in a text that is read or researched by a student. It *seems* that learning should be proportional to the amount of material imbibed, or its chronological order, but that is not necessarily so. No end of reading and research can go into creating the scenario and the drama, but pulling that background work together through action makes it memorable. Content relevant to student interest and involvement has a much higher chance of becoming part of that person's memory bank than information that is transmitted because someone else deems it important.

A few people may love reading and remembering lots of facts, but it is a mistaken notion that sacrificing quantity of information for the quality of a learning experience reduces the net impact. As you reminisce about your own educational experiences, which are the ones that are memorable for you? For example, in Nina Krebs' experience, the straight As she received in her basic college biology class do not reflect her knowledge of biology, which barely exists. She memorised lots of information, took the tests, and forgot the content. However, she vividly remembers handling the live *centuroides sculpturatus* (a variety of scorpion native to southern Arizona), which was passed around in the lecture hall populated by several hundred students. She would recognise one now, if she saw it.

Opportunities for social learning using DPS are endless. Using DPS to create scenarios related to subjects ranging from developing basic conversational skills to dating and sex education – at whatever level of authenticity the environment can tolerate – offers opportunities to explore relevant material. By illustrating personal or social issues most students think about, the school engages its responsibility for creating a community learning environment regarding the developmental tasks of adolescence or any other relevant life passage.

DPS can contribute to complex content learning as well as to psychosocial developmental issues. The following example demonstrates a rich and complex learning experience for students in a university class, Psychology of Crime. The topic that would otherwise have been included in a lecture presentation, is community conferencing as an alternative to court procedures, an approach pioneered by Australian social researchers Kathleen Daly and Hayes Hennessey.[4] Special emphasis was placed on concepts of restorative justice and retribution. Approximately 100 students in the class attended a production of *Face to Face*, a play by Australian playwright David Williamson,[5] presented by Bathurst Players and directed by Tandi Pickard.

1 *Expressive Art type*

Theatre: In the performance, when Glen, a young construction worker, rams into the back of his boss's Mercedes in a fit of anger at being sacked, he is given the opportunity to discuss his actions in a community conference, rather than going straight to court.

2 *Element*

A variation of *Imaginal Psychotheatrics*, a large group with a common interest in watching a play related to that focus, is an appropriate choice here. The topic, workplace violence and bullying, is directly relevant to this Psychology of Crime class in many ways. The play's focus on conflict resolution beyond 'might makes right' adds complexity to the drama and thus to potential learning for the students.

3 *Craft*

Rhetorical Reality Analysis was used twice in this example:

- Immediately after the play was performed the Director, Tandi Pickard and the Lecturer, Rob Allen facilitated discussion with the cast and audience.
- Later after discussing the theatrical performance, the story was extended through links added by students in small tutorial groups composed of class members, using 'what if' and 'probably' scenarios. These 'links' were then developed into a strong 'chain' reflecting the tutorial group story of the performance.

4 *Story Map*

Orientation: In this creative approach combatants are brought together in the same room with a skilled mediator, in this case acrimonious co-workers but it could also be the perpetrator and victim of a crime. They are encouraged to express themselves assertively rather than aggressively, in an attempt to achieve greater understanding.

Complication: In the case of *Face to Face*, it is a dispute involving Glen, a very angry young man with limited intellectual abilities. After being fired for assaulting the foreman, Glen slams his car into the owner, Greg's, Mercedes.

Sequence of Events: In an effort to prevent the angry young man from being sent to jail and to try to resolve the issue in the best interests of all concerned, a conference is organised with all the interested parties.

Resolution: to try and give shape, meaning and resolution to a difficult workplace issue involving abuse and humiliation, racism, poor management practices, leading to an explosive reaction resulting in Glen damaging the car of his boss. Conferencing can create a 'win/win' situation, where almost everyone involved can learn something which is beneficial and leave feeling better about the process.

Coda: Human beings are more alike than they are different and if they try they can come to understand one another, even though they have different backgrounds and different places in society.

5 *Dramatic Enactment*

7 Expressive Arts: Tutorial groups were held during the week following the formal lecture on 'violence' and then after the night of the theatrical performance. The six separate tutorial groups each consisted of about 20 students, almost equally male and female. Three career majors were prevalent: criminal justice, policing and psychology. The students in each tutorial group were asked to bring in an example from one of the Expressive Arts that reflected their experience of the theatrical performance and subject matter. All 7 of the Expressive Arts were utilised and this certainly enriched the review – examples:

Narrative – newspaper articles, poems, books
Film – TV shows, news reports, cinema
Theatre – several mentioned other performances they had experienced that related to *Face to Face* and the topic. Quite a few used theatre to portray other possibilities and had students play roles in *Face to Face* which demonstrated these different possibilities
Music – many songs were used to illustrate the experience, a few were actually original compositions
Visual Art – several students brought in examples of art work. A few even had their own creations.
Dance and Kinaesthics – several used movement and 'human sculpture' to illustrate the experience
Ritual and Epic – few utilised the ritual experience of a 'funeral' to depict the result of violence and epic through institutionalised violence such as war or genocide

6 *Meaning*

Students explored psychosocial aspects of crime, particularly learned behaviours and motivational theories, using a formal lecture and then the experience of a theatrical performance and its characters as reference points. Viewing the performance brought to life abstract issues and personalised these to improve the educational experience. This was further enhanced through small tutorial groups using experiential illustrations to explore these concepts. Overall, the students rated this experience as helpful to them in completing their essay assignment concerning violence and crime.

7 *Touchstone Story*

Each of the six Tutorial Groups in the Psychology of Crime class developed its own Touchstone Story.

Key points and themes:

- People are not treated equally in our society. They are judged on wealth, appearance, gender, culture and social class
- Treating people like stereotypes leads to misunderstanding and conflict

- Every person has reasons for the way they behave
- It seems to be part of human nature to feel superior to those less fortunate than oneself
- When people learn a little about each other, they find that they are more alike than they are different and are able to understand one another a little better
- It is natural to protect oneself and one's kin before anyone else
- Being mistreated and misunderstood leads to anger and retaliation

Teaching a lesson using DPS

Biography and Discussion

Planning is done by the Facilitator (teacher) or by Facilitator and clients (students) to determine the best approach, depending on the content to be learned. The Facilitator works with the content to determine how best to relate it to the clients.

Handouts with basic guidelines for the activity may be helpful. Action is preceded by a brief description of the process and demonstration so that clients can know what is expected of them in their roles.

1 *Expressive Art type*

In order to use DPS for educational purposes, the Facilitator (teacher) conceptualises the target learning process in context of the 'story' using one or more of the 7 Expressive Arts to illustrate this:

Narrative – oral, written, book, poem
Film – cinema, television, photographs
Theatre – formal performance or informal short scenario
Music – song, melody, composition
Visual Art – painting, drawing, collage, installation
Dance and Kinaesthetics – choreographed movement or activity
Ritual and Event – festival, ceremony (marriage), spectacle, happening (Olympics)

2 *Element*

Imaginal Psychotheatrics will usually be the choice as most educational settings will involve a group that shares a common characteristic – the particular learning objective. Sometimes *Playwright Psychotheatrics* will be appropriate if teaching and learning is focused on an individual or couple or occasionally a very small group. Rarely will *Montage Psychotheatrics* be utilised due to its extremely intensive nature – however, this is certainly appropriate to 'live' and really 'experience' the learning aspect. Using Montage Psychotheatrics in lifestyle coaching or in human resources work is very relevant (See Chapter 16 Human Resources).

3 *Craft*

The vehicle used here is designed to complement the choice of the appropriate Psychotheatrics Element utilised: Imaginal Psychotheatrics uses Rhetorical Reality Analysis; Playwright Psychotheatrics uses Expressive Writing; and Montage Psychotheatrics uses the Method of Physical Action. Next, develop and transform this with Step 4, the Story Map.

Rhetorical Reality Analysis (Imaginal Psychotheatrics): after one group member highlights the story focusing on the common purpose of the group, other group members add on aspects that directly relate. Link by link this becomes a strong chain, creating a powerful group reality learning experience.

Expressive Writing (Playwright Psychotheatrics): simply write for a brief period of time, 20 minutes to 30 minutes on a particular aspect of the learning objective.

Method of Physical Actions (Montage Psychotheatrics): The new Transformation Personality Role – behavioural, emotional and cognitive aspects are identified and then lived out in a collective setting according to the learning objectives.

4 *Story Map*

To develop the learning objectives of the story for each Psychotheatrics Element, use the Story Map. The simplest structure is to build on the Craft aspects accomplished previously:

- highlight the characters and setting
- focus on the issue or problem to be solved
- solve the issue or problem
- tie up the loose ends.

Orientation: Who – is in the story? *When* – is it happening? *Where* – is it happening? *What* – is going on in the story?

Complication: This is the trigger that will begin a chain of events – *What* challenge(s) does the main character need to overcome? *What* affects one or more of the characters in the story?

Sequence of events: Story structure – *What* events happen first, next, last? *How* do the characters react to the complication? *What* are their feelings and how do they behave? *What* are some of the key events?

Resolution: How is the issue/problem resolved or the challenge overcome? *How* will things work out? *What* issues need to be confronted? *How* will your story end?

Coda: The message or moral of the story?

5 *Dramatic Enactment*

This is the actual dramatic performance of the learning experience with a special focus on the story developed through the Craft and Story Map – NOT the whole learning experience. Pick a part of the learning experience that you would like to see in 3D action and later you can do another segment if necessary. Utilise one or more of the 7 Expressive Arts to illustrate and dramatically express the learning experience.

Narrative – students may orally discuss the situation – or write a composition and then share their work
Film – possibly illustrating the learning experience through photos actually taken (for example, digital compositions) or filming a representative illustration and perhaps relating this to an existing cinematic or television experience
Theatre – referring to a formal performance or actual informal short scenario using other students as players. This could lead to many different possibilities
Music – create or refer to a song, melody, or composition for example
Visual Art – create or refer to a painting, drawing, collage, or installation
Dance and Kinaesthetics – choreographed movement or activity
Ritual and Epic – create or refer to a festival, ceremony (rite of passage), spectacle, happening (e.g. the Olympics)

The possibilities are endless using one or more of the 7 Expressive Arts to dramatically enact the learning story. This makes learning a phenomenological intersubjective meaningful experience, 3 dimensional, alive, now and immediate and directly relevant to those involved.

6 *Meaning*

What have you learned from this process? After the Dramatic Enactment, it is a good time to review what has taken place in the developing learning story:

What is the Meaning in all this? Look for sign posts in what values and attitudes were expressed! This step is all about discovery of what the original learning story in Step 1 Expressive Art type experience and Step 3

Craft has become and what it means, when combined with Step 4 Story Map and Step 5 Dramatic Enactment!

It is now time to review the previous steps and to question what has occurred. We are then able to discover and legitimise the meaning of the illustrative learning story that has been developed through this particular Psychotheatrics Element. After this has been completed, we now have the essence for the foundation of the Touchstone Story.

7 *Touchstone Story*

Are there threads that weave into an overall major story pattern? Are there interpersonal, transpersonal or a mythic connection reflected in the work you completed? Can you summarise in a phrase or two the most salient points of the work?

Once an original learning story is transformed, a transcendence of new meanings has occurred. This tapestry is the Touchstone Story. It is expected that there will ultimately be several Touchstone Stories. Each one needs to be discovered through the Psychotheatrics 7 Step DPS.

Coalescence

Coalescence can occur through general class discussion and review. It is important that the opportunity be provided for clients to process the experience as well as the content that may not be clear to them.

Self Awareness

'The self is not something ready-made, but something in continuous formation through choice of action.' (*John Dewey 1859–1952*[6])

Consistent with the philosophy of life-long learning, DPS can be useful to individuals or groups interested in self-exploration or search for meaning.

This process is designed as one to promote personal responsibility, supporting autonomous choice and decision making. Whether through meditation, walking, expressive writing, or some other means of quieting your mind and opening up, giving yourself space to be is an essential step. When you can accomplish that, pay attention to the characters that enter your consciousness and the sequence of events. What is the complication? Can you sort through to a resolution? If you add links to the story by creating several possible perspectives, do other meanings emerge that you hadn't considered before?

The content for your story can come from your dreams, the ones you have while asleep, or from your daydreams. Your internal resources supply you with ample information for exploration. No one can take this journey but you.

This example from Nina Krebs' life serves as an illustration of the process:

My sister-in-law gave me a copy of Julia Cameron's *The Artist's Way*[7] about the time I retired. Although many times I had started working my way through self-help books, I had never actually completed one. This time I did, and it changed my life. Cameron has two requirements that continue throughout the book: 'morning pages', a form of daily expressive writing and 'the artist date'. The artist date requires the client to go out on her own excursion 'committed to nurturing your creative consciousness' approximately two hours once weekly. This event is to be solo, 'pre-planned to defend against all interlopers'. The goal is to 'take in, fill the creative well'.

Like the 'morning pages', the artist date sounds simple. It is and it isn't. The relevance here is that whether your interest is art or something else, giving yourself time and space to nurture your creative consciousness is the key to your search for meaning. If you take that time, and then work through DPS to think about it, you enrich the experience and broaden your awareness.

Here is a brief example of a personal life change that fits the DPS model:

1 *Expressive Art type*

Narrative: Julia Cameron's *The Artist's Way* – reading and then using this as a workbook to actualise the 'artist experience'. Some thoughts: I love art, would love to be an artist, but

- It is too late in life to learn complicated skills
- I am not talented
- I don't know how

2 *Element*

Playwright Psychotheatrics was utilised here.

3 *Craft*

Expressive Writing was part of this process all the way. The following steps are an oversimplified summary of decisions that were scary and uncomfortable then. During this time, I wrote morning pages nearly every day, including dreams, free associations, conscious fears, doubts and aspirations.

Putting my thoughts on paper gave me a level of objectivity I didn't have while they were slithering around in my head.

4 *Story Map*

Orientation: I am about to have more free time than I have ever had in my life. Art is something I have always admired, but accomplished only sporadically in a very amateur way.

Complication: I idealise artists. I feel like I have waited too long to learn skills that would allow me to be competent in such a rarified field. I'm not talented, and I don't know where to start.

Sequence of Events:

- Some time before I retired, I overheard Tina Heringer, then a clerk at the art store where I had taken someone else's work to be framed, say that she would be offering a class in 'composition'.
- I approached her about signing up for the class, which turned into a painting class.
- I continued working through *the Artist's Way*. It took me about a year.
- Tina's class helped me understand that I could learn to draw, compose, and paint.
- Two years into retirement, I began taking classes at a community college.

Resolution: I will see what I can learn one step at a time and try not to compare myself to other people.

5 *Dramatic Enactment*

Ritual and Epic, Visual Art: The day after I retired, I went on a daylong vision quest in the foothills where I put ribbons in the trees to create sacred space, meditate, read, write, and take photographs. I began conscientiously keeping artist dates, even when I didn't have time or feel particularly motivated. I pushed myself to visit galleries, talk to artists, try making visual art work I had no idea I could actually do. I still take classes. I did direct myself – take responsibility – to pursue the steps that have become another turn in my 'sacred journey'.

6 *Meaning*

Artists may have unconventional and aesthetically sophisticated ways of seeing the world, but they share human strength and frailty. Although some people are incredibly talented, much of making art can be taught and learned. Art is not sacred. The process of making it is.

7 Touchstone Story

I am an artist.

My life was enriched by this process and continues to be so. Opening up new psychological frontiers can be an exhilarating experience. It can also become frightening. No one changes in a vacuum, and even in the example I mention above, some environmental changes resulted: a guest room became a studio, I began attending classes using much of my discretionary time, and I redirected my financial resources. Fortunately, my husband supports these changes, but had that not been the case I would have had to deal with the possible conflict.

Conclusion

Pedagogy and educational psychology overflow with knowledge about teaching, learning, human growth and possibility, but this knowledge is rarely fully engaged. The containers, both physical and organisational, where people are supposed to learn things are often less than ideal. DPS can create a transitory container that in a short period of time provides memorable experiences for students and professionals – whether content based or focused on interpersonal processes. Because the story focus in DPS can be a small slice of life, or a very specific content focus, it is relatively easy to choose a topic for exploration.

The values and conflicts that underlie decisions in educational systems about what to teach as well as how to teach sometimes have the effect of reducing classroom experience to a low common denominator. Pressures on schools to serve incredibly diverse populations while constantly facing funding and personnel cutbacks contribute to chaotic, even combative classrooms where it is hard to accomplish anything. Because it is engaging, people at widely varied levels of ability can participate and learn from their involvement. DPS is a tool that can work well in the hands of educators who are skilled at group or interpersonal processes.

As a self-awareness tool, DPS can help interested individuals or groups clarify experience and meaning by working through the process. It provides a strong and adaptable trellis around which to grow.

18
Facilitator Skills

Active, participative *Dramatic Psychological Storytelling* (DPS) is flexible and adaptable depending on the situation and the needs of those participating. The fluid nature of the process and the number of options available for use in different situations, offer nearly limitless possibilities. Professionals who have used DPS, including the authors, have found that even when the issue or problem seems vague or inconsequential and the themes tangled, by selectively focusing and following DPS, a path can be shaped. The same is true if the issue or problem seems overly complex.

The theory that underlies this work suggests that a small slice of behaviour, or a part of a story, can represent the dynamics of the whole. Therefore, it is possible to select and simplify in order to develop the Dramatic Enactment and still have enough material to be representative and meaningful.

The process of sifting out material to frame relevant themes requires careful attention from the Facilitator and authentic input from participants. To be an effective Facilitator using DPS, one must be skilled in listening and able to help the client(s) focus. More than anything, the Facilitator is a guide for the client(s) as he or she transforms personal experience that may be hazy or overwhelming into something meaningful and more useful. In addition to knowing the model and the Psychotheatrics process, the Facilitator's main functions include the capacity to:

- Identify the main elements of the client(s) story
- Frame those elements into story form, which are true to the client(s) intent, using the Story Map
- Be sensitive to the environment in which the work occurs, such as the organisational or family system

- Guide the client(s) through the Dramatic Enactment process
- Support the client(s) in extracting Meaning and planning follow up

The foundation skills listed below are essential for work with DPS in all the applications. Each application, Clinical/Counselling, Human Resources, Education and Awareness, has special requirements regarding knowledge of its methods, standards of practice, safeguards and ethics.[1] Although DPS may be used for self-exploration, individually or in a group setting, excellent professional skills are needed to work with client(s). This is especially true with the three Psychotheatrics Elements, particularly if that process includes conflict management. DPS is designed for use by practiced Facilitators in Clinical/Counselling, Human Resource and Educational settings. 'Professional artistry' is essential, the kind of competence practitioners display in unique, uncertain and conflicted situations of practice. This is a common result of experience, 'tacit knowing-in-action that we all exhibit everyday in countless acts of recognition, judgement and skilled performance'.[2]

The Facilitator who has mastered the foundation skills as listed below, can then focus on the process and move it along. Although one person can serve as Facilitator, a two-person team for group work using Imaginal Psychotheatrics allows one Facilitator to coordinate the action and the other to track, record, and monitor the focus. Switching roles also promotes balance and variety.

Foundation skills[3]

- Listen
- Assess
- Condense and frame
- Build trust
- Support
- Contain
- Guide
- Manage conflict
- Summarise
- Support the Dramatic Enactment
- Analyse
- Interpret
- Acknowledge

Special DPS preparation

What specifically do you need to know, in addition to basic Facilitator skills, to use DPS?

- Be clear about the steps in DPS. Know what each one is designed to accomplish. Although each step does not have to be expressly used in every situation, or used in the same order for all applications, keeping them in mind as guidelines for the process keeps the Facilitator on track.
- Be clear about the 7 Expressive Art types. Do your homework by thinking about examples in each of the categories that are meaningful to you.
- Review the Psychotheatrics Element you intend to use for the Dramatic Enactment so you feel comfortable with the steps involved. Explain Psychotheatrics to a friend or colleague, so you can verify that you understand the theory and the process. Have your listener feed back to you what they heard.
- Be clear about how to facilitate the Craft step. Practise using story links and chaining for Rhetorical Reality Analysis (Chapter 12), Expressive Writing (Chapter 13) and the Method of Physical Action (Chapter 14).

Taking time to do these exercises will help your confidence, so while facilitating, your focus can be on what is happening in the room, rather than trying to recall the process. It helps if the client(s) have done some preparation as well. Although this may not always be possible, if they come to the setting having thought about examples of the Expressive Art types related to the topic(s) under consideration, the groundwork has been accomplished. Having the DPS forms as described on page 209, Expressive Art, available to complete at the beginning of a session, might be another way to accomplish this goal. Thinking about the Expressive Art types shifts client(s) into a different way of thinking about the issues.

Biography and Discussion and planning for Coalescence

DPS has the capacity to generate dramatic insight and uncover buried feelings in a short time. How outcomes that have been gained through this process will be supported depends on the readiness of the client(s) or organisation to participate fully. The decision makers must be clear that the process will provide rich data and be willing to deal with it. Negotiation for this outcome should be explicit, with the understanding that follow-up will be necessary. Proposing a new process of any sort is likely to elicit resistance and objections. Listen to these concerns, take them seriously and determine from where the threat is coming.

- Do adequate safeguards exist in the environment to make this a safe time to implement DPS?
- Can client(s) and Facilitators speak their truth without fear of retribution?
- Will change be supported?
- What support exists to maintain changes, suggested by the outcome after DPS?
- How do you know?
- If you have good answers for these questions, the client(s) is ready for the process.

Implement DPS

The guidelines given here are general, designed to stimulate your thinking, rather than to restrict it: Establish the relationship with the client(s), assemble the group or meet with the individual, and ask them to talk about the relevant issues, concerns or experience. Building trust is an essential step. The people you work with have a right to know how you are qualified to lead them through this process. Giving them a sense of your experience and qualifications is an important consideration here.

Sharing some of your own vulnerability and growth process might be appropriate as well, depending on the situation. It is essential that the process be experienced by the client as a cooperative one, not something that will be done **to** them. If you are an outsider entering an environment to direct the process with someone else's client, it is nonetheless important to do enough relationship building to give the client(s) a sense that you can be trusted with their material, whether using the model individually or in a group setting.[4]

If this is your first venture with DPS, do not pretend otherwise. Even though you are not very experienced in this process, your skills from other professional work may generalise. If possible it is best to learn from an experienced Facilitator in DPS. Learning by doing, then considering the effects and affects of the experience is a central feature of reflective practice.[5] If you are working with your own client, be clear about how DPS contributes to your on-going relationship.

Participants need enough information to comprehend the process and have assurance that it is not to be hurtful or humiliating, so they can determine whether they are willing to participate. Speaking of 'drama' is likely to inspire fear and excitement simultaneously. Prospective participants need a sense that the Dramatic Enactment is something they can handle, so that they are able to participate with a sense of excitement rather than anxiety. To impose this process on someone without informed willing consent is incongruent with the spirit of the process.

1 *Expressive Art type*

During Biography and Discussion, if possible, ask the client(s) to review the 7 Expressive Art types and create their own list on a 3-column chart noting: 1) art types, 2) personal examples and 3) comments about relevance to the current process. Then, in the first session during implementation, as client tells the 'story', listen for themes and relate them to the art selections. Especially in Imaginal Psychotheatrics, create a group composite of everyone's examples. Track recurring topics. Notice perceptual conflicts or disagreements so they can be brought into the open and acknowledged. Stop frequently to clarify the intent of the speaker. Take notes on a while board so client(s) can follow your perceptions and process. The effectiveness of the DPS process relies on honesty. Hearing accurately, or revising your perceptions to match the client(s), provides a solid foundation for the process.

2 *Element*

Generally, choosing the Psychotheatrics Element with your client is straightforward:

Imaginal Psychotheatrics is usually the choice for groups who will work with a shared characteristic or issue. Through story links and chaining, participation in the Dramatic Enactment, and the other steps of DPS, the group creates imagery that becomes accessible to all. Focus can shift from conflict to commonality.

Playwright Psychotheatrics is the usual choice for individuals or pairs as it highlights personal insight, choice making, and behaviour change. By creating and producing his/her Dramatic Enactment process the individual has a wide range of control and creative license to stretch and contract it at will.

Montage Psychotheatrics is designed for leadership training, coaching, or other situations that require role development within the collective. Through outlining roles, desired behaviours and effects, individuals can experiment with character development, using the Method of Physical Action in a collective setting. As mentioned in the chapter on Montage, only a highly skilled Facilitator should work with this element and use extreme care throughout.

It may be desirable to use Playwright Psychotheatrics with a group. In certain educational or therapeutic situations, it might make sense to employ Montage Psychotheatrics. Sometimes it may even be advantageous to use Imaginal Psychotheatrics with an individual. As you work through the DPS, you may use Imaginal at one juncture and Playwright at another. Your judgement and creativity are your guides. Client needs and material will influence your choices.

3 *Craft*

Review the appropriate Psychotheatrics Element chapter so that you are clear about how to facilitate the relevant Craft, **Rhetorical Reality Analysis, Expressive Writing** or **Method of Physical Action.**

In addition to the specific skills needed for each Craft, all the foundation skills apply. Regardless of which process is being used, the wellbeing of the client(s) and the integrity of the process are paramount.

4 *Story Map*

Assess the material you are gathering to determine whether a workable story is emerging. Finding the simplest elements of the story will help in the dramatic process. Because of the holographic nature of this model, the story elements need not be complex to authentically represent the dynamics of the scenario.

Condense and frame the elements you identify. Write these on a whiteboard, so client(s) can follow your process. It is at this point that the similarity of the client(s) story to a larger legend, myth or contemporary work may emerge. If you are noticing that similarity, make a note of it. Ask if the client has thought of a story that might relate. This identification need not be rigid or perfect.

Support individuals or group members by letting them know they are doing good work. It helps them to know what is expected of them and what will come next. Check from time to time to see if people have questions about the process. Make sure everyone understands what is going on. It is worth repeating that the story does not need to be an elaborate one to be effective and meaningful.

Contain the content and the process. This may be the hardest part of the Facilitator's work. When developing stories, people may have a tendency to wander off the main track into their own thickets and it is easy for the Facilitator to follow them. When this happens, the process collapses. Keep coming back to the main points. Develop a repertoire of supportive, guiding statements that help keep the process on track like, 'That sounds (interesting, scary, entertaining) and worth pursuing, but for now, let's stay focused on (the subject at hand)', or others that fit your style. If you realise you are off track, acknowledge it and find your way back.

Guide the client(s) by creating an outline as the process moves along. Keep track of the main points as they emerge. Support their digging deeper to maintain authenticity. Use the Story Map as an outline.

Manage conflict as it emerges. Don't bury it. Depending on whether or not the conflict is about to disrupt the process, it may be important to stop and do work on it. If this is the case, interrupt the process and develop a Dramatic Enactment which addresses the conflict. Or, it may be possible to acknowledge the conflict, spell it out and gain agreement to set it aside for attention at another time.

Summarise the story as it has unfolded. Gain agreement with client(s) about the accuracy, sequence, characters and the other sign-posts of the Story Map. Using the main characteristics and avoiding excessive detail, complete the Story Map form – preferably on a white board or some other visible tool so that all have access.

5 *Dramatic Enactment*

Assist the creative **illustration of the story** using one or more of the **7 Expressive Arts**, supporting the client(s) throughout the direction and production process.

6 *Meaning*

Analyse the findings in search of the meaning. Skill at asking client(s) about his or her experience and any understanding that has been gained comes into prominence here. Listen carefully and acknowledge the main aspects so that the client(s) can validate them. Lead the discussion so that what has been accomplished is shared. Encourage each of the client(s) to speak about his or her experience.

7 *Touchstone Story*

Interpret and refine the findings. Using your skills as a listener, help the client(s) clarify the most salient outcomes. It may not be possible to summarise one central idea, but even brainstorming a list of the most important findings or experiences can serve the purpose here. Facilitator and/or client(s) may be able to come up with a phrase, a poem or headline that reflects the core learning. When mythic perspective emerges, the Touchstone Story becomes even more memorable.

Acknowledge all who participated, by pointing out ways they added to the outcome. If some client(s) have been quiet throughout the process, acknowledge their presence, an essential part of any participative process.

Skills for applications

Clinical and Counselling

DPS as an adjunct to on-going individual, family or group therapy offers access to sensitive material that is guarded by complex defences. The Facilitator uses her/his skill in introducing the process, folding it into on-going therapy and then following through, by integrating discoveries as the therapy process continues. The number of people involved – family or group – increases the complexity of this process.

The power of DPS is that it bypasses defences by objectifying thoughts, feelings and behaviour. Since these defences exist for good reason, it is essential that Facilitators provide appropriate safeguards and integrative steps when client(s) are confronted with unconscious material revealed through DPS. It is important that the Facilitator who plans to use DPS be sophisticated in diagnostic methods and screen clients appropriately.

Clients must have enough ego strength to tolerate viewing the objectification of their material, some of which may have been unconscious up to the point of the Dramatic Enactment. Adequate object constancy should be present as well. With proper support in comprehending and integrating unconscious material uncovered through DPS, clients benefit greatly. However, people who have fragile reality contact or weak ego boundaries may not have the resilience to tolerate this feedback. For such individuals, this approach is not recommended. However, some of the other DPS steps may be useful.

Diagnostic categories vary significantly according to theoretical perspective or global location. Generally speaking though, DPS is not recommended with individuals suffering from schizophrenia, acute phases of bi-polar disorder or severe borderline personality disorder.[6]

Since people outside the therapeutic relationship may become involved in the Dramatic Enactment step, arrangements must be made to protect the confidentiality of the client(s). How this is accomplished will depend on practices within the setting.

Facilitators steeped in the foundation skills outlined above, in addition to their technical diagnostic and treatment expertise, will find DPS to be an accessible and powerful addition to their professional repertoire.

Human Resources

Consent and support by leadership of an organisation is essential if DPS is to be used. Whether the Facilitator works inside the organisation or is an outside consultant, skill and timing are required to sell, introduce and implement DPS. Deciding who will be involved and how the process will be portrayed to the participants and the organisation at large, requires the utmost assessment skills and tact. Of course the Human Resources professional encounters these issues all the time, but the additional factor here is that DPS is a non-linear, creative process that is not only revealing but enjoyable. The more rigid and linear the organisation, the more difficult it may be for the HR professional to introduce DPS.

Most organisations of any size use training videos of one kind or another. DPS is a kind of training video, only it happens to be live; and the results of going through the process will be much longer lasting than gains from passively watching a video.

Decision makers in organisations are likely to have had exposure to the arts in some form or another. Find out how that captured their imagination and link it to DPS. Help them see how de-constructing and sharing significant aspects of their organisation can lead to common understanding and problem solving. Without disclosing the specifics of the material revealed by participants, let the extended organisation know that something exciting is happening over at a particular department due to the utilisation of DPS. It follows, therefore, that as department members become involved in the DPS process, their colleagues will observe reduced skepticism.

The HR professional, using or supporting DPS, serves as the pillar against which organisational resistance is hurled. Probably the most powerful of these projectiles will be resistant to the use of time and personnel resources for any change process, let alone one that is creative. After you have had your initiation with DPS, it will be easier to withstand the 'we don't have time (money, personnel) for this!' assault because you will have experienced its efficacy. In the meantime, creating the conditions within which change can happen requires time, money and some degree of safety. Clarity about outcomes and how results will be supported will depend largely on how well these have been identified, recognised and agreed to.

Education

Guidelines for working in educational settings are similar to those for working in other organisations as outlined in the sections above. DPS can be a great teaching tool for material that can be illustrated using the 7 Expressive Arts, which is just about anything from the birth of a cell to intergalactic conflict. The main tool or skill for the teacher involved in using DPS is imagination. Skilled teachers are particularly well qualified to work as Facilitators using this model, since it is part of their daily work to:

- Create a learning environment
- Maintain focus on content and/or process
- Direct the learning process by encouraging participation and supporting risk taking.

In addition, students from kindergarten through graduate school can contribute their energy, skills and content to enliven the storytelling process. When teachers can create a supportive environment for creative experimentation, the remaining task is one of selecting the material for illustration.

DPS takes the students out of the typical classroom and increases learning by direct involvement and contribution in the process. The 'Face to Face' example in Chapter 17 Education, offers insight into this process. By viewing a theatrical production, students in a *Psychology of Crime* class had the benefit of absorbing rich material. This provided the background for a discussion of complex issues that would have taken much longer using other more traditional teaching and learning methods. Having seen the production as a class group, they were able to start from that point. The background they had received in class, also enabled them to conduct their discussion and proceed from there to work in groups, write papers and carry on other learning activities. Using the theatrical production and characters as a reference point brought to life abstract issues and personalised these to improve the educational experience, requiring no special skills from the teacher beyond those good teachers use all the time. The choice of the process is what made the difference.

Conclusion

DPS is designed so that people from various perspectives, in a wide variety of settings can benefit through its use. A skilled Facilitator who is also proficient in DPS is essential for the proper application of the process. Necessary safeguards include the respect for privacy, not asking individuals to exceed their comfort level more than they choose and adequate physical arrangements. In a Clinical and Counselling, Human Resources or Educational setting, the Facilitator evaluates the work based on previously set goals and takes the steps needed to follow through with plans made before the DPS experience. In working with Imaginal Psychotheatrics or Montage Psychotheatrics, a team of two Facilitators can be more effective in keeping group interactions dynamic and effective. Because the process helps people shift from their usual way of thinking about themselves and interacting with others, they are likely to feel safe, enjoy the experience and have some unexpected insights.

Notes

Chapter 1 Introduction: Destination or Journey

1 Beck, Renee & Metrick, Sydney, Barbara (2003) *The art of ritual* (Berkeley, California: Celestial Arts Press) p. 10.

2 Ganis, Sid (6 March 2006) President, Academy of Motion Picture Arts and Sciences (Academy Awards Ceremony Los Angeles).

3 http://www.beyondblue.org.au/index.aspx?link_id=1 Retrieved 21 March 2006. Depression and anxiety are the most common of all mental health complaints. Together they account for most of the economic, social and personal costs of mental disorders internationally. *Beyondblue* is a national, independent, not-for-profit organisation working to address issues associated with depression, anxiety and related substance misuse disorders in Australia. *Beyondblue* is a bipartisan initiative of the Australian, state and territory governments with a key goal of raising community awareness about depression and reducing stigma associated with mental illness.

4 Muller, B. 'Metacognition', *AI & Society* (Sep 2000) Vol. 14, Issue 3–4, pp. 440–53.

5 Pennebaker, J.W. (1997) *Opening up: The healing power of expressing emotions* (New York: Guilford Press).

6 Based on the work of Bormann, E.G. (1972) 'Fantasy and rhetorical vision', *Quarterly journal of speech* (Speech Communication Association) Vol. 58, 1972, pp. 396–407.

7 Pennebaker, J.W. (1997) *Opening up: The healing power of expressing emotions* (New York: Guilford Press).

8 Bormann, E.G. (1982) 'Fantasy and rhetorical vision: Ten years later', *Quarterly Journal of Speech* (Speech Communication Association) Vol. 68, 1982, pp. 288–305.

9 Based on the work of Stanislavski-Benedetti, J. (1998) *Stansislavski & the actor* (London: Metheun).

Chapter 2 Intersubjective Meaning

1 Skiffington, Ross (2002) Bell Shakespeare Company, Pamphlet, *Comedy of Errors* (Melbourne, Australia).

2 Borosh, C. (2003) 'A phenomenological research investigation into university students' experience of an action based workshop series on career decision making', Post-graduate psychology thesis (Charles Sturt University, Bathurst, Australia) Individual theses available through CSU Library.

3 Fox, J. (ed.) (1987) *The essential Moreno: Writings on psychodrama, group method and spontaneity* (New York: Springer).

4 Schutzenberger, Anne Ancelin (1991) 'Terminally ill patient: 15-year experience in application of psychodrama in cancer therapy', in P. Holmes & M. Karp (eds), *Psychodrama: Inspiration & technique* (London: Tavistock/Routledge).

5 Wilson, M. (2006). *Storytelling and theatre* (Hampshire, U.K.: Palgrave Macmillan) p. 9.
6 Holmes, P. & Karp, M. (1991) *Psychodrama: Inspiration and technique* (London: Tavistock/Routledge) p. xiii.
7 Wind, Egar (1967) *Pagan mysteries in the renaissance* (Harmondsworth, England: Penguin) p. 238.
8 Hillman, J. (1996) *The soul's code* (New York: Random House).

Houston, J. (1997) *The search for the beloved: Journeys in sacred psychology* (New York: Tarcher/Putnam).

Murdock, Maureen (1993) *The heroine's journey: Women's quest for wisdom* (Boston: Shambala).

Sandner, Donald F. and Steven H. Wong (1997) *The sacred heritage: The influence of shamanism on analytical psychology* (New York and London: Routledge).

9 http://www.who.int/mental_health/management/depression/definition/en/ Retrieved 20 January 2006.
10 Sexson, Lynda (1992) *Ordinarily sacred* (London: University Press) p. 3.
11 Doogue, Geraldine (2003, October 5) 'Psyche & soul', *Compass* (television series) (Electronic version) (Sydney: Australian Broadcasting Corporation).
12 Gilligan, C. (1994) Getting civilized. *Fordham law review*, 63, 17–31.
13 Bradley, B. (2005) *Psychology and experience* (Cambridge: Cambridge University Press) pp. 14 and 18.
14 Houston, J. (1997) *The search for the beloved: Journeys in sacred psychology* (New York: Tarcher/Putnam) p. 237.
15 Goddard, Harold (1965 *The meaning of Shakespeare, Vol. 2* (Chicago: University of Chicago Press).
16 Rushdie, S. (1997) *The Moor's last sigh* (New York: Vintage).
17 Houston, J. (1997) *The search for the beloved: Journeys in sacred psychology* (New York: Tarcher/Putnam) p. 101.
18 Hillman, J. (1996) *The soul's code* (New York: Random House).
19 Steinman, Louise (1995) *The artist as storyteller in contemporary performance* (Berkeley: North Atlantic Books) Preface.
20 Zipes, J. (2006) in M. Wilson, *Storytelling and theatre* (Hampshire, U.K.: Palgrave Macmillan) pp. xv–xvi.

Zipes, J. (1995) *Creative storytelling: Building communities, changing lives* (London: Routledge).

Zipes, J. (2004) *Speaking out: Storytelling and creative drama for children* (London: Routledge).

21 Luke, Helen (1982) *The inner story* (New York: Crossroads) p. 5.
22 Wilson, M. (2006) *Storytelling and theatre* (Hampshire, U.K.: Palgrave Macmillan) pp. 27–9.
23 Steinman, Louise (1995) *The artist as storyteller in contemporary performance* (Berkeley: North Atlantic Books) Preface.
24 'The Fred Hollows Foundation's mission draws on the values and beliefs inspired by the work and example of the late Professor Fred Hollows

(1929–1993). The Fred Hollows Foundation is a non-government organisation which seeks to eradicate avoidable blindness in developing countries and to improve the health outcomes of Indigenous Australians... A world where no one is needlessly blind and of a land where Indigenous people enjoy the same health outcomes as all Australians.' Retrieved 25 May 2006, from: www.hollows.org.

25 Bradley, B. (2005) *Psychology and experience* (Cambridge: Cambridge University Press) p. 8.

26 Zipes, J. (2006) in M. Wilson, *Storytelling and theatre* (Hampshire, U.K.: Palgrave Macmillan) p. xviii.

27 Zipes, J. (1995) *Creative storytelling: Building communities, changing lives* (London: Routledge) p. 11.

28 Wilson, M. (2006) *Storytelling and theatre* (Hampshire, U.K.: Palgrave Macmillan).

29 Neuhauser, P. (1993) *Corporate legends and lore: The power of storytelling as a management tool* (New York: McGraw-Hill Education).

30 Burns, G. (2001) *101 healing stories: Using metaphors in therapy* (New York: Wiley).

31 Wilson, M. (2006) *Storytelling and theatre* (Hampshire, U.K.: Palgrave Macmillan) pp. 20 and 24.

32 Honos-Webb, L., Sunwolf & Shapiro, J.L. (2004) 'The healing power of telling stories in psychotherapy', in J.D. Raskin & S.K. Bridges (eds), *Studies in meaning: Bridging the personal and social in constructivist psychology*, pp. 85–114. (New York: Pace University Press).

33 Klein, M. (2002) *Envy and gratitude (1946–1963)* (New York: Free Press).

Chapter 3 Expressive Arts

1 Schechner, R. (2003) *Performance theory* (London: Routledge).

2 Gardner, H. (1999) *Intelligence reframed: Multiple intelligences for the 21st century* (New York: Basic Books).

3 Mayer, J.D., Caruso, D. & Salovey, P. (2000) 'Emotional intelligence meets traditional standards for an intelligence', *Intelligence*, 27, pp. 267–98.

4 Pellowski, Anne (1997) *The world of storytelling* (New Providence, New Jersey: R.R. Bowker).

5 Baldwin, Christina (2005) *Storycatcher: Making sense of our lives through the power and practice of story* (Novato, California: New World Library) p. 3.

6 Menninger, W.C. Bibliotherapy. *Bulletin of the Menninger Clinic*, Vol. 1, No. 8, pp. 263–4.

7 White, M. & Epston, D. (1990) *Narrative means to therapeutic ends* (New York: Norton).

8 Calisch, A. 'From reel to reel: use of video as a therapeutic tool', *Afterimage*, Vol. 29, Issue 3, pp. 22–5.

9 Centre for popular education (2005) *Photo voice* (Sydney: University of Technology-Sydney).

10 Moore, Phillip (1997) *Acting out: Therapy for groups* (Hants, England: Arena).

11 Langley, D.M. (1987) *Dramatherapy and psychiatry* (London: Croom Helm) p. 41.

12 Curtis, A.M. 'Communicating with bereaved children: a drama therapy approach', *Illness, Crisis & Loss*. Vol. 7, Issue 2, pp. 183–91.

13 Boal, A. (1995) *The rainbow of desire: The Boal method of theatre and therapy* (London: Routledge).
14 Gersie, A. (1996) *Dramatic approaches to brief therapy* (London: Jessica Kingsley).
15 Emunah, R. (1994) *Acting for real: Drama therapy – process, technique and performance* (New York: Brunner Mazel).
16 Landy, R.J. (1986) *Drama therapy: Concepts and practices* (Springfield, IL: Charles C. Thomas).
17 Elson, Louis C. (1908) *Curiosities of music* (Boston: Oliver Ditson Company).
18 Jones, N.A. & Field, T. 'Music therapies accentuate frontal EGG asymmetry in depressed patients', *Adolescence,* Fall 99, Vol. 34, Issue 34, pp. 529–35.
19 Compass (2003, December 25) *Music* (Sydney: Australia Broadcasting Corporation).
20 Lefevre, M. 'Playing with sound: the therapeutic use of music with children', *Child & family social work,* Vol. 9, Issue 4, pp. 333–45.
21 www.musictherapy.org/faqs.html Retrieved 10 February 2005.
22 Newton, Stephen J. (2001) *Painting, psychoanalysis, and spirituality* (Cambridge: Cambridge University Press).
23 Whitney, J. Stellar, S. & Paige, K. 'Science, art, learning and teaching: making connections', *Teaching science – the journal of Australian Science Teachers Association,* Summer 2004, Vol. 50, Issue 4, pp. 25–8
24 Steinman, Louise (1995) *The artist as storyteller in contemporary performance* (Berkeley: North Atlantic Books) Preface.
25 Levy, F.J. (1992) *Dance movement therapy* (Reston, VA: National Dance Association).
26 Mills, L.J. & Daniluk, J.C. 'Her body speaks: the experience of dance therapy for women survivors of child sexual abuse', *Journal of counseling & development,* Vol. 80, Issue 1, pp. 77–95.
27 Chaiklin, H. & Chaiklin, S. 'Body awareness and its expression: a technique for social casework', *Social Casework,* Vol. 63, Issue 4, pp. 237–40.
28 www.medicomm.net/Consumer%20Site/am/dance.htm Retrieved 10 February 2005.
29 Turner, V. (1990) Are there universals of performance in myth, ritual and drama? In R. Schechner & W. Appel (eds), *Means of performance* (Cambridge: Cambridge University Press).
30 Coult, T. & Kershaw, B. (eds) (1999) *The Welfare State handbook* (London: Metheun) p. 3.

Chapter 4 Dramatic Psychological Storytelling

1 Rotter, J.B. (1954) *Social learning and clinical psychology* (New York: Prentice Hall).
Rotter, J.B. 'Internal versus external control of reinforcement. A case history of a variable', *American psychologist,* 45, pp. 489–93.
2 Allen, R.D. & Krebs, N. (1979) *Psychotheatrics: The new art of self-transformation* (New York: Garland).
3 Bormann, E.G. (1972) 'Fantasy and rhetorical vision', *Quarterly journal of speech* (Speech Communication Association) Vol. 58, pp. 396–407.
4 Pennebaker, J.W. (1997) *Opening up: The healing power of expressing emotions* (New York: Guilford Press).

5 Benedetti, J. (1998) *Stansislavski & the actor* (London: Metheun).
6 Anderson, M. and Anderson, K. (1998) *Text types in English* (Melbourne: Macmillan).
7 Barranger, M.S. (2002) *Theatre: A way of seeing* (New York: Wadsworth) p. 120.
8 Leith, D. (1998) *Fairy tales and therapy* (London: Daylight Press/Society for Storytelling), pp. 9 and 19.
9 Wilson, M. (2006) *Storytelling and theatre* (Hampshire, U.K.: Palgrave Macmillan), p. 107.
10 Westwood, M.J., Keats, P.A. & Wilensky, P. 'Therapeutic enactment: integrating individual and group counselling models for change', *Journal for specialists in group work*, Vol. 28, No. 2, June 2003, pp. 122–38.
11 Blaikie, W. (2004) *Sacred drama* (CD-Rom Interview). Dramatic Psychological Storytelling Institute: www.dramaticpsychologicalstorytelling.com.
12 Lazarus, A.A. & Messer, S.B. (1991) 'Does chaos prevail? An exchange on technical eclecticism and assimilative integration', *Journal of psychotherapy integration*, 1, 143–58.
13 Sunwolf & Frey, L.R. (2001) Storytelling: The power of narrative communication and interpretation. In W.P. Robinson & H. Giles (eds), *The new handbook of language and social psychology*, pp. 119–35 (Sussex: John Wiley).
14 Kelly, G.A. (1991a) *The psychology of personal constructs: Vol. 1. A theory of personality* (London: Routledge).
Kelly, G.A. (1991b) *The psychology of personal constructs: Vol. 2. Clinical diagnosis and therapy* (London: Routledge).
15 Brown, L.S. (1994) *Subversive dialogues: Theory in feminist therapy* (New York: Basic Books).
16 Beck, A.T. (1976) *Cognitive therapy and emotional disorders* (New York: International Universities Press).

Beck, A.T. (1992) 'Cognitive therapy: A thirty year retrospective', *American psychologist*, 46, 368–75.

Greenberger, D. & Padesky, C.A. (1996) *Mind over mood: Change how you feel by changing the way you think* (London: The Guilford Press).

Young, J.E., Klosko, J.S. and Weishaar, M.E. (2003) *Schema Therapy: A practitioner's guide* (New York: Guilford).

17 Kantor, D. & Lehr, W. (1975) *Inside the family* (San Francisco: Jossey-Bass).
Minuchin, S. (1974) *Families and family therapy* (Cambridge: Harvard University Press).
18 Frankl, V. (1997) *Man's search for meaning* (New York: Pocket Books).
May, R. (1994) *The discovery of being: Writings in existential psychology* (New York: W.W. Norton).
19 Dukes, S. (1984) 'Phenomenology methodology in the human sciences', *Journal of religion and health*, 23, 197–203.

Giorgi, A. (ed.) (1985) *Phenomenology and psychological research* (Pittsburgh, PA: Duquesne University Press).

Husserl, E. (1931) *Ideas: General introduction to pure phenomenology* (D. Carr, Trans) (Evanson, IL: Northwestern University Press).

Husserl, E. (1970) *The crises of European sciences and transcendental phenomenology* (D. Carr, Trans) (Evanson, IL: Northwestern University Press).

Moustakas, C. (1994) *Phenomenological research methods* (Thousand Oaks, CA: Sage).

Polkinghorne, D.E. (1989) Phenomenological research methods. In R.S. Valle & S. Halling (eds), *Existential – phenomenological perspectives in psychology* (New York: Plenum).

20 Seligman, M. (2004) *Authentic happiness: Using the new positive psychology to realize your potential for lasting fulfilment* (New York: Free Press).

Chapter 5 Narrative

1 Miller, Laura (Dec 6, 2005 & Jan 2, 2006) 'Far from Narnia: Philip Pullman's secular fantasy for children', *The New Yorker*, p. 53.

2 Mowaljarlai, David and Jutta, Malnic (1993) *Yorro Yorro: Inner traditions* (Rochester, VT) p. 107.

3 Bauman, Richard (1986) *Cambridge studies in oral and literate culture: Story, performance, and event* (London, New York, New Rochelle, Melbourne, Sydney: Cambridge University Press). Analysis of the qualities of literary qualities of orally performed verbal art, focusing on the significance of its social context. Emphasis is on the act of storytelling.

Blayer, Irene Maria F. & Monica Sanchez (eds) (2002) *Storytelling: Interdisciplinary & intercultural perspectives* (New York: Peter Lang Publishing, Inc.) This interdisciplinary collection of sixteen readings from the International Conference on Storytelling (1999), serves as a bridge between the academic and the non-academic world by incorporating essays from scholars as well as storytellers. Topics covered include education, ethnolinguistics, First Nations studies, folklore, linguistics literature, psychology, and sociology (quoted from the back cover) an incredible resource.

4 Knight, Brenda (2000) *Women who love books too much: Bibliophiles, bluestockings and prolific pens from the Algonquin Hotel to the Ya-Ya Sisterhood* (Berkeley California: Conari).

5 Stein, Howard F. (2004) *Beneath the crust of culture: Psychoanalytic anthropology and the cultural unconscious in American life* (Contemporary Psychoanalytic Studies). (New York-Amsterdam) p. ix.

6 Nelson, G. Lynn (2004) *Writing and being: Embracing your life through creative journaling* (Maui, Hawaii-San Francisco: Inner Ocean Publishing, Inc.).

Cameron, Julia (1992) *The artist's way: A spiritual path to higher creativity* (New York: Tarcher, Putnam).

Goldberg, Natalie (1986) *Writing down the bones: Freeing the writer within* (Boston and London: Shambala).

7 Mettzger, Deena (1992) *Writing for your life: A guide and companion to the inner worlds* (San Francisco: Harper San Francisco, A Division of HarperCollins) p. 7.

8 Pennebaker, James (August, 1997) *Opening up: The healing power of expressing emotions* (New York: The Guilford Press).

9 Gutowsky, Constance (October 30, 2005) (Sacramento, California) Personal conversation with Nina Krebs.

10 Conway-Dobson, J. Brigette (2005) 'Dramatic Psychological Storytelling and the Search for Meaning', Post-graduate psychology thesis (Charles Sturt University, Bathurst, Australia) p. 6. Individual theses available through CSU Library or www.dramaticpsychologicalstorytelling.com

West, P.M., Huber, J. & Min, K.S. (2004) Altering experienced utility: 'The impact of writing and self-referencing on preferences', *Journal of Consumer Research*, 31 (3), pp. 623–30.

11 Folsom, Heather (July 17, 2005) Personal Interview with Nina Krebs, San Francisco.

Heather Folsom is a psychiatrist who lives in the San Francisco Bay Area. Author of a book of short stories *Philosophie Thinly Clothed* (Cadmus Editions, 2003) and a novel *Hypohypothesis* (Cadmus Editions, 2005) she is currently writing another novel for publication in September 2007. She graduated from UCLA film school, spent six years playing professionally as a rock and roll musician before going to medical school at Yale and University of California, Davis.

Folsom, Heather (2005) *Hypohypothesis* (Cadmus Editions, San Francisco).

12 Kafka, Franz (1995 edition) 'The judgement', *Stories 1904–1924,* translated by J.A. Underwood (Abacus) pp. 43–56.

13 Rob Allen, Loraine Anderson, Karen Lattouf, Julie Simon, Carol Tutchener, and Jo (Joan) Willis: *Dramatic psychological storytelling* – 'Imaginal research project' (Charles Sturt University, Bathurst, Australia), Individual theses available through CSU Library or www.dramaticpsychologicalstorytelling.com.

Chapter 6 Film

1 Robyn Medek, artist, professional background in film and photography 'Towards Beauty's End' Bathurst Regional Art Gallery exhibition 1 April–15 May 2005 (from University of Queensland Art Museum).

2 Schechner, Richard (2003) *Performance theory* (London: Routledge).

3 Wallabies vs Springboks Metro Cinemas. 25 April 2005 (Bathurst, Australia).

4 Khoa Do, age 26, Film-maker (2005) Young Australian of the Year (April 24) 'Sunday Life', *Sun herald* (Sydney) pp. 20–1.

5 *Motorcycle diaries* http://www.motorcyclediariesmovie.com/home.html retrieved 26 August 2005.

'This movie is based on the true story that took Ernesto Guevara (Gael Garcia Bernal) and Alberto Granado (Rodrigo de la Serna) on a road trip all across and along South America in the 1950s. The script/direction elegantly avoids politics. Its focus is on the human transformation of two young Argentine professionals, a turning point in their lives, who decide to see their continent with their own eyes. This movie only covers Che Guevara's life before he became the famous Che Guevara. Most of us would agree with Che's goals but less, I guess, would agree with his means. However, the movie concentrates on how the world changed Ernesto which in turn led him to try to change the world. The movie ends at the end of their road trip. Finally, this movie ironically represents Che's ultimate goal, a unified continent: the director is Brazilian, the main actor Mexican, the main actress and supporting actor Argentinean, the script writer is from Puerto Rico and the producer, Robert Redford is American. And, the movie was filmed in Argentina, Chile and Peru.'

6 David Stratton is a former director of the North Sydney Film Festival, former film critic for the film industry magazine 'Variety' and is currently film critic for *The Australian*.

A recipient of the Australian Film Institute's Raymond Longford Award, David also served as a former President of the International Critics Jury for the Venice and Cannes Film Festivals, authored two books, and is currently lecturing in Film History at the University of Sydney. David has been the film consultant for the Australian SBS-TV from its inception and then presenter of *Movie of the Week* and *Cinema Classics* for over 22 years. Currently David is now presenter of *At the Movies* with Margaret Pomerantz on ABC-TV (Australian Broadcasting Corporation).

7 *Pierrot Le Fou,* directed by Jean-Luc Godard, De Laurentiis, Dino de Laurentiis Cinematografica, Rome Paris Films, Société Nouvelle de Cinématographie (SNC), 1965, Fox/Lorber Home Video, 1998. Nominated for Golden Lion Award, Venice Film Festival.

8 *Million dollar baby* – http://milliondollarbabymovie.warnerbros.com/intro.html retrieved 26 August 2005.

'Frankie Dunn (Clint Eastwood) has trained and managed some incredible fighters during a lifetime spent in the ring. The most important lesson he teaches his boxers is the one that rules his life: above all, always protect yourself. In the wake of a painful estrangement from his daughter, Frankie has been unwilling to let himself get close to anyone for a very long time. His only friend is Scrap (Morgan Freeman), an ex-boxer who looks after Frankie's gym and knows that beneath his gruff exterior is a man who has attended Mass almost every day for the past 23 years, seeking the forgiveness that somehow continues to elude him.

Then Maggie Fitzgerald (Hilary Swank) walks into his gym. Maggie's never had much, but there is one thing she does have that very few people in this world ever do: she knows what she wants and she's willing to do whatever it takes to get it. In a life of constant struggle, Maggie's gotten herself this far on raw talent, unshakable focus and a tremendous force of will. But more than anything, what she wants is for someone to believe in her.

The last thing Frankie needs is that kind of responsibility – let alone that kind of risk. He tells Maggie the blunt hard truth: she's too old and he doesn't train girls. But "no" has little meaning when you have no other choice. Unwilling or unable to give up on her life's ambition, Maggie wears herself to the bone at the gym every day, encouraged only by Scrap. Finally won over by Maggie's sheer determination, Frankie begrudgingly agrees to take her on.

In turns exasperating and inspiring each other, the two come to discover that they share a common spirit that transcends the pain and loss of their pasts, and find in each other a sense of family they lost long ago. What they don't know is that soon they will both face a battle that's going to demand more heart and courage than any they've ever known.

Warner Bros. Pictures Clint Eastwood, Hilary Swank and Morgan Freeman in *Million Dollar Baby*. The film is directed by Clint Eastwood and produced by Clint Eastwood, Albert S. Rudy, Tom Rosenberg and Paul Haggis. Gary Lucchesi and Robert Lorenz serve as executive producers and Bobby Moresco is the co-producer. The screenplay is by Paul Haggis, based upon stories from "Rope Burns" by F.X. Toole. The director of photography is Tom Stern; the production designer is Henry Bumstead; the film is edited by Joel Cox A.C.E.; and the music is by Clint Eastwood.'

9 *Sideways* www2.foxsearchlight.com/sideways/retrieved 26 August 2005.

'Writer-director Alexander Payne's fourth feature film (following *Citizen Ruth, Election* and *About Schmidt*) starts with two old friends setting off on a wine-tasting road trip ... only to veer dizzily *Sideways* into a wry, comedic exploration of the crazy vicissitudes of love and friendship, the damnable persistence of loneliness and dreams and the enduring war between Pinot and Cabernet.

The misadventures begin when Miles (Paul Giamatti), an un-recovered divorcé and would-be novelist with a wine fixation, decides to give his old college buddy and washed-up actor Jack (Thomas Haden Church) a celebratory trip to the vineyards of Santa Barbara wine country the week before Jack's wedding. The two couldn't be an odder couple. Jack is an over-sexed charmer; Miles is a sad-sack worrier. Jack is looking for his "last taste of freedom"; Miles is just hoping to not get even more depressed. Jack is fine with cheap Merlot; Miles pines for the perfect Pinot. Indeed, the only thing they seem to share in common is the same heady mix of failed ambitions and fading youth.

And yet, as they make their way up the coast, Miles and Jack soon find themselves drowning in wine and women (Sandra Oh and Virginia Madsen). When Jack falls head-over-heels for a local wine pourer and threatens to call off his nuptials, Miles tries to keep his friend on the straight and narrow. But Miles's own romantic encounter with a wine-savvy waitress interferes and sends them both careening headlong into reality. Now, the wedding approaches and with it the certainty that Miles and Jack won't make it back to Los Angeles unscathed or unchanged ... if they get there in one piece at all.

Sideways is written by the multiple award-winning team of Alexander Payne and Jim Taylor (About *Schmidt, Election*), based on Rex Pickett's novel of the same name.'

10 Sheehan, H. (2001) *Irish television drama: A society and its stories* (Dublin: RTE).

11 *Whale Rider* – www.whaleriderthemovie.com-html-themovie_synopsis.html.url retrieved August 17, 2005.

'A contemporary story of love, rejection and triumph as a young girl fights to fulfil her destiny, *Whale Rider* is directed by Niki Caro (*Memory and Desire*) who adapted it for the screen from the novel by award-winning New Zealand writer Witi Ihimaera (*The Matriarch, Tangi*).

Winner: Toronto International Film Festival 2002, The People's Choice Award Winner: 2003 San Francisco Film Festival VirginMega Audience

Award for Best Narrative Feature Winner: 2003 Film Festival Rotterdam Canal and Audience Award Winner: 2003 Sundance Film Festival World Cinema Audience Award.'

12 Rob Allen, Anna Bray, Mixhuca Cervantes-McBride, Brigette Conway-Dobson and Tamlyn Phillips.
Dramatic psychological storytelling – Playwright research project, Charles Sturt University, Bathurst, Australia. Post-Graduate Psychology – Individual theses available through CSU Library or www.dramaticpsychologicalstorytelling.com.
13 Pennebaker, J.W. (1997) *Opening up: The healing power of expressing emotions* (New York: Guilford Press).

Chapter 7 Theatre

1 Sonia Moore (1967) *The Stanislavski system* (New York: Pocket Books).
2 Steinman, Louise (1995) *The artist as storyteller in contemporary performance* (Berkeley: North Atlantic Books) Preface.
3 Barranger, M.S. (2002) *Theatre: A way of seeing* (New York: Wadsworth) pp. 3–7.
4 Bill Blaikie is a professional arts educator who focuses on theatre as a tool for generating original works with a particular interest in physical and masked theatre. He has studied and worked in the US, Italy, Indonesia, Malaysia and the UK. He has directed over 40 productions ranging from Euripides, through Shakespeare to Bob Ellis's latest play 'A Local Man'. Bill is a senior lecturer in Theatre/Media at Charles Sturt University, Bathurst, Australia.
5 Bathurst is Australia's first inland settlement, just three hours from Sydney over the Blue Mountains, a rich history is evident throughout Bathurst and surrounding districts. A population of just over 30,000 makes Bathurst large enough to have all the conveniences and experiences of a city, yet small enough to reflect country lifestyle.
6 Rob Allen, Loraine Anderson, Karen Lattouf, Julianne Simon-Abbott, Carol Tutchener, Joan Willis – *Dramatic Psychological Storytelling* – 'Imaginal research project' (Charles Sturt University, Bathurst, Australia) Individual theses available through CSU Library or www.dramaticpsychologicalstorytelling.com.
7 *The Jester* was written and performed by Carey Allen: September 2004 at Charles Sturt University – Bathurst, Australia:

> *Good day dear nobles, sitting high and proud. I should bow down to you; bow down to your class and stature, for I am but a fool.*
>
> *I would bow down if I had reason. If I was not blessed with the knowledge that you are all in fact nothing, insignificant, there is not a good man among you! Does that scare you, scare you I say, the thought that you are nothing, the thought that you weren't put here for any divine purpose or reason-just to live and die and never be remembered. Why look at the world from the eyes of a fool, is it all laughter that brings us in, or the truth be told that we are all in fact laughed at?*
>
> *On ya feet ya mad man. Where did I come from? No-one knows! Where am I going? To let the truth be told! Laugh, skip, dance, hop, I am the Jester, I am the Fool, the Joker cruel. I come from not here, I come from not there, but materialise from under your hair.*

There is no applause for me. I am someone you know too well. We talk about your darkest secrets in your darkest hours, you try to hide but you can not cause I'll dig you out, dig you out of your hole and bury you in a deeper one! I am your truth!

Real? Not real, not in your mind anyway.

Ahh yes, yes you remember me now. I was the one who pushed you through the dark times but also the one who brought you into them!

A trick for you master? A trick for you my lord? (does a trick) Not good enough I see, well how about this one: your wife doesn't love you, your daughter is a slut, you're going to be fired, everything is not going to be ok and you know it!

Ahhhhh the pain, the hurt. Hit me harder, kick me, and hide your feelings inside like you have always done. Everyone, all of you do this, look for someone else to blame. The fool they say, you can't blame it on me, your truth! And up again.

I asked a blind man once if he'd seen my shoe, but he hadn't seen anything at all. I asked a deaf man if he'd heard anything go by him, but he hadn't heard anything at all…so then I killed them both. You don't find that funny do you? You can only laugh so much at one person's misfortune where the whole time you should be laughing at yourself for being so shallow. Shallowness is the essence of man, or man is the essence of shallowness; tip-toeing through the weary pond sticking everything to you to feel more of a person, more of a man. Clothes, money, items, have blinded you, blinded you to your origins. You can only ever be what you are: a disdained egocentric anomaly of a materialistic society! Hurt? When you look at me do not judge me but judge yourselves!

Don't listen to him, don't listen to him. He's but a Fool, what would he know? He doesn't know me personally or any of us.

Don't I, don't I know you?

Ha, ha! In my hand I have an invisible deck of cards. Think of any card. Good, with you thinking about that hopefully you'll be able to keep your mind off my wife. And here are the cards again! Have you ever seen an invisible deck of cards disappear? Well neither have I! But stand back and prepare yourselves dear nobles. Stand back and await the final trick, the grand finale. As I reach into my pocket what will I pull out? Is it an ice-cream that I can eat, or a little puppy? Neither I am afraid. As any Fool knows the finale must go off with a bang, and what better than with a gun. (placing gun to head).

Do I kill myself now or later, you be the judge. I am the judge of you but please, my apologies. Don't let the truth get in your way. Continue on with your falsified image of the world, continue on governing yourselves by your own rules, looking for redemption in made up concepts like Karma or 'All your sins will be forgiven'. Passing all the blame and responsibility on to the higher forces, which are in fact all in your mind. A substitute you've invented to push the truth as far away as this gun is to my head.

Do you want me to do it? Do you want me to? The gun is not real, not more than you or even me. Yet as I place the cold metal against my face I can't help but see the meaning here. I am an innocent, a symbolic image of truth, happiness and evil. I don't conform to society, as I am the part of society that you pushed out. I am my own, I am my own. You may look at me as a fool but I look at you as naïve, not even you can take that away from me. Only I can end this.

This is the day happiness dies, this is the day truth dies. Ha ha (bang)...Ha Ha.
© Carey Allen 2004

8 Schechter, J. (1985) *Durov's pig: Clowns, politics and theatre* (New York: Theatre Communications Group).

Chapter 8 Music

1 Hart, Mickey & Stevens, Jay (1990) *Drumming at the edge of magic* (San Francisco: Harper) p. 43.
2 Elson, Louis C. (1908) *Curiosities of Music* (© Oliver Ditson Company, Boston) (first, 1880, J.M. Stoddart & Company) p. 7.
3 Redmond, Layne (1997) *When the Drummers were women: A spiritual history of rhythm* (New York: Three Rivers Press) p. 6.
4 Bray, A. (2005) *Dramatic psychological storytelling*: 'Exploring the meaning of the dramatic experience'. Unpublished Postgraduate Diploma of Psychology thesis (Charles Sturt University, Bathurst, Australia).
5 Peelman, R. (2005, August 21) Music – dramatic, psychological and storytelling aspects. (CD-Rom interview). Dramatic Psychological Storytelling Institute: www.dramaticpsychologicalstorytelling.com.
Roland Peelman – Artistic Director

Born in Belgium, Roland studied at the Royal Conservatorium of Music in Gent, the State University of Gent and the Statliche Hochschule fur Musik in Cologne under people such as C.A. Coppens, Rudolph Werthen, Aloys Kontarsky and Volker Wangenheim. He was very active as a pianist and teacher for several years and started appearing as a conductor with various orchestras at the Hochschule in Cologne as well as becoming the Music Director of the Brecht-Eisler Collective in Gent and Antwerp in the early eighties. In 1983 he was appointed Chorus Master at the Opera of Flanders.

Roland immigrated in 1984 to Australia and briefly settled in Mount Gambier before joining The Australian Opera in Sydney where he worked six years as chorus master, repetiteur and conductor. In 1989 he co-founded Sydney Metropolitan Opera to foster the creation of contemporary music theatre and served as its Music Director till 1995. In 1990 he was appointed Artistic Director of both The Song Company, Australia's well-known a cappella ensemble based in Sydney and The Hunter Orchestra, Australia's first professional regional orchestra based in Newcastle.

In the meantime The Song Company has developed into an international touring ensemble of the highest standard, appearing at major festivals in Australia, Asia and abroad. He has worked with most orchestras in Australia as well as Royal Flanders Philharmonic in symphonic as well as operatic repertoire.

6 Compass – ABC TV Online (2003, December 25) Retrieved from http://www.abc.net.au/tv/
7 Henderson, Moya. *I walked into my mother.* Retrieved from www.abc.net.au/arts/music/stories/mother.ram.

8 Book, Linda (2002) *Someday I'm gonna have a horse,* in concert 22 July 2002, Sacramento, California, www.lindabook.com Retrieved 10 December 2005.
9 *Sun Rings* (April 27, 2005) Kronos Quartet in concert, Mondavi Center Program pp. 27–35, www.MondaviArts.org
10 Simhan, Rasmi (April 29, 2005) 'An otherworldly night with Kronos', *Sacramento bee,* Friday Ticket, p. 14.
11 Lennon, John. http://www.brainyquote.com/quotes/authors/j/john_lennon.html accessed 23 January 2006.

Chapter 9 Visual Art

1 www.artquotes.net/quotesartists.htm retrieved September 5, 2005.
2 Sylva, Bob (2005, December 28) 'Clay is her rock: Once homeless Veronica Kyle is molding a new life, thanks to a new passion for ceramic art classes' (Sacramento): *Sacramento bee* newspaper.
3 www.artquotes.net/quotesartists.htm retrieved September 15, 2005.
4 Newton, Stephen J. (2001) *Painting, psychoanalysis, and spirituality* (Cambridge: Cambridge Press).
5 Reding, Chris (2005, August 31) Personal interview, Davis, California.

Chris Reding lives and paints in Marin County, California. Her work in various media has been featured in solo as well as juried group shows for the past two decades. An award winning designer, her sculpture, art books, and textile works, along with her paintings, portray her unique view of the world. A skillful, dedicated teacher, her sensitivity embraces students of diverse abilities and interests.

6 Rivera, Ricardo (2005, November) Personal interview. Sacramento CA.
7 Krebs, Nina (1999) *Edgewalkers* (Far Hills, New Jersey: New Horizons Press).
8 Heringer, Tina (2005, July 13) Personal interview – San Francisco.
9 Krebs, Nina (May 2003) *Portent and Portal: The soul and spirit of everywoman* (Sacramento City College: Gregory Kondos Gallery).
10 Cameron, Julia (2002) *The artist's way* (New York: Jeremy P. Tarcher/ Putnam).
11 Lecht, Suzanne (June, 2005) Personal interview by Carey Allen & Lucy Milan. Hanoi.
Suzanne Lecht, Art Director – Art Vietnam Gallery

Living and working in Asia since 1982, with a lifelong commitment to working in the arts worldwide, Art Director Suzanne Lecht is recognised as a leading authority on contemporary art in Vietnam. Dedicated to discovering exceptional artists who are singular and passionate in their expression, Suzanne has been an advocate in educating the world about the arts of Vietnam. A pioneer in her field, Suzanne has been working with Vietnamese artists since the day she moved from Tokyo to Hanoi in January 1994 – a year and half before diplomatic relations were restored between Vietnam and the US. She opened Art Vietnam Gallery in 2002 in Hanoi and has recently opened a sister gallery, the Fielding Lecht Gallery in Austin Texas. Exhibitions of Vietnamese art are mounted on a monthly basis in both locations along with a lecture series on the development of the arts in Vietnam.

Chapter 10 Dance and Kinaesthetics

1 Steinman, Louise (1995) *The artist as storyteller in contemporary performance* (Berkeley: North Atlantic Books) p. 107.
2 Moreno, Z., Blomkvist, L.D. and Rützel, T. (2000) *Psychodrama, surplus reality and the art of healing* (New York: Brunner – Routledge Taylor & Francis Group).
3 Lawson, Amy (2 October 2005) The Health Report p. 28, *Sun-Herald* (Sydney: Australia).
4 Woodruff, C. (2005) Kinaesthetics (CD-Rom Interview).
www.dramaticpsychologicalstorytelling.com
Carol Woodruff is a tertiary educator with more than 20 years of pre-service teacher preparation experience in health & physical education (H&PE). Following her initial experience as a secondary school H&PE teacher, post graduate qualifications in both health education & health promotion were achieved through the University Oregon. Her current interests are physical activity at the workplace and the potential areas of pedometer as a motivational tool for physical activity adherence. Carol is Course Coordinator of Bachelor of Human Movement/Bachelor of Teaching (Secondary), School of Human Movement Studies at Charles Sturt University, Bathurst, Australia.
5 Murphy, G. (2004) Dance (CD-Rom Interview).
www.dramaticpsychologicalstorytelling.com
Graeme Murphy, Artistic Director – Sydney Dance Company

Choreographer Graeme Murphy was appointed Artistic Director to Sydney Dance Company in 1976 – then known as The Dance Company (N.S.W.). He has since created a remarkably diverse repertoire of Dance works, including 30 full-length productions for Sydney Dance Company, as well as works for The Australian Ballet, Nederlands Dans Theater, the Royal New Zealand Ballet, the Canadian Opera Company and The Metropolitan Opera, New York.

In 1988 he was commissioned by the Australian Bicentennial Authority to create a national Dance event, *VAST*, involving 70 Dancers from four state Dance companies – Australian Dance Theatre, West Australian Ballet, The Queensland Ballet and Sydney Dance Company.

Side by side with Associate Director Janet Vernon, he has led Sydney Dance Company on more than 20 international tours in Asia, Europe, North and South America.

Graeme Murphy was awarded an AM for services to Dance in 1982. He is the recipient of three honorary doctorates – Hon. D Litt Tas (1990), Hon. D Phil Qld (1992), Hon. D Litt UNSW (1999). He was honoured at the Inaugural Sydney Opera House Honours in 1998 and was named by the National Trust of Australia as a National Living Treasure in 1999. In 2001, he was presented with the Helpmann Award for Best Choreography for *Body of Work – A Retrospective, Gala Performance*, as well as four Australian Dance Awards including Outstanding Achievement in Choreography for *Tivoli*. In 2002, he was given the prestigious James Cassius Award, in recognition of his career achievements. In 2003, he was awarded the Australian Government's Centenary Medal in honour of his contribution to the development of Dance in Australia. In 2004 he was chosen as Cultural Leader of the Year by the Australian Business and the Arts Foundation.

6 *Some Rooms*

'A room can be an extension of a personality – rooms affect people and people affect rooms. The four "rooms" are a metaphor used to explore the growth and development of human personalities and relationships. They are "living rooms" where each inhabitant is individually and ruthlessly revealed.'

Graeme Murphy, Choreographer

7 Pennebaker, J.W. (1997) *Opening up: The healing power of expressing emotions* (New York: Guilford Press).

Chapter 11 Ritual and Epic

1 Campbell, Joseph (1988) *Myths to live by: How we create ancient legends in our daily lives to release human potential* (New York: Bantam Books) p. 43.
2 *New Oxford dictionary & thesaurus of English* (2003) (Oxford: New Oxford).
3 van Gennep, Arnold (1960) *The rites of passage* (Chicago: University of Chicago Press) p. vi, Solon Kimbala.
4 Toffler, Alvin (1970) *Future shock* (New York: Bantam).
5 Rev. Margaret Voerman was born in Basra, Iraq in 1931, her father worked as Collector of Customs firstly in the British Civil Service and from 1933, for the Iraq Government. In 1933 her mother took her family (a sister and two brothers) to England so they could be educated there. Margaret's earliest spiritual encounters were in the Cathedral of St. Peter at Gloucester, and she still has loving memories of that place and its people.

In December 1940 Margaret's mother brought her children to Australia to join relatives. She was educated at Monte Sant' Angelo Mercy College, North Sydney, and at Sydney Teachers' College. Margaret lived in Sydney until after her marriage, then moved to Bathurst.

Margaret raised her four children in Bathurst. After they left home, she became increasingly drawn to pastoral ministry. In 1987 she was accepted to train for the priesthood of the Anglican church at St. Mark's College of Ministry in Canberra. Margaret returned to the Diocese of Bathurst in 1990 and was ordained Deacon in 1990 and priest in December 1992 by Bishop Bruce Wilson.

Her parish work was at All Saints' Cathedral Bathurst and Christ Church, Blayney. In Bathurst, she served as Chaplain to the Base Hospital, Macquarie Care Centre and St. Vincents' Hospital. In 1998 Margaret retired from chaplaincy but continues to serve as an Honorary Priest to the Bathurst Parishes.

6 Allen, Rob. *Labyrinth Walk at Grace Cathedral – San Francisco* (9 February 2004) (CD-Rom). www.dramaticpsychologicalstorytelling.com.
7 Pennebaker, J.W. (1997) *Opening up: The healing power of expressing emotions* (New York: Guilford Press).

8 Osmen, Sarah Ann (1990) *Sacred places: A journey into the holiest lands* (New York: St. Martin's Press) p. 40.

9 The Reverend Dr Lauren Artress, President and Founder, laurenartress@veriditas.net *Veriditas, The voice of the labyrinth movement,* 1009 General Kennedy Avenue, 1st Floor The Presidio, San Francisco, California 94129 voice: 415.561.2921 – fax 415.561-2922.

The Reverend Dr Lauren Artress is author of *Walking a Sacred Path: Rediscovering the Labyrinth* as a Spiritual Tool (2002 Putnam/Riverhead Books, New York) and serves as a Canon at Grace Cathedral. She has been with the Cathedral since 1986 when she first served as Canon Pastor until 1995 and then served as a Canon for Special Ministries until August 2004. She created Quest: Grace Cathedral Center for Spiritual Wholeness in 1987 through the Laurence S. Rockefeller's Fund for The Enhancement of the Human Spirit.

Lauren created Veriditas, centered around a 12th century mystical tool symbolic of the Path of Life that is re-introducing the walking meditation back into the Christian tradition. She travels world-wide offering workshops and lectures on the labyrinth and on Hildegard von Bingen. She creates large group events that nurture the connection between the human and Divine such as the Women's Dream Quest and Singing for Your Life (now called Symphony of Souls), a 24 hour, year-end healing event. In 1996 she created Veriditas, a non-profit dedicated to introducing people to the healing, meditative powers of the labyrinth. In addition to her ordination as an Episcopal priest she is a licensed psychotherapist in the State of California.

Lauren holds a Bachelor's Degree in Special Education from Ohio State University and a Master's of Education from Princeton Theological Seminary. She received her analytic training in Object Relations and Systems Theory at The Blanton-Peale Graduate Institute at The Institute of Religion and Health in New York City. Her Doctor of Ministry degree was granted in 1986 from Andover Newton Theological School in Boston Massachusetts in Pastoral Psychology.

Lauren serves on the Board for the International Transpersonal Association as well as the Transpersonal Institute. She is a Diplomate in the American Association for Pastoral Counsellors and a Clinical Member in the American Association for Marriage and Family Therapists and licensed in the State of California.

10 Suzuki, David & McConnell, Amanda (2002) *The sacred balance: Rediscovering our place in nature* (Vancouver, Canada: Greystone Books).

11 Allen, Rob (2005, 21 August) *Kelso High School fire* (CD-Rom). www.dramaticpsychologicalstorytelling.com.

12 Kelso High School, Bathurst, NSW, Australia. Fire occurred on 20 August 2005.

13 Pennebaker, J.W. (1997) *Opening up: The healing power of expressing emotions* (New York: Guilford Press).

14 Bormann, E.G. (1972) 'Fantasy and Rhetorical Vision', *Quarterly journal of speech,* Speech Communication Association, Vol. 58, 1972, pp. 396–407.

15 Beck, Renee & Metrick, Sydney, Barbara (2003) *The art of ritual* (Berkeley, California: Celestial Arts Press) p. 2.

Chapter 12 Imaginal Psychotheatrics

1 Bormann, E.G. (1972) 'Fantasy and Rhetorical Vision', *Quarterly journal of speech*, Speech Communication Association, Vol. 58, pp. 396–407.
Bormann, E.G. (1982) 'Fantasy and Rhetorical Vision: Ten Years Later', *Quarterly journal of speech*, Speech Communication Association, Vol. 68, pp. 288–305.
2 Bormann, E.G. (1972) 'Fantasy and Rhetorical Vision', *Quarterly journal of speech*, Speech Communication Association, Vol. 58, p. 398.

Chapter 13 Playwright Psychotheatrics

1 Rich, Adrienne (1986) *'Dreams before waking', in your native land, your life: Poems by Adrienne Rich* (WW Norton & Company, Inc.) http://thewitness.org/archive/julyaug00/poetry.html.
2 Cameron, Julia (2002) *The artist's way* (New York: Jeremy P. Tarcher/Putnam).
3 Goldberg, Natalie (1986) *Writing down the bones: Freeing the writer within* (Shambhala, Boston) p. 116.
4 Pennebaker, J.W. (1997) *Opening up: The healing power of expressing emotions* (New York: Guilford Press).

Chapter 14 Montage Psychotheatrics

1 McCrae, R.R. & Costa, P.T. (1990) *Personality in adulthood* (New York: Guilford Press).

Costa, P.T. & McCrae, R.R. (1991) *NEO-PI-R: Professional manual – revised NEO personality inventory (NEO-PI-R) and NEO Five factor Inventory (NEO-FFI)* (Odessa, Florida: Psychological Assessments Resources).

McCrae, R.R. & Costa, P. (1997) 'Personality test structure as universal', *American psychologist*, 52, pp. 509–16.

2 Benedetti, J. (1998) *Stansislavski & the actor* (London: Metheun).
3 Westen, D., Burton, L. & Kowalski, R. (2006) *Psychology: Australian and New Zealand*, p. 403 (Sydney: John Wiley).

Chapter 15 Clinical and Counselling

1 Gilligan, Carol (2002) *The birth of pleasure: A new map of love* (New York: Vintage Books) p. 22.
2 Frankl, Viktor (1977) *Man's search for meaning* (Boston: Beacon Press) (First published in Austria (1946) under the title *Ein Psycholog erlebt das Konzentrattonslager*).
3 May, Rollo (1978) *The courage to create* (New York: Norton).
4 Woodman, Marion (1982) *Addiction to perfection: The stil unravished bride* (Toronto: Inner City Books) p. 74.
5 Blake, William (1965) *Milton*, in David Erdman (ed.), *Poetry and prose* (Garden City: Doubleday) pp. 290–3.

6 Modified from Ernst Bormann's work: Bormann, E.G. (1972) 'Fantasy and rhetorical vision', *Quarterly journal of speech* (Speech Communication Association, Vol. 58, 1972) pp. 396–407.
7 Pennebaker, J.W. (1997) *Opening up: The healing power of expressing emotions* (New York: Guilford Press).
8 Allen, R.D. & Krebs, N. (1979) *Psychotheatrics: The new art of self-transformation* (New York: Garland).
9 Masterson, James, F. (1985) *The real self: A developmental, self, and object relations approach* (New York: Brunner/Mazel Publishers).
10 Benjamin, Jessica (1998) *Shadow of the other: Intersubjectivity and gender in psychoanalysis* (Oxford: Routledge).
11 Atwood, George E. and Stolorow, Robert D. (1984) *Structures of subjectivity: Explorations in psychoanalytic phenomenology* (Oak Lawn, Illinois: The Analytic Press).
12 Beck, J. (1995) *Cognitive therapy: Basics beyond* (New York: Guilford Press).
13 Young, J.E., Klosko, J.S. and Weishaar, M.E. (2003) *Schema Therapy: a practitioner's guide* (New York: Guilford Press) p. 7.
14 LeDoux, J. (1996) *The emotional brain* (New York: Simon & Schuster) p. 239.
15 Boal, A. (1995) *The rainbow of desire: The Boal method of theatre and therapy* (London: Routledge).
16 Barranger, M.S. (2002) *Theatre: A way of seeing* (New York: Wadsworth).
17 White, M. & Epston, D. (1990) *Narrative means to therapeutic ends* (New York: Norton).

Chapter 16 Human Resources

1 http://www.brainyquote.com/quotes/authors/p/peter_f_drucker.html retrieved April 7, 2006.
2 'Every great institution is the lengthened shadow of a single man. His character determines the character of the organisation.' Ralph Waldo Emerson http://www.brainyquote.com/quotes/quotes/r/ralphwaldo108801.html – retrieved 3–27–06.
3 Bochner, S. (2003) 'Organisational culture and climate', in M. O'Driscoll, P. Taylor & T. Kalliath (eds), *Organisational psychology in Australia and New Zealand* (New York: Oxford University Press) pp. 302–22.
4 Bales, R. (1970). *Personality and interpersonal behaviour* (New York: Holt, Rinehart and Winston).
5 Anderson, M. & Anderson, K. (1997) *Text types in English 1* (South Yarra: Macmillan).
6 Houston, J. (1987). *The search for the beloved: Journeys in mythology and sacred psychology* (New York: Jeremy P. Tarcher/Putnam).
7 Bormann, E.G. (1982) 'Fantasy and rhetorical vision: Ten years later', *Quarterly journal of speech*, Speech Communication Association, Vol. 68, 1982, pp. 288–305.
8 Anderson, M. & Anderson, K. (1997) *Text types in English 1* (South Yarra: Macmillan).
9 Houston, J. (1987) *The search for the beloved: Journeys in mythology and sacred psychology* (New York: Jeremy P. Tarcher/Putnam).

10 Boyce, M.E. (1995) 'Collective centring and collective sense-making stories – storytelling in one organisation', *Organisation studies*, 16, 107–37.
11 Hughes, J. (1998) 'Resistance and expression: Working with women prisoners and drama', in J. Thompson (ed.), *Prison theatre: Perspectives and practices* (London: Jessica Kingsley Publishers).
12 Allen, Rob (November 2005) *Leadership skills using Montage Psychotheatrics* (CD-Rom). www.dramaticpsychologicalstorytelling.com.
13 Note: This is a composite case study and main themes were extracted from representative sessions. Quotes used are composite examples and also reflect comments by organisational clients in general. In order to protect confidentiality, no real clients have been used for the purpose of this illustrative example.
14 McClelland, D.C. (1985) *Human motivation* (Glenview, IL: Scott Foreman).
15 Barrack, M.R. & Mount, M.K. (1991) 'The big five personality dimensions in job performance: a meta-analysis', *Personnel psychology*, 44, pp. 1–26.
16 Bass, B.M. (1990) *Bass and Stagdill's handbook of leadership* (3rd edn) (New York: Free Press).
17 Anderson, C.R. & Schneier, C.E. (1978) 'Locus of control, leader behaviour and leader performance among management students', *Academy of Management journal*, 2, pp. 690–8.

Rotter, J.B. (1966) 'Generalised expectancies for external vs internal control of reinforcement', *Psychological monographs*.

18 Zaccaro, F.J., Foti, R.J. & Kerry, D.A. (1991) 'Self-monitoring and trait based variance in leadership. An investigation of leader flexibility across multiple group situations', *Journal of applied psychology*, 76, pp. 305–15.
19 Bandura, A. (1977) 'Self-efficacy – towards a unifying theory of behaviour change', *Psychological review*, 84, pp. 191–225.
20 Costa, P.T. & McRae, R.R. (1994) *NEO personality inventory* (Lutz, FL: Psychological Assessment Resources).
21 Muchinsky, P.M. (2000) *Psychology applied to work* (6th edn) (Stamford, CT: Wadsworth Thomas Learning).
22 Benedetti, J. (1998) *Stansislavski & the actor* (London: Methuen).

Chapter 17 Education and Awareness

1 Dewey, J. (1897) 'My pedagogic creed', *The school journal*, pp. 77–80.
2 Fulghum, R. (2004) *All I really need to know I learned in kindergarten* (New York: Ballantine).
3 Stein, H. (2003) 'Beneath the crust: psychoanalytic anthropology and the cultural unconscious in American Life', in David Gabbard and Kenneth J. Saltman, *Education as enforcement: The militarization and corporatization of schools* (London: Routledge Falmer) pp. 21–50.
4 Daly, K. & Hennessey, H. (2001) 'Restorative justice and conferencing in Australia', *Trends & issues in crime and criminal justice #186* (Canberra: Australian Institute of Criminology).
5 Williamson, D. (2002) *Face to face: A conversation* (Sydney: Currency Press).

6 Dewey, J. retrieved April 7, 2006 http://www.quotationspage.com/quotes/John_Dewey/ Dewey
7 Cameron, Julia (2002) *The artist's way: A spiritual path to higher creativity* (New York: Tarcher, Putnam).

Chapter 18 Facilitator Skills

1 Knapp, S.J. & VandeCreek, L. (2005) *Practical ethics for psychologists: A positive approach* (Washington D.C.: American Psychological Association).
Just an example – Clinical/Counselling, Human Resources and Education, all have professional associations with detailed ethical guidelines for practice.
2 Schon, D. (1987) *Education the reflective practitioner* (San Francisco: Jossey-Bass), p. 22.
Cited in Bradley, B. (2005) *Psychology and experience* (Cambridge: Cambridge University Press) p. 28.
3 Egan, E. (2006) *The skilled helper: A problem management and opportunity development approach to helping* (Belmont, CA: Wadsworth).

This work has very good but also very basic minimum standards of practice necessary to be an effective Facilitator. It is assumed that all Facilitators using DPS will be recognised as fully qualified by their relevant professional association(s) to provide services in their discipline area.

4 Corey, M.S. & Corey, G. (1997) *Groups: Process and practice* (5th edn) (Pacific Grove, CA: Brooks/Cole).

Tyson, T. (1998) *Working with groups* (Melbourne: Macmillan Education Australia).

5 Bradley, B. (2005) *Psychology and experience* (Cambridge: Cambridge University Press).
6 American Psychiatric Association (2000) *Diagnostic and statistical manual of mental disorders DSM-IV-TR* (Washington, D.C.: American Psychiatric Publishing).

Neimeyer, R.A. (2000) Narrative disruptions in the construction of self. In R.A. Neimeyer & J.D. Rashkin (eds), *Constructions of disorder: Meaning-making frameworks for psychotherapy*, pp. 207–42 (Washington, D.C.: American Psychological Association).

Bibliography

Allen, R., Anderson, L., Lattouf, K., Simon-Abbott, J., Tutchener, C. & Willis, J. – *Dramatic psychological storytelling* – 'Imaginal research project' (Charles Sturt University, Bathurst, Australia) Individual theses available through CSU Library or www.dramaticpsychologicalstorytelling.com.

Allen, R., Bray, A., Cervantes-McBride, M., Conway-Dobson, B. & Phillips, T., *Dramatic psychological storytelling* – Playwright research project, Charles Sturt University, Bathurst, Australia. Individual theses available through CSU Library or www.dramaticpsychologicalstorytelling.com.

Allen, R.D. & Krebs, N. (1979) *Psychotheatrics: The new art of self-transformation* (New York: Garland).

American Psychiatric Association (2000) *Diagnostic and statistical manual of mental disorders DSM-IV-TR* (Washington, D.C.: American Psychiatric Publishing).

Anderson, C.R. & Schneier, C.E. (1978) 'Locus of control, leader behaviour and leader performance among management students', *Academy of management journal.*

Anderson, M. & Anderson, K. (1997) *Text types in English 1* (South Yarra: Macmillan).

Anderson, M. and Anderson, K. (1998) *Text types in English* (Melbourne: Macmillan).

Atwood, G.E. and Stolorow, R.D. (1984) *Structures of subjectivity: Explorations in psychoanalytic phenomenology* (Oak Lawn, Illinois: The Analytic Press).

Baldwin, C. (2005) *Storycatcher: Making sense of our lives through the power and practice of story* (Novato, California: New World Library).

Bales, R. (1970) *Personality and interpersonal behaviour* (New York: Holt, Rinehart and Winston).

Bandura, A. (1977) 'Self-efficacy – towards a unifying theory of behaviour change', *Psychological review*, 84, pp. 191–225.

Barrack, M.R. & Mount, M.K. (1991) 'The big five personality dimensions in job performance: A meta-analysis', *Personnel psychology*, 44, pp. 1–26.

Barranger, M.S. (2002) *Theatre: A way of seeing* (New York: Wadsworth).

Bass, B.M. (1990) *Bass and Stagdill's handbook of leadership* (3rd edn) (New York: Free Press).

Bauman, R. (1986) *Cambridge studies in oral and literate culture: Story, performance, and event* (London: Cambridge University Press).

Beck, A.T. (1976) *Cognitive therapy and emotional disorders* (New York: International Universities Press).

Beck, A.T. (1992) 'Cognitive therapy: A thirty year retrospective', *American psychologist*, 46, 368–75.

Beck, J. (1995) *Cognitive therapy: Basics beyond* (New York: Guilford Press).

Beck, R. & Metrick, S. (2003) *The art of ritual* (Berkeley, California: Celestial Arts Press).

Benedetti, J. (1998) *Stansislavski & the actor* (London: Metheun).

Benjamin, J. (1998) *Shadow of the other: Intersubjectivity and gender in psychoanalysis* (Oxford: Routledge).

Blaikie, W. (2004) *Sacred drama* (CD-Rom Interview). Dramatic Psychological Storytelling Institute: www.dramaticpsychologicalstorytelling.com

Blake, W. (1965) *Milton*, in David Erdman (ed.), *Poetry and prose* (Garden City: Doubleday).

Blayer, I., Maria, F. & Sanchez, M. (eds) (2002) *Storytelling: Interdisciplinary & intercultural perspectives* (New York: Peter Lang Publishing, Inc.).

Boal, A. (1995) *The rainbow of desire: The Boal method of theatre and therapy* (London: Routledge).

Bochner, S. (2003) 'Organisational culture and climate', in M. O'Driscoll, P. Taylor & T. Kalliath (eds), *Organisational psychology in Australia and New Zealand* (New York: Oxford University Press) pp. 302–22.

Book, L. (2002) *Someday I'm gonna have a horse*, in concert 22 July 2002, Sacramento, California, www.lindabook.com retrieved 10 December 2005.

Bormann, E.G. (1972) 'Fantasy and rhetorical vision', *Quarterly journal of speech* (Speech Communication Association) vol. 58, 1972, pp. 396–407.

Bormann, E.G. (1982) 'Fantasy and rhetorical vision: Ten years later', *Quarterly journal of speech* (Speech Communication Association) Vol. 68, 1982, pp. 288–305.

Borosh, C. (2003) 'A phenomenological research investigation into university students' experience of an action based workshop series on career decision making', Post-graduate psychology thesis (Charles Sturt University, Bathurst, Australia) Individual theses available through CSU Library.

Boyce, M.E. (1995) 'Collective centring and collective sense-making stories – storytelling in one organisation', *Organisation studies*, 16, 107–37.

Bradley, B. (2005) *Psychology and experience* (Cambridge: Cambridge University Press).

Bray, A. (2005) *Dramatic psychological storytelling*: 'Exploring the meaning of the dramatic experience'. Unpublished Postgraduate Diploma of Psychology thesis (Charles Sturt University, Bathurst, Australia).

Brown, L.S. (1994) Subversive dialogues: Theory in feminist therapy (New York: Basic Books).

Burns, G. (2001) *101 healing stories: Using metaphors in therapy* (New York: Wiley).

Calisch, A. 'From reel to reel: Use of video as a therapeutic tool', *Afterimage*. Vol. 29, Issue 3, pp. 22–5.

Cameron, Julia (2002) *The artist's way* (New York: Jeremy P. Tarcher/Putnam).

Campbell, J. (1988) *Myths to live by: How we create ancient legends in our daily lives to release human potential* (New York: Bantam Books).

Centre for popular education (2005) *Photo voice* (Sydney: University of Technology-Sydney).

Chaiklin, H. & Chaiklin, S. 'Body awareness and its expression: a technique for social casework', *Social casework*. Vol. 63, Issue 4, pp. 237–40.

Compass (2003, December 25) *Music* (Sydney: Australia Broadcasting Corporation).

Corey, M.S. & Corey, G. (1997) *Groups: Process and practice* (5th edn) (Pacific Grove, CA: Brooks/Cole).

Costa, P.T. & McCrae, R.R. (1991) *NEO-PI-R: Professional manual – revised NEO personality inventory (NEO-PI-R) and NEO Five factor inventory (NEO-FFI)* (Odessa, Florida: Psychological Assessments Resources).

Costa, P.T. & McRae, R.R. (1994) *NEO personality inventory* (Lutz, FL: Psychological Assessment Resources).

Coult, T. & Kershaw, B. (eds) (1999) *The Welfare State handbook* (London: Metheun).

Curtis, A.M. 'Communicating with bereaved children: A drama therapy approach', *Illness, Crisis & Loss*. Vol. 7, Issue 2, pp. 183–91.

Daly, K. & Hennessey, H. (2001) 'Restorative justice and conferencing in Australia', *Trends & issues in crime and criminal justice #186* (Canberra: Australian Instititute of Criminology).

Dewey, J. (1897) 'My pedagogic creed', *The school journal*, pp. 77–80.

Doogue, G. (2003, October 5) 'Psyche & soul', *Compass* (television series) (Electronic version) (Sydney: Australian Broadcasting Corporation).

Dukes, S (1984) 'Phenomenology methodology in the human sciences', *Journal of religion and health*, 23, 197–203.

Egan, E. (2006) *The skilled helper: A problem management and opportunity development approach to helping* (Belmont, CA: Wadsworth).

Elson, L.C. (1908) *Curiosities of music* (© Oliver Ditson Company, Boston) (first © 1880, J.M. Stoddart & Company).

Emunah, R. (1994) *Acting for real: Drama therapy – process, technique and performance* (New York: Brunner Mazel).

Folsom, H. (2005) *Hypohypothesis* (Cadmus Editions, San Francisco).

Fox, J. (ed.) (1987) *The essential Moreno: Writings on psychodrama, group method and spontaneity* (New York: Springer).

Frankl, V. (1997) *Man's search for meaning* (New York: Pocket Books).

Fulghum, R. (2004) *All I really need to know I learned in kindergarten* (New York: Ballantine).

Ganis, S. (6 March 2006) President, Academy of Motion Picture Arts and Sciences (Academy Awards Ceremony Los Angeles).

Gardner, H. (1999) *Intelligence reframed: Multiple intelligences for the 21st century* (New York: Basic Books).

Gersie, A. (1996) *Dramatic approaches to brief therapy* (London: Jessica Kingsley).

Gilligan, C. (1994) Getting civilized. *Fordham law review*, 63, 17–31.

Gilligan, C. (2002) *The birth of pleasure: A new map of love* (New York: Vintage Books).

Giorgi, A. (ed.) (1985) *Phenomenology and psychological research* (Pittsburgh, PA: Duquesne University Press).

Goddard, H. (1965) *The meaning of Shakespeare, Vol. 2* (Chicago: University of Chicago Press).

Goldberg, N. (1986) *Writing down the bones: Freeing the writer within* (Boston and London: Shambala).

Greenberger, D. & Padesky, C.A. (1996) *Mind over mood: Change how you feel by changing the way you think* (London: The Guilford Press).

Hart, M. (1990) *Drumming at the edge of magic* (San Francisco: Harper).

Henderson, M. *I walked into my mother* Retrieved from www.abc.net.au/arts/music/stories/mother.ram

Hillman, J. (1996) *The soul's code* (New York: Random House).

Holmes, P. and Karp, M. (1991) *Psychodrama: Inspiration and technique* (London: Tavistock/Routledge).

Honos-Webb, L., Sunwolf & Shapiro, J.L. (2004) 'The healing power of telling stories in psychotherapy', in J.D. Raskin & S.K. Bridges (eds), *Studies in meaning: Bridging the personal and social in constructivist psychology*, pp. 85–114 (New York: Pace University Press).

Houston, J. (1987). *The search for the beloved: Journeys in mythology and sacred psychology* (New York: Jeremy P. Tarcher/Putnam).

Houston, J. (1997) *The search for the beloved: Journeys in sacred psychology* (New York: Tarcher/Putnam).

Hughes, J. (1998) 'Resistance and expression: Working with women prisoners and drama', in J. Thompson (ed.), *Prison theatre: Perspectives and practices* (London: Jessica Kingsley Publishers).

Husserl, E. (1931) *Ideas: General introduction to pure phenomenology* (D. Carr, Trans) (Evanson, IL: Northwestern University Press).

Husserl, E. (1970) *The crises of European sciences and transcendental phenomenology* (D. Carr, Trans) (Evanson, IL: Northwestern University Press).

Jones, N.A. & Field, T. 'Music therapies accentuate frontal EGG asymmetry in depressed patients', *Adolescence*, Fall 99, Vol. 34, Issue 34, pp. 529–35.

Kantor D. & Lehr, W. (1975) *Inside the family* (San Francisco: Jossey-Bass).

Kelly, G.A. (1991a) *The psychology of personal constructs: Vol. 1. A theory of personality* (London: Routledge).

Kelly, G.A. (1991b) *The psychology of personal constructs: Vol. 2. Clinical diagnosis and therapy* (London: Routledge).

Klein, M. (2002) *Envy and gratitude (1946–1963)* (New York: Free Press).

Knapp, S.J. & VandeCreek, L. (2005) *Practical ethics for psychologists: A positive approach* (Washington D.C.: American Psychological Association).

Knight, B. (2000) *Women who love books too much: Bibliophiles, bluestockings and prolific pens from the Algonquin Hotel to the Ya-Ya Sisterhood* (Berkeley California: Conari).

Krebs, N. (1999) *Edgewalkers: Defusing boundaries on the new global frontier* (Far Hills, New Jersey: New Horizons Press).

Landy, R.J. (1986) *Drama therapy: Concepts and practices* (Springfield, IL: Charles C. Thomas)

Langley, D.M. (1987) *Dramatherapy and psychiatry* (London: Croom Helm).

Lazarus, A.A. & Messer, S.B. (1991) 'Does chaos prevail? An exchange on technical eclecticism and assimilative integration', *Journal of psychotherapy integration*, 1, 143–58.

LeDoux, J. (1996) *The emotional brain* (New York: Simon & Schuster).

Lefevre, M. 'Playing with sound: The therapeutic use of music with children', *Child & family social work*, Vol. 9, Issue 4, pp. 333–45.

Leith, D. (1998) *Fairy tales and therapy* (London: Daylight Press/Society for Storytelling).

Levy, F.J. (1992) *Dance movement therapy* (Reston, VA: National Dance Association).

Luke, H. (1982) *The inner story* (New York: Crossroads).

Masterson, J.F. (1985) *The real self: A developmental, self, and object relations approach* (New York: Brunner/Mazel Publishers).

May, R. (1978) *The courage to create* (New York: Norton).

May, R. (1994) *The discovery of being: Writings in existential psychology* (New York: W.W. Norton).

Mayer, J.D., Caruso, D. & Salovey, P. (2000) 'Emotional intelligence meets traditional standards for an intelligence', *Intelligence*, 27, pp. 267–98.

Menninger, W.C. Bibliotherapy. *Bulletin of the Menninger Clinic*, Vol. 1, no. 8, pp. 263–4.

Metzger, D. (1992) *Writing for your life: A guide and companion to the inner worlds* (San Francisco: Harper San Francisco, A Division of HarperCollins) p. 7.
McCrae, R.R. & Costa, P.T. (1990) *Personality in adulthood* (New York: Guilford Press).
McCrae, R.R. & Costa, P. (1997) 'Personality test structure as universal', *American psychologist*, 52, pp. 509–16.
McClelland, D.C. (1985) *Human motivation* (Glenview, IL: Scott Foreman).
Miller, L. (Dec. 6, 2005 & Jan. 2, 2006) 'Far from Narnia: Philip Pullman's secular fantasy for children', *The New Yorker*, p. 53.
Mills, L.J. & Daniluk, J.C. 'Her body speaks: The experience of dance therapy for women survivors of child sexual abuse', *Journal of counseling & development*, Vol. 80, Issue 1, pp. 77–95.
Minuchin, S. (1974) *Families and family therapy* (Cambridge: Harvard University Press).
Moore, P. (1997) *Acting out: Therapy for groups* (Hants, England: Arena).
Moore, S. (1967) *The Stanislavski system* (New York: Pocket Books).
Moreno, Z., Blomkvist, L.D. & Rützel, T. (2000) *Psychodrama, surplus reality and the art of healing* (New York: Brunner – Routledge Taylor & Francis Group).
Moustakas, C. (1994) *Phenomenological research methods* (Thousand Oaks, CA: Sage).
Mowaljarlai, D. & Jutta, M. (1993) *Yorro Yorro: Inner traditions* (Rochester, VT).
Muchinsky, P.M. (2000) *Psychology applied to work* (6th edn). (Stamford, CT: Wadsworth Thomas Learning).
Muller, B. 'Metacognition', *AI & society* (Sep. 2000) Vol. 14, Issue 3–4, pp. 440–53.
Murdock, M. (1993) *The heroine's journey: Women's quest for wisdom* (Boston: Shambala).
Neimeyer, R.A. (2000) 'Narrative disruptions in the construction of self', in R.A. Neimeyer & J.D. Rashkin (eds), *Constructions of disorder: Meaning-making frameworks for psychotherapy*, pp. 207–42 (Washington, D.C.: American Psychological Association).
Nelson, G.L. (2004) *Writing and being: Embracing your life through creative journaling* (Maui, Hawaii-San Francisco: Inner Ocean Publishing, Inc.).
Neuhauser, P. (1993) *Corporate legends and lore: The power of storytelling as a management tool* (New York: McGraw-Hill Education).
Newton, S.J. (2001) *Painting, psychoanalysis, and spirituality* (Cambridge: Cambridge University Press).
Osmen, S.A. (1990) *Sacred places: A journey into the holiest lands* (New York: St. Martin's Press).
Peelman, R. (2005, August 21) Music – dramatic, psychological and storytelling aspects. (CD-Rom interview). Dramatic Psychological Storytelling Institute: www.dramaticpsychologicalstorytelling.com.
Pellowski, A. (1997) *The world of storytelling* (New Providence, New Jersey: R.R. Bowker).
Pennebaker, J.W. (1997) *Opening up: The healing power of expressing emotions* (New York: Guilford Press).
Pickard, T. (2002) 'Dramatic themes in a modern workplace: Post-graduate psychology thesis', Charles Sturt University, Bathurst, Australia.
Polkinghorne, D.E. (1989) 'Phenomenological research methods', in R.S. Valle & S. Halling (eds), *Existential – phenomenological perspectives in psychology* (New York: Plenum).

Redmond, L. (1997) *When the Drummers were women: A spiritual history of rhythm* (New York: Three Rivers Press).
Rich, A. (1986) 'Dreams before waking', in *Your native land, your life: Poems by Adrienne Rich* (WW Norton & Company, Inc.) http://thewitness.org/archive/julyaug00/poetry.html
Rotter, J.B. (1954) *Social learning and clinical psychology* (New York: Prentice Hall).
Rotter, J.B. (1966) 'Generalised expectancies for external vs internal control of reinforcement', *Psychological monographs*, 80.
Rotter, J.B. (1990) 'Internal versus external control of reinforcement. A case history of a variable', *American psychologist*, 45, pp. 489–93.
Rushdie, S. (1997) *The Moor's last sigh* (New York: Vintage).
Sandner, D.F. & Wong, S.H. (1997) *The sacred heritage: The influence of shamanism on analytical psychology* (New York and London: Routledge).
Schechner, R. (2003) *Performance theory* (London: Routledge).
Schechter, J. (1985) *Durov's pig: Clowns, politics and theatre* (New York: Theatre Communications Group).
Schutzenberger, A.A. (1991) 'Terminally ill patient: 15-year experience in application of psychodrama in cancer therapy', in P. Holmes & M. Karp (eds), *Psychodrama: Inspiration & technique* (London: Tavistock/Routledge).
Seligman, M. (2004) *Authentic happiness: Using the new positive psychology to realize your potential for lasting fulfilment* (New York: Free Press).
Sexson, L. (1992) *Ordinarily sacred* (London: University Press).
Sheehan, H. (2001) *Irish television drama: A society and its stories* (Dublin: RTE).
Skiffington, R. (2002) Bell Shakespeare Company, Pamphlet, *Comedy of errors* (Melbourne, Australia).
Stein, H. (2003) 'Beneath the crust: Psychoanalytic anthropology and the cultural unconscious in American life', in David Gabbard and Kenneth J. Saltman, *Education as enforcement: The militarization and corporatization of schools* (London: Routledge Falmer) pp. 21–50.
Stein, H.F. (2004) *Beneath the crust of culture: Psychoanalytic anthropology and the cultural unconscious in American life* (Contemporary Psychoanalytic Studies). (New York-Amsterdam) p. ix.
Steinman, L. (1995) *The artist as storyteller in contemporary performance* (Berkeley: North Atlantic Books).
Sunwolf & Frey, L.R. (2001) 'Storytelling: The power of narrative communication and interpretation', in W.P. Robinson & H. Giles (eds), *The new handbook of language and social psychology*, pp. 119–35 (Sussex: John Wiley).
Suzuki, D. & McConnell, A. (2002) *The sacred balance: Rediscovering our place in nature* (Vancouver, Canada: Greystone Books).
Toffler, A. (1970) *Future shock* (New York: Bantam).
Turner, V. (1990) 'Are there universals of performance in myth, ritual and drama?' in R. Schechner & W. Appel (eds), *Means of performance* (Cambridge: Cambridge University Press).
Tyson, T. (1998) *Working with groups* (Melbourne: Macmillan Education Australia).
van Gennep, A. (1960) *The rites of passage* (Chicago: University of Chicago Press).
West, P.M., Huber, J. & Min, K.S. (2004) Altering experienced utility: 'The impact of writing and self-referencing on preferences', *Journal of consumer research*, 31 (3), pp. 623–30.

Westen, D., Burton, L. & Kowalski, R. (2006) *Psychology: Australian and New Zealand*, p. 403 (Sydney: John Wiley).

Westwood, M.J., Keats, P.A. & Wilensky, P. 'Therapeutic enactment: Integrating individual and group counselling models for change', *Journal for specialists in group work*, Vol. 28, No. 2, June 2003, pp. 122–38.

White, M. & Epston, D. (1990) *Narrative means to therapeutic ends* (New York: Norton).

Whitney, J. Stellar, S. & Paige, K. 'Science, art, learning and teaching: Making connections', *Teaching science – The journal of Australian Science Teachers Association*, Summer 2004, Vol. 50, Issue 4, pp. 25–8.

Williamson, D. (2002) *Face to face: A conversation* (Sydney: Currency Press).

Wilson, M. (2006) *Storytelling and theatre* (Hampshire, U.K.: Palgrave Macmillan).

Wind, E. (1967) *Pagan mysteries in the Renaissance* (Harmondsworth, England: Penguin).

Woodman, Marion (1982) *Addiction to perfection: The stil unravished bride* (Toronto: Inner City Books) p. 74.

Young, J.E., Klosko, J.S. & Weishaar, M.E. (2003) *Schema Therapy: A practitioner's guide* (New York: Guilford).

Zaccaro, F.J. Foti, R.J. & Kerry, D.A. (1991) 'Self-monitoring and trait based variance in leadership. An investigation of leader flexibility across multiple group situations', *Journal of applied psychology*, 76, pp. 305–15.

Zipes, J. (1995) *Creative storytelling: Building communities, changing lives* (London: Routledge).

Zipes, J. (2004) *Speaking out: Storytelling and creative drama for children* (London: Routledge).

Zipes, J. (2006) in M. Wilson, *Storytelling and theatre* (Hampshire, U.K.: Palgrave Macmillan).

Name Index

Subject Index